— Economic —
Abundance

Economic
Abundance
An Introduction

William M. Dugger and James T. Peach

M.E.Sharpe
Armonk, New York
London, England

HB
801
.D83
2009

Library of Congress Cataloging-in-Publication Data

Dugger, William M.
  Economic abundance : an introduction / William M. Dugger, James T. Peach.
    p. cm.
  ISBN 978-0-7656-2340-9 (cloth : alk. paper)—ISBN 978-0-7656-2341-6 (paper : alk. paper)
  1. Supply and demand. 2. Resource allocation. 3. Scarcity. I. Peach, James T. II. Title.

  HB801.D83 2009
  338.5'21—dc22   2008033384

Printed in the United States of America

EB (c)	10	9	8	7	6	5	4	3	2	1
EB (p)	10	9	8	7	6	5	4	3	2	1

Contents

List of Tables, Figures, and Box

Tables

Figures and Box

Preface

Why We Wrote This Book

We were both educated in the institutionalist tradition of economics that once thrived at the University of Texas (see Phillips 1995) and wrote this book for our students, for the next generation. Economics as it is usually taught is the economics of scarcity, defined as the study of the allocation of scarce resources among alternative wants. We were taught that this definition is wrongheaded because the most important resource humanity has is its joint stock of knowledge. That stock is not scarce, unless people make it so. Knowledge can be used over and over again. If I learn something, you can learn it too, unless I keep you from doing so.

The scarcity definition of economics has profound implications. To define economics as the study of scarcity is to assume, wrongly, that the current institutional arrangements that promote scarcity cannot change. This is scarcity economics. It denies the possibility of abundance.

What We Mean By Abundance

Abundance does not mean that goods are available free. That would be impractical in the extreme. In fact, it would be contradictory. If abundance meant free goods, abundance also would mean unlimited waste. If everything were free, everything would be wasted. Then, of course, nothing would be abundant any more. Instead of free, abundance means adequacy. Supplies of goods cannot be free, but they can be adequate. Abundance does not mean that everyone can eat all they want for nothing—free chocolate for everybody. It means that everyone has adequate food, not free food, and the meaning of *adequate* is related to the state of human knowledge. Back in the Stone Age, people knew how to use stone tools and related technologies so the level of adequacy corresponded to that Stone Age context. If everybody can participate in the use of the community's Stone Age knowledge, then they can produce an adequate level of goods and services for that knowledge base. The level of adequacy back then meant something different than it does today. In the Space Age of today, human abilities are improved and enlarged by expanded knowledge. So, too, is the level of adequacy. In other words, adequacy depends upon the knowledge context in which people are operating. It was low in the Stone Age, much higher in the Space Age. Abundance does not mean that everyone is satiated. It means that everyone has enough within the limits of knowledge of society. It does not mean unlimited goods without regard to context, but it does mean sufficient goods, within a particular context. Our working definition of abundance is the full participation of all in the use of the community's joint stock of knowledge. And knowledge is not scarce in the sense that one person's use of it precludes anyone else's use.

Redefining Economics

We have always been struck by the peculiar contrast between economics defined as the study of scarcity and the spectacular facts of modern economic growth. Scarcity does exist. Everyone faces a twenty-four-hour day and must choose how to spend those precious hours. Devoting more time to the study of economics means less time reading nineteenth-century French literature. Opportunity cost—the cost of the next best alternative—is indeed a meaningful short-run concept, and everyone faces short-run trade-offs.

Trade-offs and opportunity costs are real. Nevertheless, the evidence is overwhelming that the study of scarcity in the short run obscures rather than illuminates the most important facts, trends, and issues of modern economies. Scarcity economics ignores the possibility of abundance. It misses the remarkable technological and institutional changes associated with what is often called the industrial revolution. That revolution is ongoing. The world's capacity to produce goods and services has increased dramatically over the last few centuries and is continuing to increase. The modern world is different from preindustrial society. The modern world needs an economics based on modern notions of widespread abundance and equality rather than concepts of scarcity and inequality. Scarcity economics is too narrow. Economics should include the study of abundance.

The social world inherited from the past is made up of institutions. Some of those hand-me-down institutions make some aspects of the modern world just as mean, ugly, and brutal as in the preindustrial world. Some people still go to bed hungry or cold or wet, while others are warm and dry and fat. Some people still die from preventable disease, while others live longer than was once imagined possible. Some husbands still beat their wives. Some people still live out their existence in ignorance. In some places, warlords still burn, pillage, and rape their way through their communities. However, the institutions that make up the social world are not immortal. They are handed down from previous generations. One generation does not have to hand down to future generations the same rotten institutions. Future generations do not have to accept such poisoned hand-me-downs. Future generations can reconstruct the institutions that need to be fixed. The mistakes of the past need not be repeated in the future. People do not have to reproduce an economy of scarcity. People should accept a moral obligation to the future, so it need not suffer the same things as were suffered in the past. The future is not inevitable. The future is contestable (Dugger and Sherman 2000).

We do not have to define economics as the allocation of scarce resources to meet unlimited wants. We can replace the science of scarcity definition of economics with Allan Gruchy's definition of economics as "the science of the social provisioning process" (Gruchy 1987, 4–7, 21). The social provisioning definition of economics does not exclude the study of scarcity. It makes room for the study of abundance. Gruchy's approach is more comprehensive and dynamic than the scarcity approach. In the social provisioning approach, scarcity is not assumed by definition, so abundance becomes a meaningful concept.

Our book is intended to expose students to a broader and more adequate conversation about economics. Our book is not intended as a replacement for a textbook. We do not cover everything that students should explore. However, our book does provide essential material that is not found in the textbooks.

Distinctive Features of This Book

Five features distinguish this book from other supplemental texts. First, we provide a serious treatment of abundance. We define abundance as the full use of the community's joint stock of knowledge. We emphasize that knowledge is not scarce in the sense that one person's use of it precludes anyone else's use. We discuss a number of famous economists who argue that abundance is not utopian. We show why it has not been attained and how it could be.

The second distinctive feature of our approach is that we tie equality and abundance to each other. In the conventional wisdom, inequality must be tolerated today in order to earn abundance tomorrow. We disagree. Allowing the underdogs of our society to be ground down today is not the way to achieve abundance tomorrow. The problem is that today's economic underdogs are not able to participate fully and equally in economic activity, and that is why they will continue to be poor tomorrow. Something is holding them down.

What is holding the poor down? What keeps abundance out of reach? Our answer is the third distinctive feature of the book. We present a unified theory of inequality and scarcity by using the negative-sum game concept from game theory. We explain that racism, sexism, classism, and nationalism are negative-sum games whose combined impacts simultaneously hold the social underdogs down and deprive society of abundance.

This deprivation brings in the fourth distinctive feature of our book: we invite readers to join us in empirical estimation of the costs of negative-sum games. We show students how it is done and urge them to go further with their own empirical explorations. In the process, we urge the next generation of economists to reconstruct the Queen of the Social Sciences as an empirical science instead of the dismal science. We also show them how the empirical data can be mistreated, can be tortured till it confesses to the conventional wisdom. We urge students not to torture the data themselves and not to believe the data that has been tortured by others.

Our advocating of universal employment is the fifth distinctive feature of the book. Instead of the natural rate of unemployment or full employment, we propose driving the unemployment rate down closer and closer to absolute zero. Provide universal employment and the increased production will provide the wherewithal to put abundance within our grasp. Furthermore, if everyone had a job that pays a living wage, the desperation that pushes people into playing negative-sum games would be virtually gone.

Three Parts of the Book

The first part of the book, a practical guide to abundance, contains chapters on the intellectual history of abundance, the meaning of abundance, population, and resources and the environment. The second part of the book explains why abundance escapes us. This part focuses on the inequality "games" people play: classism, nationalism, sexism, and racism. The third and last part of the book focuses on changing these games by pursuing the goal of universal employment. The final chapter sums up and devotes the last word to Veblen's game—a game that we play with each other that can re-create scarcity within any level of output, no matter how high.

Abundance does not mean that people will ever be able to sit back and do nothing but pluck juicy apples off the tree. There is much work that needs to be done in the world, products to make and services to perform. Nevertheless, a good portion of the work goes undone even while the International Labor Office estimates that there are nearly 200 million unemployed workers in the world. We can simplify the whole book down to this: If all 200 million unemployed people went to work at a living wage, abundance would be within the global community's grasp. At modern-day technological levels of productivity, 200 million worker-years of additional production would transform the global economy in a generation. That is the promise of abundance, and the challenge, too.

Dedication and Acknowledgments

The book is dedicated to the memory of Wendell C. Gordon, Professor of Economics at the University of Texas. He was our teacher and friend. He was a World War II soldier, an intellectual maverick, and an institutional economist. We should have come closer to meeting the standards he set for us. But we take heart; there is a new generation of mavericks coming.

Pauline J. Dugger provided computer technical assistance and formatted the manuscript. William Waller, John Henry, and F. Tomasson Jannuzi commented on earlier parts of the manuscript. Lynn Taylor and Katie Corasaniti at M.E. Sharpe were very supportive. Kathleen Brook and Kaitlin Peach provided much needed advice and comment.

Abundance

A Practical Guide

1

An Intellectual History of Abundance

Putting Abundance in Context

The purpose of the following exercise in the history of economic thought is to demonstrate that the concept of scarcity has no right to a monopoly position in economics. While scarcity has dominated economic analysis for nearly two centuries, many of the great economists wrote convincingly about the possibility of an economy of abundance. The leading "abundance economists" include Adam Smith, Karl Marx, Thorstein Veblen, John Maynard Keynes, and many others from diverse schools of thought and diverse perspectives.

Abundance is the antithesis of scarcity. Abundance means that everyone has adequate health care, nutrition, education, transportation, recreation, housing, self-expression, and personal security. Abundance does not mean that goods are free. Abundance means adequacy, not satiation. The level of adequacy is not constant, but is relative to the community's know-how. When members learn how to do more, their advance in knowledge lifts the level of adequacy. Such an advance in knowledge is technological progress, and it has propelled the human community from the Stone Age to the Space Age. In a Stone Age community there is a lower level of adequacy than in a Space Age community. In the Stone Age, adequacy may not have included enough food to allow everyone to grow to modern humans' stature and to enjoy a long and healthy life span. The Space Age level of adequacy is higher because such a higher standard is practical with improved technology.

Scarcity, on the other hand, means that some members of the community suffer from inadequate health care, nutrition, education, transportation, recreation, housing, self-expression, or personal security—relative

3

to their community's level of technology. And the appropriate level of technology today is that of the Space Age, regardless of where one happens to live on the planet.

Unfortunately, the level of adequacy in a community is not determined solely by what is practical, given the community's level of technology. The modern community's standard of adequacy is severely distorted by questions of status. Thorstein Veblen argued that the status dimension is introduced into a community's standard of adequacy by the division of people into rich and poor groups. Veblen used the term *leisure class* to characterize a group that becomes rich enough that it does not have to work. Instead of working, rich people can show off their wealth and make others envious, touching off competition for status through conspicuous consumption (Veblen [1899] 1975). This competition quickly becomes irrational as each person tries to consume more than everyone else. No matter how much people can produce, however, everyone cannot consume more than everyone else. The attempt to do so is irrational—indeed, logically impossible. Nevertheless, people still try and are left feeling envious, ashamed, or dishonored when they fail. As a result, the modern community's standard of adequacy is distorted and impractically high, and people come to think that scarcity is the natural condition of humanity.

There will never be enough for each person to have more than everyone else. This is the problem of relative scarcity—what we will call Veblen's game. We will return to this important issue after discussing absolute scarcity—when there is not enough for everyone to have a sufficient share. Relative scarcity and absolute scarcity are different. Relative scarcity always will exist.

With absolute scarcity, people are condemned to conflict and poverty. The absolute scarcity lens suggests that the distribution question (who gets how much) is a dominant theme in economics because slicing the pie is a more important and difficult question when the pie is too small. From this absolute scarcity perspective, the poor are poor because there is just not enough to go around and there never will be. Can absolute scarcity be resolved, or not? This issue will be the focus of most of our book.

Suppose we break away from the grip absolute scarcity has on our thinking. Suppose we take a different approach—the abundance approach. Viewing the world from the abundance perspective leads us to examine a different set of problems. How can all people, no matter who they are, achieve a standard of living adequate to the Space Age economy instead of the Stone Age economy or something in between the two? That is, how does everybody get up to the very edge of the moving technological frontier? That means everybody—women, men, minorities, foreigners, illegal aliens, Christians, Muslims, Jews, Hindus, Buddhists, Druids, and atheists, too. What do people do with the abundance of goods and services the world economy is capable of producing with its Space Age technology? What is the meaning of work in an abundant society? What does Space Age abundance imply for people's obligations to their home—the planet earth? Does abundance imply a moral obligation to stop global warming? How does economics change if distribution is no longer a central focus? If the poor are not poor because there is too little to go around, then why are they poor?

The scarcity point of view has a virtual monopoly on orthodox economics. In fact, economics is taught in the schools as if it were the science of scarcity. More specifically, economics is commonly defined in textbooks as the study of the allocation of limited resources to meet unlimited human wants. The scarcity point of view does not have a complete monopoly, however. Institutional economists offer an alternative definition of economics that does not assume scarcity at the outset. In what follows, we adopt the institutionalist's definition of economics as "the science of the social provisioning process" (Gruchy 1987, 4–7, 21). In institutional economics, scarcity is not assumed by definition, so abundance becomes a meaningful concept.

Adam Smith Plus Malthus, Ricardo, and Mill

We begin our intellectual history of abundance with the great optimist Adam Smith. However, we cannot avoid a digression on the great pessimist David Ricardo, nor can we skip over either the great moralist Thomas Malthus or the brilliant progressive John Stuart Mill. Smith, Ricardo, Malthus, and Mill are all grouped tightly together in the history of economic thought.

Adam Smith (1723–1790) is called the father of modern economics. He was Scottish and an optimistic promoter of the free market system. Although even he discussed the possibility of a distant stationary state, his famous book *An Inquiry into the Nature and Causes of the Wealth of Nations* was one of the first systematic attempts to explain the possibilities of economic growth (Smith [1776] 1937). Adam Smith's optimistic assessment was based on the increases in output stemming from specialization and division of labor. The only limit to the division of labor and, hence, the only limit to growth was the extent of the market. His argument was historically grounded, powerfully written, and easy to understand.

Smith saw three main benefits of specialization: (1) increases in the skill or dexterity of a worker performing the same task repeatedly, (2) the time saved by not shifting from one task to another, and (3) the possibility that a specialized worker might invent labor-saving machines. The combination of the three benefits of specialization resulted in greatly increased output per worker.

Smith described an economy of abundance: "It is the great multiplication of the productions of all the different arts, in consequence of the division of labour, which occasions, in a well-governed society, that universal opulence which extends itself to the lowest ranks of people" (Smith [1776] 1937, 9). Although he emphasized that the process of economic growth could be slowed or halted by monopolistic restrictions on trade or by other factors that might limit the extent of the market, he envisioned almost no limit to the increases in output that could result from specialization and division of labor. Furthermore, he believed that the increases in output should be widely distributed to include the poorest people. The economy he envisioned was clearly an economy of abundance, not an economy of scarcity.

Thomas Malthus (1766–1834) was English. He strongly opposed the optimism and egalitarianism of the French Revolution of 1789 and he disagreed with Adam Smith on the prospect of growth (Dugger 1990). He first published his famous *Essay on the Principle of Population* in 1798. In it, he countered Smith's optimism with the specter of overpopulation. Malthus argued that since the population could grow geometrically while the food supply grew only arithmetically, all ameliorative schemes of equality or redistribution to the poor were doomed to failure. As Mark Blaug points out, "Malthus always went out of his way to antagonize all those who believed in the amelioration of social conditions" (Blaug 1978, 69).

Adam Smith's insight regarding universal opulence was almost forgotten by economists after Malthus raised the issue of overpopulation. To make intellectual matters even worse, Englishman David Ricardo (1772–1823) continued the attack on economic abundance. His famous *Principles of Political Economy and Taxation* was first published in 1817. He provided an analytical framework for what he termed the "stationary state" (Ricardo [1817] 1963, 54) and what contemporary growth theorists now call the "steady state." Ricardo presented several analytically elegant arguments on why the economy would, at some point, inevitably reach the steady state. Only one of these arguments will be described here.

Ricardo, like Malthus, assumed that there was an inevitable tendency for the population to increase. For Ricardo, it was also obvious that land, especially arable land, was a finite resource. Ricardo assumed that the combination of an increase in population and a finite supply of fertile land must result in increased food prices: "As population increases, these necessaries will be constantly increasing in price" (Ricardo [1817] 1963, 49). Ricardo also assumed that rising food prices must mean an increase in wages. His logic on this point, called "The Iron Law of Wages," was simple and brutal. Because of the supply and demand for labor, wages were always at a subsistence level, barely high enough to keep workers and their families alive, and that is where wages stayed. If food prices decreased, children would be better fed because nominal wages could buy more food (real wages rose). So more children would live into adulthood, adding to the labor supply and driving real wages back down to a subsistence rate once again. If food prices increased, nominal wages would have to increase by the same proportion or the worker would "soon be totally deprived of subsistence" (49).

Ricardo is well known for arguing that the institution of land rent reduces profit and accumulation. He also assumed that at any given time, the output of the economy was fixed. If this were the case, any increase in wages could occur only by reducing the share of output going to profit. If profits fell, so would the incentive to invest. With little or no investment, capital accumulation would cease and the economy would enter the stationary state. When it arrived, there would be no possibility of an economy of abundance. But even the pessimistic Ricardo admitted that he thought the stationary state was "far distant" (54). Ricardo's assessment is consistent with that of more recent growth theorists such as Evsey Domar, who states, "And yet I fail to see any indications that the world is any closer now to a stationary state than it was, say, a hundred years ago" (Domar 1957, 14).

Englishman John Stuart Mill (1806–1873) wrote what became the standard economics textbook for many years. His *Principles of Political Economy*, first published in 1848, influenced many other late nineteenth-century economists. Mill supported liberty and the rights of women. More optimistic about the possibility of abundance than Ricardo, Mill

cited the "unlimited growth of man's power over nature," "greater security of property," "improved business capacities," and "the continual
growth of the principle and practice of cooperation" as reasons to expect
"an indefinite increase of capital and production" (Mill 1848, 211–214).
But, analytically, Mill could not quite abandon Ricardo's steady state.
In Mill's words, "We have now been led to recognize that this ultimate
goal [the steady state] is at all times near enough to be fully in view; that
we are always on the verge of it" (260). But Mill's steady state was a far
different thing than Ricardo's: "It is scarcely necessary to remark that a
stationary condition of capital and population implies no stationary state
of human improvement" (264).

Karl Marx

Karl Marx (1818–1883) was born in Prussia and became its most famous
son by promoting the working-class revolution from his exile in England. He is both the most hated and the most revered of all economists.
His most famous work, *The Communist Manifesto*, was first published
in 1848. He clearly recognized the significance of abundance. He lured
intellectuals away from the pessimism of Malthus and Ricardo and back
into thinking that abundance was possible. Marx was neither the first nor
the last of the great economists to recognize the possibility of abundance,
but the system of thought named after him is still a powerful alternative
to the belief in scarcity. Marx used the concept of surplus to formulate
his theory of exploitation. Extracted from the economy by the capitalist's
exploitation of the workers, the surplus reproduces the capitalist system
through capital accumulation. However, properly allocated to meet the
needs of society under socialism, the surplus could produce an economy
of abundance.

Marx differed significantly from Smith over the desirability of capitalism, and his thoughts on scarcity and abundance were complex. He
believed that modern technology was capable of producing an economy
of abundance, but could not do so under capitalism. The institutions
of capitalism that were woven into bourgeois society held back the
abundance that would otherwise exist. Those institutions included the
private ownership of the means of production (capital) and the hiring of
workers by capitalists in order to make a profit selling the goods they
made on the market. As Marx put it, "The conditions of bourgeois society
are too narrow to comprise the wealth created by them" (Marx [1848]

1988, 61). Marx and his followers developed several related lines of argument into a multifaceted theory of this contradiction in bourgeois society (Sherman 1991).

Thorstein Veblen Plus Paul Sweezy, Joseph Schumpeter, and John R. Commons

American economist and social critic Thorstein Veblen (1857–1929) emphasized the significance of abundance in his famous *Theory of the Leisure Class*, published in 1899. He is America's most creative economist. His influence is apparent in the works of Paul Sweezy, Clarence Ayres, Stuart Chase, and John Kenneth Galbraith. Veblen recognized that the modern industrial economy was very productive—"The mechanical industry of the new order is inordinately productive" (Veblen [1921] 1965, 8)—yet was always operating below, probably far below, its capacity to produce.

For Veblen, there were two important aspects of the modern economy: the machine process and business enterprise. Veblen argued that the machine process could be very productive because of the community's joint stock of knowledge and the state of the industrial arts. Under modern industrial conditions, it could be so productive that it overwhelmed the business enterprise's ability to sell everything it could produce (Veblen [1921] 1965). But business enterprise was another matter altogether. For Veblen, "the motive of business is pecuniary gain" (Veblen [1904] 1975, 16). This motive did not necessarily correspond to a smoothly functioning industrial system. Veblen recognized that it was the extraordinarily productive nature of the machine process that allowed business people to engage in the "conscientious withdrawal of efficiency." However, two aspects of the machine process were particularly important because they made the extraordinarily productive system also extraordinarily prone to derangement. The first aspect was the unavoidable interdependence of industries: "no plant or works would be a producer in the absence of all the rest" (Veblen [1919] 1964, 54). As a result, a disturbance in one plant or industry was likely to affect other industries. The second aspect of the machine process was "an unremitting requirement of quantitative precision and accuracy in the timing and ordering of industrial events" (Veblen [1904] 1975, 10).

In combination, these two characteristics imposed the need for "interstitial adjustments between the several sub-processes of industry"

(Veblen [1904] 1975, 21). Veblen argued that this adjustment process offered the business community the opportunity for pecuniary gain without contributing to increases in output. Quite the contrary, business could make a profit whether or not the industrial system was functioning smoothly. What Veblen called "free income" (income derived from intangible assets rather than a return for productivity) could be derived from patents, trade secrets, monopoly, or other legal devices designed to restrict output. In brief, for Veblen, the business community deliberately restricted output below what the industrial system was capable of producing. Business manipulation of the industrial system made it function poorly, made it go through unstable cycles of boom and bust. Because it was sabotaged by business, the economy of abundance was limited to a thin stratum of the community that Veblen described as the leisure class. Of course, even members of the leisure class did not really enjoy abundance. Instead, they pursued an irrational competition in conspicuous consumption (Veblen [1899] 1975).

Paul Sweezy (1910–2004) was the dean of independent Marxist thinkers in the United States for nearly half a century (O'Hara and Sherman 2004). Sweezy's most famous book, *Monopoly Capital*, was written with Paul Baran and published in 1966. Sweezy emphasized the importance of the economic surplus. In his treatment, the absorption of the rapidly growing economic surplus becomes an important contradiction of modern capitalism. The modern capitalist economy has become so incredibly productive that its capacity to produce outpaces its capacity to absorb production. Modern capitalism is faced with a perpetually deepening realization crisis because it produces faster than it can sell. It can produce fully but it cannot realize a profit at full production, so it falls into crisis. In spite of considerable limitation of competition through consolidation and monopolization, the crisis has to be met with frenzied sales efforts on the part of the private capitalists and with frenzied efforts to stimulate the economy on the part of the public authorities.

Veblen's leisure class, in its stimulation of conspicuous consumption, plays a crucial role in the absorption of the surplus. The example of the leisure class spurs the underlying population (everyone else who has to work because they are not financially independent) to strive for more and more conspicuous consumption of their own. Workers try to surpass the consumption achieved by their neighbors and coworkers. No one can cease the effort to get ahead in the modern rat race; an orgy of waste and invidious behavior is required to keep up with the always rising competitive level. The scramble is wildly irrational, but does help absorb the incredible capacity of the economy to produce. If the surplus is not absorbed, unemployment will soar. But too much unemployment cannot be allowed lest it foster revolt (remember Marx). So the rat race must run full tilt, and abundance will stay forever outside people's grasp. People will never have enough because they cannot all surpass their neighbors. Workers must push others down in order to thrust themselves above. At best, people are trapped in what economists call a zero-sum game (more about this later). My gain is your loss. The only way out of this Veblenian nightmare, Sweezy argued, is a conversion to democratic socialism (Baran and Sweezy 1966).

Joseph Schumpeter (1883–1950) was born in Austria but enjoyed an illustrious career at Harvard. His *Capitalism, Socialism, and Democracy* was first published in 1942. He is one of the most complicated of all economists. A staunch supporter of Paul Sweezy while both were at Harvard, he was an anti-Marxist Marxist. Schumpeter was a close student of Marx whose analysis of capitalism led him to agree with Marx's conclusion that capitalism was doomed. However, unlike Marx, who cheered on the demise of capitalism, Schumpeter lamented its demise. Marx applied positive adjectives where Schumpeter applied negative ones. Schumpeter's heavy emphasis on sociological and political factors in economics clearly placed him close to Veblen, whom he disdained. Schumpeter was profoundly conservative. Yet he expressed the possibility of abundance very clearly and directly: "If capitalism repeated its past performance for another half-century starting with 1928, this would do away with anything that according to present standards could be called poverty, even in the lowest strata of the population, pathological cases alone excepted" (Schumpeter [1942] 1950, 66). The basis of Schumpeter's claim rested on the best estimates at the time that the U.S. economy had been growing at about 2 percent per year in real terms for the previous half century. If such a growth rate could be continued for another fifty years, Schumpeter claimed that it would provide enough total output that "ample provision for the unemployed in particular would not only be tolerable, but a light burden" (69). Although Schumpeter disliked the waste of resources resulting from unemployment, he clearly thought society could provide for the unemployed even if the unemployment rate was 10 percent. The usually cautious and analytical Schumpeter went further: "It is easy to see that all the desiderata that have so far been espoused by any social reformers, practically without exception, even including the greater part of the cranks either would be fulfilled automatically or could be filled without significant interference with the capitalist process" (69).

What is especially remarkable about Schumpeter's claims is that the U.S. economy performed better than his lofty expectations. Between 1928 and 1978, U.S. real gross domestic product (GDP) grew by 3.7 percent per year rather than the 2 percent per year assumed by Schumpeter. Indeed, per capita real GDP increased by 2.4 percent per year during this time period. No, these years were not particularly strange years. And, yes, these years included the Great Depression of the 1930s and the alleged stagnation of the 1970s! Schumpeter, however, was no fool. He understood well that historical growth rates did not necessarily imply future growth rates.

John R. Commons (1867–1945) was an American economist who gave considerable thought to abundance. Along with Thorstein Veblen, he was the cofounder of institutional economics. His most famous book was *Institutional Economics*, first published in 1934. He realized that abundance was a profound threat to the status quo. According to Commons, the industrial revolution divided economic history into three periods—the scarcity, abundance, and stabilization periods. The scarcity period, before the conquest of abundance made possible by the industrial revolution, was characterized by the ages-old problem, caused by unproductive technology, of not enough to go around. The abundance period was the accidental and temporary outbreak of abundance brought on by the industrial revolution; this era was characterized by unprecedented increases in production caused by the new industrial technology. The stabilization period was the collective response to the threat of abundance after the industrial revolution. The industrial revolution raised per capita output so much that it threatened to destroy the relations of power and privilege that were embedded in the industrializing economies. The destruction was being wrought by overproduction, cutthroat pricing, and grinding deflation, which were promoting cycles of widespread financial collapse punctuated by brief periods of recovery. The ghost of Marx seemed to lurk just around the corner of the next financial collapse.

Commons developed his own thoughts into a unique analytical system. Nevertheless, his view of these three periods relates quite easily to the emphasis Veblen placed on the productive power of industrial technology and to the emphasis Baran and Sweezy placed on the rise of monopoly capitalism. The powerful new technology, Commons believed, drove prices down so quickly that the financial values on which the system of money and credit rested were destroyed. To protect themselves against cutthroat pricing, individual capitalists formed great combinations, first as trusts and then as huge corporations. The huge combinations ushered in a new era of stabilized prices. This era was labeled monopoly capitalism by Sweezy and Baran. Commons, explaining the same broad range of problems, called it the era of stabilization. It was based on an inappropriate collective response to industrial abundance. Instead of sharing abundance with everyone and destroying power and privilege in the process, Veblen's vested interests were protected by stabilizing a system that kept abundance from becoming widespread.

Commons called the system bankers capitalism. It stabilized the price system on which bank credit rested, but also kept abundance from accidentally breaking out. This understanding of abundance as a threat to the status quo was one of the most profound contributions made by John R. Commons. It is totally ignored to this day by his followers in transaction cost economics and is often overlooked by institutional economists as well (Commons 1934, 748–875).

John Maynard Keynes, Plus Stuart Chase, Clarence Ayres, Walt Rostow, John Kenneth Galbraith, and Amartya Sen

Englishman John Maynard Keynes (1883–1946) was the most famous economist of the twentieth century. Keynes is best known for *The General Theory of Employment, Interest, and Money*, published in 1936 during the Great Depression. Keynes offered an alternative to the classical assumption that full-employment equilibrium is the natural state of a capitalist economy. Instead, Keynes suggested the possibility of a less than full-employment equilibrium. For more than a generation, Keynes's *General Theory* dominated discussions of macroeconomic policy.

Keynes also had a great deal to say about future economic conditions, including the possibility of economic abundance. He set out his views on abundance in an essay titled "Economic Possibilities for Our Grandchildren." Writing at the beginning of the Great Depression when there was a "bad attack of economic pessimism," Keynes (1963, 358) argued that a perspective based on the long run justified economic optimism. In Keynes's view, real economic progress started only about the sixteenth or seventeenth century. By the early twentieth century, the effects of technological progress and capital accumulation were clearly visible. Keynes suggested that the "miracle" of compound interest affected both technical progress and capital accumulation. The result had been an eightfold increase in per capita living standards in the previous hundred years (1830–1930). Keynes explained that these trends were likely to continue. As a result, in another hundred years the world's peoples could fall into "the lap of economic abundance" (368). Keynes concluded that, "assuming no important wars and no important increase in population, the economic problem may be solved, or be at least within sight of solution, within a hundred years. This means that the economic problem is not—if we look into the future—the permanent problem of the human race" (365–366).

American Stuart Chase (1888–1985) was an engineer and accountant rather than an economist, but he wrote numerous articles and books on economics. Chase was profoundly influenced by Thorstein Veblen. Chase's book *The Economy of Abundance* is an eloquent, if not sophisticated, treatment of the topic. According to Chase, "The Economy of Abundance is self defined. It means an economic condition where an abundance of material goods can be produced for the entire population of a given community, a condition never obtaining anywhere until the last few years" (1934, 10).

Ultimately, Chase's argument that the economy of abundance is attainable is based on the increasing use of inanimate energy. Comparing the energy resources available to the typical American in 1830 and in 1930, he concluded that American workers in 1930 had about forty times as much energy to do their work as did their 1830 counterparts. Chase's examination of energy resources, the trend of technology, and the structure of the economy led him to conclude that future workers would have much more energy per worker and thus be able to do much more work.

The second aspect of Chase's argument demonstrates how much he was influenced by Veblen. Output was constrained not by the availability of energy resources, other resources, or technology, but by wasteful inefficiency in many forms. Inefficiency, and a reduction in useful output, occurs because the economy is wasting energy producing the wrong kinds of consumer goods—goods designed to satisfy the desires of consumers for status or invidious comparison. Chase, like Veblen, was also impressed by what he thought were the wasteful activities of business enterprise.

Clarence Ayres (1891–1972) constructed a theory of economic development based in part on Thorstein Veblen and John Dewey. His most famous book was *The Theory of Economic Progress*, published in 1944. Ayres explicitly recognized the possibility of abundance: "No one any longer doubts the physical and technological possibility of a world-wide economy of abundance" ([1944] 1962, 232). Ayres analyzed in detail the process that could lead to abundance.

For Ayres, two forces determined the path of progress. "Thus what happens to any society is determined jointly by the forward urging of its technology and the backward pressure of its ceremonial system" (ix). The ceremonial system was the set of institutionalized beliefs that was backward-oriented and resisted new ways of thinking and doing. Opposed to it was the dynamic force of technology, defined broadly. Ayres said that technology "must be understood to include all human activities involving the use of tools—all sorts of tools" (vii). Ayres also presented a tool-combination theory of technological development:

> But all inventions and discoveries result from the combining of hitherto separate tools, instruments, materials and the like. These are capable of combination by virtue of their physical existence. The combining is of course performed by man, and especially by bright and restless men. But no one ever made a combination without there being something to combine. Furthermore, the more there is to combine in any given situation the more likely inventions and discoveries become—unless the inveterate restlessness of human hands and brains is severely curbed. (vii–viii)

For Ayres, the restraint on the possibility of progress was not the physical limitations of a finite world, but ceremonial behavior. This kind of behavior is determined by the institutional structure of a community. In Ayres's words, "This system of behavior is static and inhibitory of change" (viii). Ayres was not certain that the dynamic force of improving technology would succeed in the face of institutional resistance to change: "What is to be the outcome of the confrontation of the irresistible force of the technological process by the seemingly immovable obstacle of a population that is vast and dense and saturated with a pre-industrial culture? . . . We do not know" (xx–xxi). But Ayres did know that the institutional structure was holding back technological capabilities.

Walt Rostow (1916–2003) was an American economic historian and adviser to presidents John Kennedy and Lyndon Johnson. He finished up his long career teaching economics and history at the University of Texas. Rostow is widely known for his work on the process of economic development. His most famous book was *The Stages of Economic Growth*, published in 1960. Rostow's stages theory of development began with a simple taxonomy: "It is possible to identify all societies, in their economic dimension, as lying within one of five categories: the traditional society, the pre-conditions for take-off, the take-off, the drive to maturity, and the age of high mass consumption" (1960, 4). According to Rostow, the traditional society is characterized by mass poverty and almost no investment or technological change. The preconditions for take-off occur when an outside force (such as invasion by a colonial power) disturbs the traditional equilibrium. In this stage, Rostow postulated the beginnings of a shift from agriculture to other industries. The take-off occurs when investment increases from 5 to 10 percent of GDP. The drive to maturity occurs when "a society has effectively applied the range of (then) modern technology to the bulk of its resources" (59). The age of high mass consumption occurs after the drive to maturity has produced a level of income high enough that the major concerns of society can be shifted away from further increases in real income to other purposes. In other words, the age of high mass consumption was Rostow's definition of the economy of abundance.

Rostow regarded the five stages as absolutes. All societies would inevitably pass through all five stages. Occasionally, there might be a chance to speed up the process (e.g., by an advanced nation invading a traditional society and shocking it out of its complacency or by a rich nation providing the funds necessary to make the transition from the preconditions stage to the take-off stage), but such chances did not alter Rostow's basic conclusion that the economy of abundance was eventually going to happen for all nations. His optimism was unshakable.

John Kenneth Galbraith (1908–2006) was one of the most widely read economists of the last half of the twentieth century. He published *The Affluent Society* in 1958. Galbraith followed in the intellectual tradition of abundance established by Marx, Veblen, and Keynes. To Galbraith, however, abundance was not something achievable in the future. Galbraith believed that it had already arrived. As he stated in his conclusion to *The Affluent Society*, "To furnish a barren room is one thing. To continue to crowd in furniture until the foundation buckles is quite another. To have failed to solve the problem of producing goods would have been to continue man in his oldest and most grievous misfortune. But to fail to see that we have solved it, and to fail to proceed thence to the next task, would be fully as tragic" (1969, 268).

Indian intellectual Amartya K. Sen (1933–) won the 1998 Nobel Prize in Economics. He discusses what we have called the economics of abundance in many of his works. His recognition of the economy of abundance is straightforward: "We live in a world of unprecedented opulence, of a kind that would have been hard even to imagine a century or two ago" (1999, xi). Now at Harvard, he published his influential *Development as Freedom* in 1999. For Sen, the capacity to produce is not the central question. Development is the central issue. Sen defines development in terms of various freedoms that may or may not coincide with increased output. These include the right to a long and healthy life; the absence of discrimination, particularly against women; the right to live in a healthy environment; and the right to political freedoms. Sen notes, "Development requires the removal of major sources of unfreedom: poverty as well as tyranny, poor economic opportunities as well as systematic social deprivation, neglect of public facilities as well as intolerance or overactivity of repressive states" (3).

Three More Thinkers: R.H. Tawney, John A. Hobson, and Erich Zimmermann

The thoughts of an Englishman from India (Tawney), an English economic heretic (Hobson), and a geographer from Germany by way of Texas (Zimmermann) round out our selective intellectual history of abundance. These three are not easily placed among the four groups discussed so far, but even a selective treatment of our subject must discuss their contributions.

R.H. Tawney (1880–1962) was born in Calcutta and became influential in the United Kingdom after World War I, when he enjoyed a distinguished career at the London School of Economics. Nevertheless, his ideas were rejected by neoclassical economists. According to his book *The Acquisitive Society*, published in 1920, industrial efficiency required that the avarice of the property owner be replaced by the professional pride, personal zeal, and trained proficiency of the worker. Tawney's view was quite similar to Veblen's view in *The Engineers and the Price System*. Tawney believed that the economy of abundance required converting industry into a profession that would serve the public good through pursuing professional goals instead of personal profit. He urged the replacement of property with profession. He also insisted that new values must be promoted. Society, Tawney argued, "must persuade its members to renounce the opportunity of gains which accrue without any corresponding service, because the struggle for them keeps the whole community in a fever. It must so organize industry that the instrumental character of economic activity is emphasized by its subordination to the social purpose for which it is carried on" ([1920] 1948, 184).

John A. Hobson (1858–1940) greatly admired Veblen. For Hobson, the central problem of economic life was maldistribution, not scarcity; he argued that underconsumption due to the maldistribution of income held back the achievement of abundance. His most famous book, *Imperialism*, was first published in 1902. Hobson largely was ignored by neoclassical economists. After all, in the textbooks a market economy cannot suffer from underconsumption, but it does suffer from scarcity. Hobson disagreed, arguing that underconsumption and unemployment kept market economies far below their productive potential and led to economic inequality within nations and to economic imperialism between nations. Hobson's 1976 autobiography, *Confessions of an Economic Heretic*, provides a lively introduction to his ideas.

When reinforced by Keynesian analysis, Hobson's insight exposes the lack of aggregate demand that constrains the production of all market economies. Outside of episodes of prolonged mobilization for the conduct of total war, full employment and full production are never achieved. Hobson understood and Keynes explained that the constraint that truly limits the human community is inadequate aggregate demand, not scarcity. With Keynes and Hobson, the intellectual history of abundance makes a complete circle by returning to the insight of Adam Smith. Although he may have worried about the distant stationary state, it was still Smith who argued that the only limit to the universal opulence promised by his system of natural liberty was the extent of the market. Today, we understand that to mean the insufficiency of aggregate demand.

However, scarcity supporters have another argument. There is still the Malthusian problem in modern form: there is only a certain amount of any natural resource and that amount limits economic growth. The amount of useful resources like copper or fossil fuel is limited, and the amount of storage space available for toxic items like carbon dioxide or mercury is limited. Eventually the world will run out of useful natural resources or of storage space, making abundance impossible. Even if societies removed the aggregate demand constraint and achieved full employment and full production, limited natural resources would ultimately restore scarcity.

Resource scarcity is where the work of Erich Zimmermann becomes important. Zimmermann's theory of resources is an antidote to the modern Malthusian argument. Unfortunately, Zimmermann had little influence on the economics profession. Zimmermann (1888–1961) was born in Mainz, Germany. He taught for years at the University of Texas. His most famous book, the textbook *World Resources and Industries*, was first published in 1933; it was so popular that an enlarged version of it was published in 1951. But it has been largely forgotten.

Zimmermann taught that resources are functional rather than natural (Zimmermann 1951; Hunker 1964). True enough, he emphasized, there is only a limited amount of resources such as coal or crude oil in the earth's crust. The amount in existence is given by nature and is limited by nature. However, the human ability to utilize any particular form of energy is a function of human culture and can change when culture changes. For example, the ability to move people and goods about using oil is a function of the culture's joint stock of knowledge, of its technology. Societies can be advanced enough to use huge tankers, pipelines, railroads, buses, subways, mass transit of all forms, agreeing on international protocols and careful urban planning. Or people can remain culturally primitive and rely on individual trucks, freighters, and private sport utility vehicles to move themselves and their things around within a legal framework of unbridled self-interest. Of course, people could even replace oil with something else. The crucial or limiting factor is an aspect of culture, not nature, and culture evolves. (Nature does, too.)

Differences Among These Abundance Economists

The recognition that abundance is possible, or that it is already here, has made for some strange bedfellows. Jeffrey D. Sachs, for example, is a globetrotting economist who advises nations on how to apply American ideas to develop their economies. His advice is usually heavily loaded with free market sermons. Nevertheless, his recent book, *The End of Poverty*, puts Sachs in bed with abundance economists. Up to this point, we may have left the reader with the false impression that the economists we discussed are in substantial agreement on additional issues in economics. Nothing could be further from the facts in the case. The economists we have discussed do share the recognition that abundance is possible, but they share little else.

A few reminders are in order. Walt Rostow's theory of predetermined stages is in stark disagreement with Thorstein Veblen's theory of open-ended social evolution. John Hobson's theory of underconsumption is a far cry from sophisticated Keynesian theory. Marx and his followers disagree sharply with Veblen and his followers over the labor theory of value. Schumpeter and Ayres disagree sharply over the significance of the entrepreneur in the process of technological progress. Many other disagreements could also be cited to warn against taking the argument in this chapter beyond the fact that these economists recognized the possibility of abundance and said so. That fact is important, but should not be used to argue that these economists shared much else.

Conclusion

Regardless of their many differences, a significant number of economists have taught that an economy of abundance is already here or is within the grasp of the human community. The economic problem of not enough to go around can be solved. There is no valid reason for the economics of absolute scarcity to continue monopolizing the study of economics. The economics of abundance should be included as well in a modern economics curriculum. Students deserve it. Truth demands it. With this book, we start the correction of the imbalance between scarcity and abundance in the economics curriculum. The correction is long overdue.

$$\boxed{2}$$

The Meaning of Abundance

Abundance and Technology

To individuals, economic abundance means the wherewithal to participate fully in all community activities and to share in all community values involved in the social provisioning process. Remember that abundance does not mean free goods for everybody. That would be absolute abundance and it is impossible. Every person cannot have everything. This is just as impossible as everyone having more than everyone else. The impossible is not meaningful. When we discuss abundance, we mean full access to the knowledge, skills, tools, and materials used in the community. Abundance is relative, not absolute. Abundance is relative to the technological level of the community. The meaning of abundance changes as technology changes. It means one thing in the Stone Age, another in the Space Age.

To Stone Age hunters, abundance meant a good shelter from the snow, wind, and sun. It meant enough animals to hunt and enough raw materials and tools to make the stone-tipped arrows and spears used to hunt them. It meant enough useful plants and herbs to gather and the knowledge needed to identify them. It meant also the tools, skills, and knowledge to make animal carcasses and plants into nourishing meals and to make animal skins into warm clothing. It meant knowledge of fire, wood, and other Stone Age materials and implements. Since Stone Age people were not Robinson Crusoes, living isolated and alone, abundance also meant living in a vibrant community of people willing to share skills and tools and to bear the collective burdens of life—to work with and care for each other, to raise and teach children. (A number of works flesh out the details needed for a thorough understanding of the issues just touched upon here. See Childe 1942; Diamond 1997, 2005; Forde 1963; Sherman 2006.)

Abundance to the Space Age office worker has the same general meaning—sufficient access to the materials, skills, and tools used by the community. Of course, the specifics are different because the technology of the Space Age is very different from that of the Stone Age. Where the Stone Age hunter needed access to the stone and wood required for making arrows and spears, the Space Age office worker needs access to the personal computer, the Internet, and the materials required for making reports and presentations. Stone Age hunters needed to be taught how to hunt the woolly mammoth, while Space Age office workers need to be taught how to use the Internet and spreadsheet programs. Stone Age hunters were taught the skills they needed by family members and community elders; Space Age office workers participate in years of formal education, earn certificates and degrees, and have their skills graded by a whole army of teachers and testing service workers.

In sum, to enjoy abundance, mammoth hunters had to have the knowledge, tools, skills, materials, and human support networks appropriate to the level of technology used by their community of mammoth hunters. Office workers have to have the knowledge, tools, skills, materials, and human support networks appropriate to the level of technology used by their community of office workers. Office workers also have to have access to far more sophisticated community learning structures than hunters. They each need one more thing. The Stone Age hunter needed access to a hunting ground where game could be had. The Space Age worker needs access to a job where income can be earned.

Technology is the key to abundance. Technology is the knowledge of how to do things. Knowing how to do things always involves tools, skills, and human networks provided by an ongoing community. Driving a car is an example of technology at work. You need a tool—the car—and you need the special experience and training required to operate it safely. You buy the car from the internationally organized automobile industry that is part of the ongoing community of the modern world. You get the money to buy the car from your job or your bank. You get the skill from driver's training class at school and from your parents, also parts of the ongoing community of the modern world. You pass a driving test before the community gives you a driver's license. You drive the car on a system of streets and highways provided by the community, and you follow a set of rules determined and enforced by a network of safety and law enforcement agencies within the community. If you live in the United Kingdom, you drive on the left; if you live in the United States, you drive on the right. If you pay for your car, register it properly, and follow the rules of the road, you can enjoy driving unhindered. If you drive too fast, you get a speeding ticket. If you drink a six-pack of beer and drive your car, you go to jail. If you stole the car in the first place, you go to jail.

You could not possibly drive a car unless you have a share in the joint stock of knowledge, tools, and skills passed on to succeeding genera-tions by the community through the learning processes it supports (Ayres [1944] 1962; Conner 2005). The community provides the reservoirs needed to hold the joint stock of knowledge and provides the means of dispensing, testing, and expanding it. For these purposes, communities support libraries, museums, special archives, research institutes, seminars, schools, families, apprenticeship programs, job training programs, and colleges and universities of all kinds. Communities also provide CDs, DVDs, tapes, books, magazines, journals, newspapers, television and radio broadcasts, films, commercial and community theaters, ballet, opera, concerts, art exhibits, the Internet, lobbyists, televangelists, spe-cial interest groups, ministries of propaganda, and advertising agencies. Preserving and distributing the community's joint stock of knowledge are vital to the modern community. Abundance is served by the widest possible distribution and the most complete possible preservation of the existing stock of knowledge.

Enlarging the joint stock is vital to a progressive community, a com-munity that wants to learn and do more. Members of the community add to this stock by discovering or inventing new ways of doing things, new things to do, and new ways of doing old things better. Again, driving a car provides an example. We added fuel injection to the carburetion system. The motor ran better. We added power steering and power brakes. The car handled better. We put in an automatic transmission. The driver controlled the vehicle better. We added air conditioning. The driver was more comfortable. We replaced regular with safety glass in the windows. Driver injuries declined. We added seatbelts and air bags. Fatalities de-clined. We replaced or supplemented parental teaching of driving skills with formal classes in school. Driver skills improved. Because of the cumulative impact of these discoveries and inventions, drivers of the early cars would hardly recognize the technological marvels that we drive today and the skill we use to drive them.

Technological advance is communal, not individual. Although students are taught to attribute discoveries and inventions to great men—the invention of the light bulb to Thomas Edison, the European discovery of North America to Leif Eriksson—it was the community's joint stock of knowledge that led to the breakthrough. Edison would never have invented the light bulb if he had been a member of Leif Eriksson's community, since the Vikings knew nothing about electricity. The same is true for Leif Eriksson and the European discovery of America (the Amerindians knew about it all along). If he had been living during the time of Alexander the Great, he could never have reached the New World with the shipbuilding and sailing technology of the classical Greeks. The North Atlantic would have been an impossible barrier. New discoveries and inventions may be made by particular people, who frequently try to claim as much credit for themselves as they can, but those particular men and women always begin with the joint stock stored up and handed down to them by their communities.

Individuals may try to get as much as possible for themselves out of the discovery or invention by using the legal and organizational tools provided them by their community. In the modern community they use the corporate form of business, the law firm, the tax exemption, the patent, copyright, and trademark, the court system, the stock market, the bank, the trust agreement, the North American Free Trade Agreement, the International Monetary Fund, the World Bank, and the World Trade Organization, along with many other community-provided tools of acquisition. Without these tools, individual inventors and discoverers would reap little from their work. Although they may claim to be self-made, they are not. Rather, they are community-made.

Although writers are not generally considered as inventors, they do "invent" their books. In the nineteenth century, English writer Charles Dickens created some of the greatest novels of the English language. But he never earned a penny in royalties for the millions of copies of his books that were printed and sold in the United States. He bitterly protested the fact, but since the U.S. government did not enforce foreign copyrights during his lifetime, his protests yielded him nothing. Nonetheless, this did not stop him from making his wonderful contribution to English literature.

Without the community's joint stock of knowledge, inventors and discoverers would have nothing to invent or discover with in the first place. Not only does the community provide the knowledge needed to make new inventions and discoveries; the community also provides the way to collect money for making them (Veblen [1904] 1975). But this does not mean that invention would stop. Dickens did not stop writing *A Tale of Two Cities* halfway through because he did not receive royalties from the U.S. sale of his earlier novels. Shakespeare wrote *Hamlet* without the benefit of effective copyright. The Romans invented concrete without patent protection. The alphabet has never been patented.

Whether or not enriched by patents, copyrights, or trademarks, people make their own new technology, but always with the technology handed down to them from their communities as the starting point. Then, their addition to the joint stock serves as the new starting point for the next generation. They stand on the shoulders of those who came before them. The next generation will stand on their shoulders. And so it will continue, unless humanity ends the cumulative process by blowing itself to hell—absent the appropriate community guidance, a distinct possibility. (Further discussion of technological progress is in Ayres [1944] 1962 and Conner 2005.)

Stone Age technology could support a certain amount of meat, fur clothing, shelter, and so forth for each member or household of the community. Privy to the community's knowledge, hunters could produce a life of Stone Age abundance; deprived of it, they could not. People denied the knowledge would be unable to feed, clothe, or shelter themselves or anyone else. Such a deprived individual would have been a helpless wretch back in the Stone Age. And such a deprived individual would also be a helpless wretch in the Space Age. Any person, in any age, who is deprived of access to the community's stock of knowledge, is doomed to a wretched existence—the experience of scarcity. Scarcity is the opposite of abundance and now you know its principal cause.

Technological progress lifts the level of abundance that the community can support among its members. The level is much higher in the Space Age than it was in the Stone Age. Access in the Space Age requires more than in the Stone Age: education in a modern school system, a job that pays an adequate income, treatment (both restorative and preventive) in an advanced health care system, the nutrition made possible by a modern agricultural and food-processing system, the clothing made possible by a modern textile system, housing in safe and sanitary neighborhoods, and more. Denied access, a member of the Space Age community reverts back to being a helpless wretch, unable to participate in the production of abundance.

Abundance requires and provides the full participation of the members of the community in the technology of the community. Abundance, meaning access for all and participation of all, enables community members to become far more than miserable wretches. Furthermore, the withholding of the community's technology from any one of its members is the denial of abundance. It pushes the denied members of the community below their potential, and if all are not working up to potential, the community itself is weakened. The potential production of those denied access to the joint stock is lost to the community.

Access to the community's joint stock of knowledge in the Space Age requires something new as opposed to the Stone Age. Stone Age hunters did not have jobs in the sense that people do today. They did not work for money and they were not employees. They did not even use modern money. In the Space Age, however, access to the community's joint stock requires having an income, an ability to pay. No money, no honey. Most people in the Space Age get money for their honey by finding a job, by becoming an employee. So understanding abundance in the Space Age requires not only understanding the growth and distribution of technology, but also the growth and distribution of jobs and income. Who gets the jobs and what do the jobs pay? Who fails to get a job and what do they lose? Why?

Abundance and Equality

Abundance is not only a technological, but also a distributional phenomenon. Abundance is linked, unavoidably, to equality. Abundance and equality are linked together through full access to and use of the community's joint stock of knowledge. The linkage is two-sided. On one side, the negative side, both abundance and equality are denied, simultaneously, when some members of the community do not obtain full access to the community's joint stock of knowledge. On the other side, the positive side, both abundance and equality are affirmed, simultaneously, when everyone does obtain full access.

Scarcity and Inequality

The conventional wisdom about inequality is wrong. Many people believe that being helpful to the poor and the unemployed is misguided; it only coddles them, making them weak and dependent on continued handouts. Many people have been taught that being softhearted is wrongheaded. That is not true. Providing family support services and wide ranges of schools and employment programs to ensure full access to everyone is more than charitable and kind. It is smart. Participating people are productive. Nonparticipating people are not. On this point, being kind is also being smart because helping people participate in the social provisioning process makes them productive.

A concrete example will illustrate this fundamental point. In the state of Oklahoma, the funding of public schools ranks among the lowest of all the fifty states in the United States. Many young people in Oklahoma fail to get the kind of education required to become employed in today's Space Age economy. Health care and family support services are also inadequate. So Oklahoma lags behind many of the other states in employment, income, and production. The lag represents the economic cost of failing to provide full access to the community's joint stock of knowledge. The abundance and full access that could be enjoyed are not. Instead, Oklahomans suffer from unnecessary ignorance, poor health, weak families, low productivity, and scarcity (Maril 2000).

The problem does not stop with Oklahoma. The United States is the most powerful nation-state in the world, capable of waging devastating war against anyone, anywhere, anytime. Yet, throughout the nation, millions of school-age children still have inadequate schools, health care, nutrition, and family support due to racial, gender, ethnic, and economic discrimination—also due to sheer neglect. Millions are left out (www. childrensdefensefund.org.). These children will suffer scarcity and poverty. Their plight as adults will perpetuate gross inequality and low worker productivity as well as low workforce participation in the richest and most powerful nation in the world.

Communities also can fail to provide job programs for everyone. Oklahoma fails there too, as does the entire United States. Important work is not being done. Millions are unemployed while global warming continues, virtually ignored. The richest and most powerful nation in the world fails to put its unemployed to work on reducing global warming. It fails to match the millions without jobs to the millions of jobs that need to be done, not just to combat global warming. Fire and police protection are inadequate all across the country. Ambulance service and emergency care are difficult to obtain in wide areas of rural America. Traffic jams and commuting times get longer and longer in cities, burning up time and carbon-based fuel. The country certainly could use some road work, bridge work, mass transit work, and environmental work, not to mention the need for more teachers, nurses, physicians, dentists, and other care providers, as well as more and better schools, day care centers, hospitals, assisted living facilities, nursing homes, hospices, drug rehabilitation programs, and battered spouse shelters. Municipal water treatment plants could use some attention, as could community recreation facilities, senior citizen centers, and veterans' hospitals.

In 1996, the United States canceled its primary federal program for supporting indigent families. The old program was Aid to Families with Dependent Children (AFDC). The new program is called Temporary Assistance to Needy Families (TANF). President Bill Clinton's administration claimed to "end welfare" by replacing AFDC with a far more restrictive program of federal grants to individual states. "Welfare," in the American conventional wisdom, was antifamily. Welfare made families dependent on the government and unable to fend for themselves. Welfare was supposed to be a kind of addiction. The sooner the addicts got off the drug, the sooner they would recover their dignity and their ability to find a job and fend for themselves. Only then could their family be on the road to recovery. At least that was how the "end welfare" supporters sold their policy.

After AFDC was eliminated, each state was freed to administer its own program, within very broad federal guidelines and financed by very restricted federal grants. As a result, in the late 1990s many poor families with small children either lost all their government support or suffered major cuts in their benefits. What the "end to welfare" actually accomplished was not a strengthening of the family. It was a creation of scarcity for those whose benefits were slashed and who were unable to find good jobs. (Further discussion and empirical analysis is in Widerquist, Lewis, and Pressman 2005.)

The United States seems to be better at exclusion than inclusion. Its government keeps many people from using the joint stock of knowledge. Examples will help. The United States attempts to keep illegal aliens from crossing its borders. Many who cross over would like to get jobs in the United States. They would like their children to go to U.S. schools across the border. Many of the adults would gladly participate in vocational training programs that lead to good jobs. They would love to join the U.S. community. So, at considerable risk, they sneak across the border to work and study. The United States spends billions of dollars chasing them down, rounding them up, sorting them out, and shipping them back. The problem is improperly framed by saying that illegal alien workers take jobs from U.S. citizens. They probably do. The problem, properly framed, is that the U.S. job pool does not grow fast enough to accommodate everyone who is willing to work—even though there is lots of work that goes undone. Both the U.S. and the global job pools are not growing fast enough.

Successful exclusion is the equivalent of a community intentionally cutting off its right hand. On the other hand, unsuccessful inclusion is the equivalent of a community accidentally smashing the thumb on its remaining hand. Both are costly because both generate inequality and scarcity. This insight is profoundly important. We will elaborate on it at length throughout the following chapters. Inequality and scarcity are not natural; that is, they are not an inherent part of the world. They are caused either by a community recklessly smashing its thumb—failing to include everyone in the use of the joint stock of knowledge, or by a community intentionally chopping off its hand—succeeding in excluding those deemed to be undeserving from using the community's joint stock.

Another example will help. El Paso, Texas, is located in a beautiful area, with the Rio Grande flowing between it and Ciudad Juárez, Mexico. The climate is dry and mild in the winter, dry and hot in the summer. The growing season is long. Beautiful mountains rim much of the city. Human communities have inhabited the area for thousands of years, providing those with the skills and the knowledge of irrigation and agriculture the opportunity of raising fine crops of corn, beans, and peppers. The area is also rich in copper and other minerals. Significant oil and natural gas fields are nearby; the coal at Piedras Negras is not far away. Even better, the sun shines almost every day, providing enormous potential for solar power, and numerous mountain and ridge locations are ideal for wind farms. Today, multicultural El Paso has about 400,000 residents over the age of twenty-five. However, about 150,000 of them have not completed high school. In the Space Age, most of those 150,000 people are condemned to a life of poverty. They will never be the beneficiaries of the country's high-tech economy. These worthy citizens of El Paso are denied access to the technology of the Space Age. They have been sorted out of the good life by a faulty educational system. Their personal loss is also a social loss to the city of El Paso, to the state of Texas, and to the United States of America because the rest of the citizens are deprived of these workers' full potential in the production of goods and performance of services. This loss does not include the lost potential of hundreds of thousands of hardworking folks right across the border in Ciudad Juárez.

The Importance of Policy

All communities make policies that influence how things are done. Such decisions do not just spontaneously emerge. Human beings decide what to do about their problems. They make choices. They seldom just submit to fate. In the Space Age they decide on economic policy, educational policy, foreign policy, environmental policy, immigration policy, and much else. The policies they implement affect all sorts of things, including access to and use of the joint stock of knowledge and skills.

Stone Age communities also made policies, although their methods seem quite informal to modern peoples, and many of their policies affected the access to and use of their joint stock. Use of the various hunting and gathering grounds had to be arranged and taught in conjunction with competing or cooperating communities (tribes or clans). Hunting and gathering policies, when followed regularly, became the established ways of doing things. They became what each community expected of the other. There were policies giving each tribe of hunters and gatherers particular territorial rights. Policy decisions also assigned individual members of the community particular roles to play within the group. When followed regularly, these assignments became the traditional ways of doing things. They evolved into institutions, but they always started out as human decisions, as policies.

Men frequently were assigned or assumed (which amounts to the same thing) the easier task of hunting, perhaps because they were considered the weaker sex or perhaps because they were lazy. Women frequently were assigned or assumed the harder work of gathering plants and useful materials while taking care of the infants and the infirm and preparing the food, perhaps because they were considered the stronger sex or because they were industrious. Whatever the reason for the original decisions, human roles were institutionalized by human choices and policies, not by the operation of forces outside of the control or knowledge of humans. They chose; therefore they were. We choose; therefore we become.

By making different decisions and implementing different policies, communities could institutionalize the teaching of the young in a number of different ways. Reliance could be placed on the family or on organized men's groups or women's groups. The nature of the groups could vary. They could be open to all and be transparent, or selective and secret; they could be secular or spiritual. The skills and knowledge of different communities were passed down in numerous ways, establishing different oral and ceremonial traditions. Such is the stuff of anthropology and it is well worth careful study. (For an introduction that is full of insight and humor, see Harris 1974 and 1977.)

Arguments and disputes arose over the decisions and the policies. Who should be taught what? Who should teach them? How? Who could hunt and where could they hunt? Who could gather and where could they gather? Who should get credit for this successful hunt or for finding this useful plant? Who should get the choice cut from the carcass or the best part of the plant? Settlement of disputes within the community became institutionalized, perhaps as an elder or a group of elders passed down the traditions of the community, making policies that established the right way to do things and the right way to give credit for things that were done. Settlement of disputes between communities with conflicting traditions was and still is much more difficult than settlement of disputes within the same community. Shared traditions can more easily provide a common ground for compromise and agreement.

In some communities, many of the decisions implemented as policies were good ones, and the institutions that evolved became successful ways of providing all the members of the community with full access to and use of the joint stock of skills and knowledge. To the extent that they were successful, the institutions fostered abundance. Other communities implemented bad policies. The institutions that evolved out of the bad policies were unsuccessful in providing full access, and those institutions fostered scarcity. The policies of different communities took them down different evolutionary paths. Results ranged from the highly successful to highly unsuccessful. The worst policies led to extinction. Such communities died out or were absorbed into more successful ones.

Let us imagine a Stone Age community where some of the people had blond hair. Suppose the blonds gained control of community policy-making and used their control to restrict the teaching of skills and knowledge about food gathering and animal-hunting to blond children only. The brunettes and redheads were left out. Imagine another Stone Age community where some of the people believed in the great god Mog, while others believed in the great goddess Mag. Suppose the former group gained control over the teaching society of their community and decided to teach only the children of fellow Mog worshippers. In each community, lots of folks would have been excluded from access to and use of the joint stock. The economic cost of inequality in each community would depend on the actual extent of exclusion in each, with the most exclusive customs providing the greatest retardation and distortion in the community practicing them. These examples are easy to understand because they are clearly outrageous.

Let us now turn our attention to a more realistic example—a Space Age community in North America that sits on an important north-south pass along an important trade route that crosses over the Rio Grande. If the schooling of children from the south bank of the river is neglected, simply because they are or appear to be from the south bank, then the job of providing access to the joint stock of Space Age knowledge and skill will be poorly done. It is poorly done, as 150,000 folks from El Paso, Texas, can testify. When poorly done, scarcity rather than abundance is the result, whether in the real Space Age or imagined Stone Age.

The most important question facing us at this point is why any community would implement policies that evolve into institutions that foster scarcity. Why shoot ourselves in the foot? Policies can be changed. Institutions can be changed. Why accept unsuccessful ones? Why not change them? Mistakes are made, of course. But why not fix them? The answer is simple. However, the answer is also painful and therefore hard to accept. Communities choose policies or fail to change unsuccessful policies that cause scarcity because powerful members of those communities benefit. The answer is painful because it means that community leaders sometimes betray their communities for their own benefit. The knowledge of their betrayal is painful to the other community members.

Another example may help clarify the importance of institutionalized policies. Why was slavery introduced into the American South back in the seventeenth century? Did a whole chorus of voices—through the democratic process, demand it? No. It provided large landowners with a desperately needed supply of workers. Slavery benefited the slave owners. It was profitable to them. Nevertheless, the brutality used to enforce it and the racism used to justify it harmed everyone else in the southern community and caused terrible harm in Africa. In terms of community interest, slavery was a mistake, but it took the Civil War to change it. Slavery is gone now, but slavery curses us still, 150 years later. The United States is still not free. It is still shackled by racism. (An excellent treatment of slavery is Davis 2006.)

The Space Age community has institutionalized its way of life through the policies it has chosen to implement and allowed to evolve into the established way things are done. Formal and informal rules have been established to choose what to do about the recurring problems and regular procedures of life. Specialized individuals and whole groups of people do nothing but decide what the rules are and how they should apply to particular cases. The individuals are called judges and the whole groups are called courts. The courts are flooded with lawyers and their clients disputing this or that rule. Some of the most important economic rules are known as property rights. They are not fixed for all time. They evolve as policy evolves. Access to needed materials and knowledge is determined by an elaborate system of these property rights.

For example, farmers cannot just go out and plant a crop of corn on some choice land they happen upon. Property rights determine use of the land. Someone owns that land and must sell or lease it before the farmer can plant a crop. Someone else owns the needed seed and must be paid for it. Then there is the small matter of the tractor and the farm implements, the water, fertilizer, pesticide, and herbicide. Further considerations include bank liens and mortgages, insurance premiums, government taxes, and marketing arrangements.

For another example, students cannot just learn anything anywhere they want. They have to go to school. Not just anyone can go to any school. Only a selected few can attend Harvard or Yale. They need not be blonds or worshippers of Mog, but if they happen to be the offspring of alumni, it helps. Other students go to big state universities or junior colleges. Many young people do not go to college at all.

Human choices determine how the joint stock of knowledge will be preserved and enlarged. Disputes arise and are resolved by more human choices. The rules for choosing evolve as they are passed from generation to generation. Who gets credit for this invention of a new computer memory chip? Who gets credit for that discovery of a new cancer drug? Patent law, patent attorneys, and the courts decide. After they have decided, the new chip and the new drug may become available, but not to just anyone; they must be paid. The owner's property rights, duly instituted by the lawyers, the judges, the courts, and the very law itself, must be respected. Do our institutions succeed in providing full access to and use of our joint stock of Space Age knowledge and skill? (See Commons [1924] 1968).

The Importance of Abundance to the Study of Economics

Abundance can be institutionalized by creating full access to and use of the community's joint stock. Scarcity also can be institutionalized by creating partial access to and use of the joint stock. Since the human community has institutionalized scarcity, economics has come to mean the allocation of scarce resources to meet unlimited human wants. Other possible meanings of economics are devalued because they are outside the expected and normal range of experience. Deviant meanings of economics are considered illegitimate and unscientific. The idea that economics is the study of the social provisioning process is not acceptable when scarcity has been institutionalized. Nevertheless, that is what economics means to us, the intrepid authors of this book, because we do not believe that scarcity is inevitable.

We will show in the rest of this book that humans have considerable choice between scarcity and abundance. People cannot choose to pull rabbits out of their hats. However, they have the ability to make different choices, to implement different policies. Bad choices have institutionalized scarcity in the Space Age community, but it is possible to institutionalize abundance, instead. We do not believe that utopia is in the future, but we do believe that people can do much better than they have. Goods will never be free to everybody. Nevertheless, abundance is possible.

The Meaning of Equality

By equality we do not mean dragging everyone down to a shared level of poverty. In fact, we mean quite the opposite. Equality is institutionalized abundance. Equality is full access to and use of the community's joint stock of knowledge and skill—its technology. Abstract discussions and definitions of equality are not very helpful, since they usually lead to the splitting of hairs and the grinding of ideological axes. Equality is best understood instrumentally instead of abstractly. That is, equality is always best discussed in terms of concrete policies. Should the income tax be made more progressive by cutting the effective tax rates paid by poor families? Should the income tax be made less progressive by cutting the effective tax rates paid by rich families? Should more private scholarship money go to poor students and less to the children of alumnae? Should the minimum wage in the United States be raised? Should a global minimum wage be introduced? Should health care be free for all children? Should prescription drugs be subsidized for all retirees? Should college tuition be free for all students? Should grade school be free for all students? Should grade school students in Pakistan be paid to go to school? These questions are meaningful. They can be debated in concrete terms. They are the content of meaningful discussions of equality. They make it real.

Policies that increase or decrease equality are institutional rather than individual in nature. They involve changing the institutionalized processes that provide or deny access to the community's technology—to its joint stock. What each individual learns and does is important, of course. Abundance and equality are all about learning and doing. Nevertheless, individual knowing and doing take place or fail to take place within a common system of institutionalized processes—the school system, the political system, the financial, health care, and judicial systems. These systems of institutionalized processes are built up by human choices working through the collective actions of governments, corporations, schools, churches, unions, labor market, banks, and courts. These institutions are common to all people and are the subjects of their common policies. It is in these institutions that equality lives or dies, in the shared system of institutionalized processes that each generation uses, amends, and passes to the next generation. It is in them that people can institutionalize equality through the policies they choose. To choose equality does not mean to force individuals into some predetermined mold. To choose equality means to reconstruct the shared system of institutionalized processes—schools, governments, markets, banks, and courts—in ways that enlarge and ensure access to the community's joint stock (Tool 1996).

The Institutional Approach to Policy

Institutional reconstruction has major advantages over individual reproach. Society will not get very far on the road to equality and abundance by identifying particular individuals who are naughty or mistaken and then chastising them. Doing so may satisfy an all-too-human desire for revenge, but it does little to improve the way things work. In particular, it does not improve the institutionalized system that each generation passes on to its children. People get more improvement in the way things work by identifying the institutions that are faulty and choosing policies that correct the shortcomings or by building new institutions.

Two examples will illustrate the advantage of institutional reconstruction over individual reproach. In the U.S. political system, the most effective way to reduce the corruption of government officials is to reform the election process, not to reproach individuals for being naughty. Punishing individual corporate executives for giving bribes and individual politicians for taking them is necessary in a just society. Nevertheless, it is not the best method for improving people's lives. It is better to rely on systematic reconstruction rather than individual repentance, better to pass legislation that takes the corrupting influence of money out of politics than pass harsh laws that put more executives and politicians in prison. The way forward is clear. Elections should be publicly financed. Bribes, now called campaign contributions, should be replaced by a system of public financing, open for all to see. Then the United States would have fewer reasons to lock up individual politicians and executives.

In the troubled U.S. educational system, a focus on institutions also is better than a focus on individuals. Today, poor and minority students are served by poorly performing schools. The individual approach emphasizes the use of vouchers, which allow individual students (actually, their parents) to try to buy their way into better schools, either private or public. These schools need to be improved, but the actual size of the vouchers would have to be very large to be successful. Otherwise, how could other schools do a good job for the poor or problem students? They need special attention—tutorial assistance, remedial reading and math teachers, summer school sessions, smaller class sizes, better trained teachers, cultural enrichment programs, longer school years, free lunches and snacks, expanded after-school programs, expanded school nurse and physician programs, and more reliable and safe transportation to and from school. All of these impose higher costs on the schools that the voucher kids would be trying to get into. Just how welcome would they be in schools that insist on doing a good job? Even if the vouchers are very large—in the range of $10,000 to $12,000 worth of purchasing power in 2007 per student per year—there are no guarantees that the schools the kids finally get into will use the funds to provide the special attention they need. New, for-profit schools could pop up like toadstools after a rain to take advantage of the voucher kids and their parents. To make the vouchers work, such predatory schools would have to be controlled by some kind of inspection and licensing system. The schools that the voucher kids got into would have to be reformed. But that is what should have been done in the first place with the schools—the institutions—that the voucher kids originally attended.

People can pass on to the next generation an institutional system that promotes equality if they focus on changing institutions rather than on changing individuals. Furthermore, they can avoid endless debates if they focus on concrete policies that promote full access and use of technology rather than focus on abstract definitions of equality itself.

Abundance Denied

Abundance threatened to break out in the last century. In 1919 American economist Thorstein Veblen asked some questions that still go to the heart of the matter:

> Why do we, now and again, have hard times and unemployment in the midst of excellent resources, high efficiency and plenty of unmet wants? Why is one-half our consumable product contrived for consumption that yields no material benefit? Why are large coordinations of industry, which greatly reduce cost of production, a cause of perplexity and alarm? Why is the family disintegrating among the industrial classes, at the same time that the wherewithal to maintain it is easier to compass? Why are large and increasing portions of the community penniless in spite of a scale of remuneration which is very appreciably above the subsistence minimum? Why is there a widespread disaffection among the intelligent workmen who ought to know better? (Veblen 1919, 312–313)

In the last century, John Maynard Keynes, scion of the conservative English intellectual aristocracy (see Chapter 1), became convinced that abundance was within humanity's grasp, at least for his grandchildren's generation. He clearly was correct. Nevertheless, on the very brink of abundance, we lost it. Three disastrous world wars (World War I, World War II, and the Cold War), numerous revolutions, regional wars, and civil wars along with the Great Depression of the 1930s cursed humanity with scarcity and inequality, not to mention death and destruction.

Now, in the next century with its Space Age technology, abundance and equality are still denied. What if peace and prosperity broke out, as it were? Let us look at the United States. The United States is a wealthy nation. In recent years its gross domestic product has consistently and easily exceeded $10 trillion, and personal income per capita has been $30,000 or above. More than 16 million new motor vehicles are sold in the United States every year, adding their share to traffic congestion and air pollution. On average, each person in the United States eats more than sixty pounds of sugar and another sixty or more pounds of high-fructose corn syrup annually and washes them down with over twenty gallons of beer and nearly fifty gallons of carbonated soft drinks. Needless to say, slightly more than 20 percent of the inhabitants are obese (*Statistical Abstract of the United States, 2004–2005*, 124th ed. 2004, 128).

The United States could produce products that are more healthful, including ones that do not promote global warming or human obesity. It also could produce more products and perform more services in general—healthful ones or not. In 2007, 4.9 percent or 7.6 million members of the U.S. civilian labor force were unemployed. An additional 4.9 million persons were not in the labor force but "currently want a job." Those who want a job but are not currently looking for work are not counted as part of the labor force by the U.S. Department of Labor. Altogether, about 12.5 million people in the United States did not have a job but wanted one. In addition, about 4.5 million persons who were working part-time would have preferred to work full-time. In total, the data suggest that at least 17 million people in the United States are not fully employed (U.S. Department of Labor 2007).

Not even the wealthy United States should allow that much waste—the lost production of 17 million (or more) potential workers. After all, 20 million people in the United States were designated as living below the official poverty line in 2003 (*Statistical Abstract of the United States, 2004–2005*, 124th ed. 2004, 451). Abundance is not a fact of life for them.

Perhaps a simple table will provide insight into the tragedy of abundance denied in America. Table 2.1 shows the enormous amounts of major grains grown in the United States. If many of the nation's inhabitants are denied food abundance, it is not because of a shortfall in grain production. With production results like these, no one should be left behind in America, but many are. About 3.8 million families in the United States suffered from hunger in 2002 (*Statistical Abstract of the United States, 2004–2005*, 124th ed. 2004, 129).

Bangladesh is not a wealthy nation. About 80 percent of the population lives on two dollars or less per day (UNDP 2006, 293). Abundance is not a meaningful concept for most Bangladeshis. The denial of abundance, even in Bangladesh, is not necessary. Bangladesh, like America, could and should produce more. Furthermore, contrary to the conventional wisdom that depicts the planet as a famine-haunted world of lagging food production, world food production per person has actually been going up. Bangladesh has shared in the rising output, but still millions of Bangladeshis have not.

Bangladesh is not unique. Many of the world's 6.5 billion people

Table 2.1

U.S. Grain Production: Corn, Wheat, and Rice, Per Capita, 1940–1999

Decade	Corn	Wheat	Rice
1940s	18	7	21
1950s	17	6	28
1960s	20	6	38
1970s	27	8	48
1980s	30	9	58
1990s	32	9	65

Source: For grain production, U.S. Department of Agriculture, National Agricultural Statistics Service, *Historical Track Records,* 2002; for population, U.S. Bureau of the Census, *Statistical Abstract,* various years.

Notes: The population figure used to calculate per capita output was the population in the last year of the decade. For corn and wheat, production is given in bushels per person. For rice, the production figure is in pounds per person. All production figures are averages for the decade.

Table 2.2

World Rice Production, Per Capita, 1961–2000 (in pounds)

Region	1961[a]	1970	1980	1990	2000
China	188	300	316	366	329
India	264	250	256	292	282
Indonesia	276	349	441	545	540
Bangladesh	594	568	545	541	595
Vietnam	584	513	499	635	633
Thailand	817	857	815	681	910
Myanmar	701	653	843	753	965
Philippines	327	358	367	361	348
World	158	189	198	217	219

Source: For rice production, the Food and Agriculture Organization of the United Nations, FAOSTAT (Food and Agriculture Organization Statistics); for population, Population Division of the Department of Economic and Social Affairs of the United Nations Secretariat, *World Population Prospects: The 2000 Revision,* 2002.

[a] The population in 1960 was divided into rice production in 1961, due to data availability. The result probably overstated slightly the per capita production in 1961.

live in grinding poverty. None of it is necessary. Abundance should be a meaningful concept to everyone, no matter where they happen to live.

For most of the inhabitants of our planet, rice is the staple food and has been for many generations. The world's ability to produce rice has increased dramatically in the last two generations, rising far faster than the planet's human population. Table 2.2 lists the world's leading rice-producing countries as of the year 2000. The table gives rice output per person, per selected country, and for the world as a whole. Table 2.2 indicates that, if food abundance is still denied to many people on the planet, it is not because of falling rice production.

These tables are not definitive. They do not "prove" that scarcity is unnecessary. They only indicate that grain production is not really the problem. Given humanity's joint stock of knowledge and skill, scarcity is not a fact of nature in the modern economy. Scarcity is made by humans, not by nature.

3

Population and Abundance

Population Is Not the Problem

Neither the size nor the growth rate of population is a major obstacle to the achievement of abundance. We do not believe that the evidence supports the conclusion that population is a barrier to economic abundance. Instead, we believe that abundance is possible with a population even larger than the world's 2005 population of 6.5 billion people. (Unless otherwise stated, population data in this chapter have been obtained from the United Nations' *World Population Prospects* [United Nations 2005].)

We reject both the population pessimists (exemplified by the writings of Thomas Robert Malthus) and the population optimists (exemplified by the writings of Adam Smith). The pessimists argue that higher population will, at some point in time, reduce economic output per person, while the optimists argue that higher population will increase output. Both emphasize population as cause and economic output as effect. Neither approach takes into account the high degree of variability in key demographic and economic variables. Furthermore, neither side seriously considers that economic output per person can have an effect on the population itself through altering the choices available to women. In this chapter we discuss an additional view of population and economy dynamics. Then we add a discussion of world demographic trends with a particular focus on those trends in the United States and Mexico. We wrap up with reflections on what demographers call the fertility rate.

The Population Pessimists

One version of the conventional wisdom is that the world is faced with an insurmountable obstacle to the spread of higher standards of living.

That obstacle is either some cataclysmic population explosion or some equally cataclysmic environmental deterioration brought about mainly by a population that has grown too large. Because of that alleged obstacle, people cannot grow abundant food and fiber, provide adequate health care for everybody, send every child to a good school, and live in comfortable dwellings in safe villages, cities, and neighborhoods. Humanity simply cannot overcome the obstacle, at least not permanently and at least not for everyone. The precise nature of the obstacle varies from one account to another. But the pessimistic argument always suggests the inevitability of scarcity imposed by a growing population pressing on the allegedly limited resources of a finite planet. This obstacle is always taken as a given, a fact of nature, unchangeable and unavoidable. The world's people would like to enjoy abundance, but it is impossible. Or so we are told.

Thomas Robert Malthus (1766–1834) remains the most famous advocate of the view that population growth prohibits abundance. The simplicity of his argument probably accounts for its widespread appeal. Because the basic argument has changed little in the last two centuries, it is important to understand Malthus. He began with the straightforward, noncontroversial proposition that food is necessary for humans to stay alive. His second and more controversial proposition was that human population tends to grow faster than "the power in the earth to produce subsistence" ([1798] 1965, 13). Malthus was very specific about the relative growth rates of population and the food supply. He argued that population tended to grow in a geometric progression (1, 2, 4, 8, 16, 32, 64, 128, 256, . . .) while the food supply tended to grow at an arithmetic rate (1, 2, 3, 4, 5, 6, . . .). In the first edition of his essay, he presented no evidence to support either of these growth rates. In later editions, Malthus attempted to provide such evidence, but even his admirers admit that the evidence was weak. We will return to this point later, but first we need to complete the Malthusian argument.

To complete his argument, Malthus added two more points, which he thought were obviously true. He argued that the effects of "these two unequal powers" (14) (population growth and growth of the food supply) must be kept equal, meaning that at least in the long run the population could not exceed the available food supply. Further, since, in his view, people would not voluntarily limit the size of the population, the "positive checks" (25) of war, famine, and disease would ultimately bring the size of the population into an uneasy equilibrium with the size of the food supply.

Box 3.1

Malthus on Population

Malthus's *Essay on the Principle of Population* became so popular and controversial that it went through six editions. The *Essay* was revised significantly between the first (1798) and second (1803) editions. The following quotations are from the first edition.

I think I may fairly make two postulata (11).

First, That food is necessary to the existence of man (11).

Secondly, That the passion between the sexes is necessary and will remain nearly in its present state (11).

Assuming then my postulata as granted, I say, that the power of population is indefinitely greater than the power in the earth to produce subsistence for man (13).

Population, when unchecked, increases in a geometrical ratio. Subsistence increases only in an arithmetical ratio. A slight acquaintance with numbers will shew the immensity of the first power in comparison of the second (14).

By that law of our nature which makes food necessary to the life of man, the effects of these two unequal powers must be kept equal (14).

This implies a strong and constantly operating check on population from the difficulty of subsistence. This difficulty must fall somewhere and must necessarily be severely felt by a large portion of mankind (14).

This ratio of increase, though short of the utmost power of population, yet as the result of actual experience, we will take as our rule, and say, that population, when unchecked, goes on doubling itself every twenty-five years or increases in a geometrical ratio (20–21).

In the next twenty-five years, it is impossible to suppose that the produce could be quadrupled (22).

Taking the population of the world at any number, a thousand millions, for instance, the human species would increase in the ratio of—1, 2, 4, 8, 16,

(continued)

Box 3.1 *(continued)*

32, 64, 128, 256, 512, etc. and subsistence as—1, 2, 3, 4, 5, 6, 7, 8, 9, 10, etc. In two centuries and a quarter, the population would be to the means of subsistence as 512 to 10: in three centuries as 4096 to 13, and in two thousand years the difference would be almost incalculable, though the produce in that time would have increased to an immense extent (25).

The constant effort towards population, which is found to act even in the most vicious societies, increases the number of people before the means of subsistence are increased. The food therefore which before supported seven millions must now be divided among seven millions and a half or eight millions. The poor consequently must live much worse, and many of them be reduced to severe distress (29–30).

That population does invariably increase where there are the means of subsistence, the history of every people that have ever existed will abundantly prove (37).

That the increase of population is necessarily limited by the means of subsistence.
Man cannot live in the midst of plenty. All cannot share alike the bounties of nature (179).

Source: Thomas Robert Malthus. [1798] 1965. *First Essay on Population with notes by James Bonar.*

Malthus never demonstrated that his argument was correct and no one else has done so either. The simple arithmetic of his predictions is obviously incorrect. The best estimate of demographers is that in 1800, about the time Malthus was writing, the world's population was about 1 billion people. If Malthus's population-doubling time of approximately every twenty-five years had been correct, the world population would now be about 256 billion and would reach 512 billion by the year 2025. Instead, the world population at the beginning of the twenty-first century is about 6.5 billion people. But these apparently contradictory observations and computations do not disprove the Malthusian position.

It is not possible to confirm or reject Malthus's original theory by the usual standards of verification or falsification. It is not possible to categorically reject the theory that, some day, population pressure will reduce output per person. The theory is simply not testable because

Malthus always qualified his statements in such a way that they cannot be rejected by a comparison with observable facts. Consider the exercise in arithmetic above. The fact that world population has not grown at the rate (or to the level) Malthus suggested does not provide enough evidence to reject his theory. Any positive population growth rate that is greater than the growth rate of the food supply will result in food shortages if the time period considered is long enough. Besides, advocates of the Malthusian view could respond by saying that Malthus's preventive (voluntary sexual restraint) or positive checks (war, famine, poverty, and disease) have been hard at work and a slower population growth rate was perfectly consistent with the original theory.

Could a high rate of population growth for some fairly long time period confirm Malthus's theory? The answer is no. Malthus argued that a high rate of population growth would ultimately be halted by food shortages. We cannot even confront Malthus's theory by examining the history of population growth over the last 200 years. As Mark Blaug states, "The Malthusian theory cannot be refuted because it cannot be applied to any actual or any conceivable population change: it purports to say something about the real world but what it says is true by definition in its own terms" (1962, 63).

There have been other criticisms of Malthus's propositions. An important point is that Malthus ignored the possibility of technological change and the potentially large increases in agricultural output that became possible with the growth of humanity's joint stock of knowledge. But modern Malthusians respond that technological change only delays the onset of the ultimate population-induced disaster.

Although it stretches the imagination to take the Malthusian predictions literally, his basic argument that population growth will someday be greater than the ability to provide food is still taken seriously by many so-called neo-Malthusians (Daly 1996; Ehrlich 1968; Meadows et al. 1974). Their current dire warnings could have been written by Malthus more than two centuries ago. A basic difference, perhaps the only difference of any importance, between the original Malthusian position and more recent neo-Malthusians is that the latter generally endorse the use of birth control methods other than abstinence, while Malthus did not (Weeks 1999).

Many prominent contemporary environmentalists, ecologists, and demographers (Czech 2000; Weeks 2000) add environmental degradation, extinction of species, and the undeniable problem of global warming to the basic Malthusian doomsday scenario. Even though global warming is not a function of population growth, it is a problem that must be addressed, and the temptation is strong to emphasize the significance of global warming by linking it with dire population predictions.

In short, Malthusians (neo or otherwise) continue to assert that humanity is ultimately doomed by population growth to a low per capita standard of living and perhaps famine and severe degradation of the environment. The Malthusian perspective is embodied in the principles found in economics textbooks, such as the concept of the steady state, the vertical long-run aggregate supply curve, and, at a more advanced level, what economists call growth theory. In all cases, the clear implication is that, as Malthus (25) said, "Man cannot live in the midst of plenty. All cannot share alike the bounties of nature."

We reject the Malthusian view of the world for three reasons. First, as we have already discussed, the Malthusian theory cannot be tested. Second, the Malthusian and neo-Malthusian propositions are not useful guides to understanding past, current, or future demographic and economic trends. Third, the Malthusian theory is not a useful guide to public policy because it suggests the inevitability of a population-induced disaster no matter how hard people try to avoid it.

It is more useful to view the interaction of demography and economics as a complex, subtle process that requires a more sophisticated understanding than that offered by Malthus and his modern disciples. Demographic and economic interaction and long-term trends will be discussed after we examine the perspectives of the population optimists.

For now, we note that the Malthusian catastrophe has not occurred more than two centuries after his original prediction. We strongly suspect, but cannot prove, that humanity will not face that catastrophe during the next few centuries, either.

The Population Optimists

There is an optimistic view of the relationship between population and abundance. The population optimists regard population growth as an essential requirement of economic progress or, at worst, as a benign accompaniment. Adam Smith stated, "The most decisive mark of the prosperity of any nation is an increase in the number of its inhabitants" ([1776] 1937, 70). Smith's benign view of population growth was based on two assertions. First, a large population provided opportunities for technological advances through the specialization and division of labor. Second, since economic expansion could be limited by the extent of the market, a growing population expanded the market and permitted economic growth to continue.

Although we reject the pessimistic theory of Malthus, we do not necessarily accept the optimistic theory of Smith. Smith's argument linking growing economic output to population growth is difficult to test in any meaningful context. Smith's reasoning is circular. A larger population opens the door to greater specialization and technological change, but these effects are not automatic. At the same time, Smith thought it was obvious that a population could not grow without a growing economy. So what comes first: the cause or the effect? A high (or low) correlation between per capita income and population growth rates neither confirms nor refutes Smith's position. Yet his circular reasoning gives an interesting insight into the possibility of circular causation. We will explore this clue later in the chapter.

Julian Simon is perhaps the most widely known contemporary population optimist (1996). In many respects, Simon's arguments are a modern version of Smith's. Both argue that population growth contributes positively to per capita productivity through the beneficial effects of population growth on technological change. Both are ardent supporters of the market economy, although Smith supported the market system before it had become firmly institutionalized while Simon supported the market after it was already well established. Adam Smith worked from an antiestablishment position. The establishment of his day favored not the free market, but mercantilism. Smith was an economic rebel, Simon an economic apologist. Smith incorporated his population view into an argument against the mercantilist status quo. Two hundred years later, Simon incorporated his population view into an argument in favor of what had become the capitalist status quo.

Simon's optimism regarding population is the central focus of his numerous works. Simon describes the various benefits of population growth, including technological change and market size, while attempting to debunk various arguments that population growth is harmful to economic activity. Simon repeatedly argues that if the size of the population were creating scarcity, then the prices of commodities derived from so-called "natural resources" would rise. His reasoning is very simple: in the scarcity scenario, growing population would raise the demand for natural resource commodities and their prices would rise because they would become increasingly scarce—there was a limit to their amount in nature. Yet when Simon examined the prices of natural resources over the long run, he found that key commodity prices had been falling in real (inflation-adjusted) terms.

Declining commodity prices led Simon to completely dismiss concerns about resource scarcity. Simon was so confident that increased population would not result in higher resources prices that in 1980 he made a famous bet with doomsday environmentalist Paul Ehrlich. The terms of the bet allowed Ehrlich to pick $1,000 worth of any five metals. If by 1990 (ten years later) the inflation-adjusted value of the metals was higher than $1,000, Simon would owe Ehrlich the difference. If the value of the metals was less than $1,000 in 1990, Erlich would owe Simon the difference. Ehrlich lost the bet and paid Simon $576.07.

Simon's argument, as expressed in his bet with Ehrlich, is plausible but hardly convincing evidence that resource prices will not rise at some point as the result of population pressure. Like the pessimistic Malthusians, the optimistic Simon assumes that past trends will continue indefinitely. Other population optimists point out that all of the world's population could easily be housed in the state of Texas in three-bedroom houses and still leave enough room for streets and parks. Again, such computations do not prove the point.

The optimists fall into the same logical trap as the pessimists. Malthusians believe that continued population growth ensures catastrophe. For the optimists, continued population growth ensures prosperity. They are both sure that the population will keep growing. We approach the population-economy connection with no such assurance. The historical record does not provide much evidence for such assurance. The evidence supports uncertainty about the future. The population could keep growing, or it could start declining.

In parts of Europe and Japan, zero and even negative population growth is emerging. There has been a great deal of recent discussion of a potential decrease in total and per capita output in a world characterized by a declining population (Eberstadt 1997; Rostow 1998). In parts of industrialized Europe, the crude birth rates have fallen so low that populations have begun to actually decline. Populations have also begun to age. That is, their average age has risen and the proportion of elderly people in the population has increased. If population and productivity move up and down together, population and output would begin declining simultaneously. This result could easily cause some people to yearn for the good old days when their chief worry was an impending Malthusian catastrophe. Even this scenario of stagnation and decline does not make the case for the optimists. In the next section, we present a perspective on population that differs significantly from the naive views of both the pessimists and the optimists.

Alternatives to Malthusian Pessimism and Smithian Optimism

More than one alternative to the extreme views of Malthus and Smith on the consequences of population change is possible. Our alternative perspective begins with some basic demography. Changes (either growth or decline) in population size in any given geographic area depend on the three fundamental demographic processes: fertility, mortality, and migration. Any introductory textbook on demography provides an explanation and elaboration of this point (Weeks 1999 is a good example). Second, we note that rates of change in fertility, mortality, and migration are highly variable over time and from place to place. We will discuss this point below. Third, we recognize that the three basic demographic processes are powerfully influenced by cultural and economic forces. Biology may set upper (and perhaps lower) limits on birth rates, but observed birth rates among humans are rarely near the biological maximum. We discuss the facts and implications of demographic uncertainty below.

Demographic Uncertainty

In 1798, when Malthus wrote his essay on population, he could argue that population tended to grow at a geometric rate with little fear of being contradicted by the facts of population growth. He was not even the first to make the suggestion. Benjamin Franklin had suggested the same proposition much earlier, in 1755, and others in England had made similar assertions (Pasinetti 1974, 86–89). Except for a very few isolated censuses, there were simply no data to test his hypothesis of a geometric growth rate. As Malthus correctly asserted, the effects of compound annual growth rates are indeed powerful: an annual population growth rate of 3 percent a year will double the initial population in about a quarter of a century. It is also true that world population has grown considerably in the last 200 years, but not as fast as Malthus suggested.

Malthus's particular growth rate is not a necessary part of his argument. The only essential ingredients in his argument are finite resources and a positive population growth rate. If we drop the assumption of finite resources, Adam Smith's position also requires only a positive growth rate. In sharp contrast to both positions, the historical record indicates a great deal of variability in key demographic variables. That is why they are called variables instead of constants. Selected examples of this demographic variability are discussed below.

A simple summary measure of the state of the world's population is its annual rate of growth. The United Nations (2005) reported that world population (for the years 2000 to 2005) grew at about 1.2 percent a year. A growth rate of 1.2 percent a year implies a doubling of the world's population in about sixty years. (Approximate doubling times can be calculated by a simple application of the so-called rule of 72. Divide the growth rate into 72 and the result is approximately the number of years it takes to double the population. In this case, 72 divided by 1.2 equals 60.)

However, a single, worldwide growth rate hides a great deal of variability. Population growth rates vary considerably from nation to nation. Somalia, an African nation with 8.2 million persons in 2005, has one of the highest growth rates in the world (3.24 percent per year). In contrast, Estonia, a European nation with 1.4 million people, has a negative rate of population change (–0.45 percent). The United Nations reports that, "In 2005, the 65 countries where total fertility was below replacement level accounted for 43 per cent of the world's population, or 2.8 billion people" (6).

More nations are expected to join the low-fertility club soon. But the variation in national population growth rates is not expected to end in the near future. In particular, the United Nations expects the more developed nations of the world to grow very slowly or not at all, while the supposedly less developed nations will continue to grow at a higher rate.

A similar pattern of variability in population growth rates can be observed in subnational areas. For example, in the United States and other geographically large nations, population growth rates exhibit a great deal of variation among states and counties. The U.S. Bureau of the Census reports that from July 1, 2002, to July 1, 2003, the U.S. population grew by 1.0 percent. In the same time period, Nevada had the highest population growth rate of 3.4 percent while North Dakota had a growth rate of 0 percent. Thirty of the fifty states had a growth rate of less than 1 percent. Population growth rates among metropolitan areas and counties are even more variable than those for states.

Population growth rates are also highly variable when examined over time. The population histories of the United States and Mexico, two of the world's most populous nations, provide a convenient example. In 1790, the population of Mexico (then New Spain) of 4.7 million persons (INEGI 1990) was about 20 percent larger than the census-reported figure for the United States of 3.9 million persons (U.S. Bureau of the Census 1998). During the nineteenth century, Mexico's population increased threefold to roughly 14 million people in 1900. Over the same time period, the U.S. population increased some nineteenfold to about 75 million people in 1900. Some perspective on these numbers is needed. Mexico's nineteenth-century population growth occurred at approximately the same rate as U.S. population growth during the twentieth century. If the U.S. population had grown at the same rate in the twentieth century as it did in the nineteenth, the U.S. would now have a population of 1.1 billion, greater than India's (1.0 billion) but somewhat smaller than China's population (1.3 billion). In contrast, the current U.S. population is about 0.3 billion or 300 million.

By 1900, the U.S. population of 75 million people was nearly six times as large as Mexico's 13.6 million, but twentieth-century population growth in the two nations did not follow the patterns of the nineteenth century. Indeed, twentieth-century population growth rates by decade varied considerably in the United States and Mexico. Between 1910 and 1921, Mexico's population decreased by 5.4 percent, although there is considerable criticism of Mexico's 1921 population census. Mexico's population growth rates began to accelerate in the 1930s after the government adopted a deliberately pronatalist population policy. Mexico's postrevolutionary population policy reflected, in part, a fear of the aggressive tendencies of its northern neighbor. An underpopulated Mexico, it was argued, would be a tempting target for U.S. aggression. Mexican policy makers also thought that a growing population would stimulate economic growth (Alba 1984). Mexico reversed its population policy in the mid-1970s. Birth rates and total population growth rates in Mexico since the 1970s reflect this policy change. Mexico's total fertility rate (TFR) in 1950 was 6.82. That figure fell to 2.40 by 2005 (United Nations 2005). (A brief explanation of various measures of fertility and mortality appears at the end of this chapter.)

U.S. population growth rates have also been highly variable in the twentieth century. During the 1930s, the U.S. population increased by 7.4 percent. At the end of the baby boom in the 1960s, the U.S. population increased by 18.4 percent. The U.S. TFR fell from 3.45 in the 1950s to 1.99 in the late 1990s and then increased slightly to 2.04 between 2000 and 2005 (United Nations 2005).

Why are rates of population change so highly variable? In a direct sense, the answer is simple: there is a great deal of variation in the rates of change of the components of population change. That is, fertility, mortality, and migration, no matter how they are measured, are also highly variable.

One explanation of this variability is the theory of demographic transition. This idea originated in the demographic experiences of European nations. In a preindustrial nation with high birth and death rates, for example, crude birth and death rates might be thirty-five or forty per thousand persons. With high birth and death rates, the population growth rate of such a nation would be relatively low. Then, as economic growth takes hold, death rates begin to fall—perhaps rapidly, due to the spread of better nutrition, housing, and sanitation. According to the standard model of the demographic transition, this initial decline in mortality occurs before a decline in birth rates. The result of the lower death rate and continued higher birth rate is rapid population growth. Eventually, however, with increases in income, urbanization, and advances in health care, birth rates too begin to decline. Ultimately, demographic transition theory suggests that both birth and death rates will tend to settle at some new and much lower level, with a correspondingly low rate of population growth.

The demographic transition offers one explanation of why population growth rates vary over time and from nation to nation—because individual nations are in different stages of the demographic transition. However, the details of the demographic transition vary from one account to another, and the theory itself has generated a high level of controversy arising from several questions. The demographic transition theory may describe European experience. Nevertheless, important questions remain about the future population trajectory for other nations. Are all nations destined to go through the demographic transition? If so, will it take the same time as it did for European nations? What are the causes of the transition in other nations? Will the sequence of events be a decline in death rates and then a decline in birth rates? Is the transition permanent or is it reversible? Exactly what does this model suggest for the future?

Demographers and economists do not have definitive answers to many of these questions (see the discussion in Lee 2003). Nevertheless, the demographic transition model is important because it focuses attention on demographic variability and the relationship between demographic variability and economic and social changes. Even a cursory look at the data suggests a strong relationship between demographic and economic variables.

Table 3.1 displays some key demographic indicators and gross domestic product (GDP) per capita for the twenty most populous nations. The world population is not evenly distributed between nations. About 200 nations now share the planet, and 10 percent of them account for 73 percent of the total population. The nations of the world include a small number of very large ones and a large number of very small ones. Even more striking evidence of population concentration exists. Among the top twenty nations, two supergiants stand out—China and India. They, alone, account for 37 percent of the world's population. An accurate description of the population distribution among the nation-states of the world is that two supernations loom over a handful of large nations and scores and scores of Lilliputian nations. Among the twenty largest nations, the percent change in population varies from Nigeria's 2.53 percent per year to Russia's –0.57 percent per year.

The most important thing to remember, among all this variation, is that population optimists and pessimists both consider population as cause and economic output as effect. In a simple world of straight-line cause and effect, this might be true: a variable is either a cause or an effect, but not both. However, Adam Smith's thinking was circular and seemingly confused. We still think that Smith was confused, but for a very good reason: he was dimly aware that the world is not simple but extremely complex. We take Smith's circular reasoning as a clue that the relation between population and economic output could involve circular causation. That is, population is not merely a cause and economic output not merely an effect; population is also an effect and economic output is also a cause. In the complex world, a variable can be both cause and effect.

Now back to Table 3.1. Nations with high GDP per person have short-term population growth rate projections below the world average of 1.2 percent. Nations with low GDP per person have short-term population growth rate projections above the world average of 1.2 percent. Some notable exceptions exist. Russia is a poor country, yet its population is declining, as it was even before the breakup of the Soviet Union. The reasons for this decline in Russia's population are numerous and complex. China is a poor country, yet its population is growing at a rate significantly below the world average. Apparently its one-child-per-family policy is working. Then there is Thailand, another poor country with a below-average population growth rate.

Crude birth rates (CBRs) also vary greatly from nation to nation. Among the twenty largest nations, Nigeria's CBR of 39.1 per thousand is nearly five times as large as Japan's 9.2 per thousand. A similar pattern can be seen in TFRs, which vary from Pakistan's 5.08 to Russia's 1.14. CBRs among the largest nations vary from a low of 7.0 in China to a high of 14.6 in Russia. If something seems familiar here, it should. With few exceptions, fertility rates (both CBRs and TFRs) tend to be low in nations with high incomes and high in nations with low incomes.

Both crude birth and crude death rates depend greatly on the age distribution of the population. As Table 3.1 shows, those nations with a high median age tend to have a lower CBR, while those with a low median age tend to have a high CBR. Many factors other than age, such as income, urbanization, and education—particularly women's education—also influence demographic variables. As will be explained below, high per capita income levels tend to be associated with low birth rates. Generally speaking, the more urban a nation is, the lower is its birth rate. In a similar fashion, higher educational levels, particularly among women, are associated with lower birth rates. Generally speaking, the more educated a population is, the lower is its birth rate. These relations are discussed at more length below.

Demographers and economists (and probably you, the reader) can add other variables to this list. The completeness of the list is not important. The important conclusion to reach is that the basic demographic processes are powerfully influenced by cultural and economic conditions.

With few exceptions, populations in rich countries grow slowly or even shrink while populations in poor countries grow fast. All other things considered, does this suggest that abundance could be an effective population control? We do not want to claim too much for the beneficial effects of abundance. Nevertheless, we wonder, and we would be negligent not to point out this intriguing possibility. In particular, could high economic output be the cause of low population growth? We think that it could, but we are open to counterargument. Here is the way we see it, tentatively.

Table 3.1

Demographic Characteristics of Selected Nations, 2000

Nation	Population[a]	Percent change[b]	Crude birth rate[c]	Total fertility rate[d]	Crude death rate[c]	Median age	GDP per capita
China	1,275.2	0.73	14.5	1.83	7.0	30.0	825
India	1,016.9	1.51	23.8	3.01	8.5	23.4	463
United States	285.0	1.03	14.5	2.11	8.3	35.2	31,730
Indonesia	211.6	1.26	20.7	2.35	7.3	24.6	1,015
Brazil	171.8	1.24	19.7	2.21	7.1	25.4	4,626
Russia	145.6	-0.57	8.6	1.14	14.6	36.8	2,944
Pakistan	142.7	2.44	35.9	5.08	9.6	18.8	516
Bangladesh	138.0	2.02	28.9	3.46	8.5	20.0	373
Japan	127.0	0.14	9.2	1.32	8.2	41.3	44,799
Nigeria	114.7	2.53	39.1	5.42	13.7	17.3	274
Mexico	98.9	1.45	22.4	2.50	5.0	22.9	3,803
Germany	82.3	0.07	8.7	1.35	10.6	39.9	32,695
Vietnam	78.2	1.35	20.2	2.30	6.4	23.1	370
Philippines	75.7	1.79	25.3	3.18	5.1	20.9	1,173
Turkey	68.3	1.42	20.9	2.43	6.0	24.2	3,048
Egypt	67.8	1.99	26.6	3.29	6.2	21.3	1,217
Iran	66.4	1.24	20.3	2.33	5.3	20.6	1,658
Ethiopia	65.6	2.46	42.5	6.14	17.7	16.9	116
Thailand	60.9	1.01	17.3	1.93	7.1	27.5	2,828
France	59.3	0.47	12.8	1.89	9.3	37.6	30,097
World	6,070.6	1.22	21.3	2.69	9.1	26.4	5,654

Source: All data, except GDP per capita, are from United Nations Population Division, World Population Prospects, 2002 Revision, http://esa.un.org/undp/p2k0data.asp.
GDP per capita is from World Bank, World Development Indicators, WDI Online: https://publications.worldbank.org/ecommerce/products.

Notes: The data above are from the "medium fertility variant" of the UN publication. [a] Population is expressed in millions of persons; [b] percent change is expressed on an annual basis; [c] the crude birth (death) rate is expressed as births (deaths) per thousand persons; [d] the total fertility rate is expressed as total births per woman.

Some Reflections on the Fertility Rate: Is Population an Effect and the Economy a Cause?

The dynamic known as the demographic transition is a special case of circular causation, of effect becoming cause and cause becoming effect. Circular causation itself is discussed in Gunnar Myrdal's *American Dilemma*, in which he presents his theory of cumulative causation and contrasts it with the offsetting causation of equilibrium systems ([1944] 1962, Appendix 3). In the demographic transition, as we discussed above, population is no longer cause and economy effect. Instead, population becomes effect and economy, cause. That is, changes in economic production cause changes in population, and the two working together eventually brought the birth and death rates down more or less in balance for the industrializing European countries and for their offshoots.

Now we wish to look at another case of circular causation. The question we investigate is simple: how does high economic output per person cause a reduction in the fertility rate? There are several closely related processes at work. Even though there is still much to be learned, demographers and economists have accumulated substantial evidence on these processes and their consequences. Here, we provide only a hint of the complexity of declining fertility rates.

Along with increased output, there have been substantial shifts in industrial structure—most notably a shift from agriculture to industry and services. In an agricultural setting, children are a distinct asset. They can be put to work at an early age and contribute to the income of the household. In an urban, industrial setting, children are not an asset. Indeed, they are very expensive to raise and educate. Worldwide, it has been noted that the shift from a rural agricultural setting to an industrial (and now service-oriented) economy is accompanied by a decline in fertility rates. In the language of supply and demand, the income elasticity of children is negative. That is, as incomes rise, people choose to have fewer children. Technically, this means that children are "inferior" goods. An inferior good is simply a good that people consume less of as incomes rise.

The simplified process just described is reinforced by increases in longevity and decreases in infant mortality. Economists and demographers frequently speak of the social security hypothesis in referring to declining fertility rates. When many children die in infancy or at a young age, parents need to have a lot of kids so that some of them may be alive when the parents are old and need care from their children. As incomes rise, parents do not need as many children to ensure that one or more of them will be around to take care of the parents in old age. Further, within the last century, rising incomes have allowed social security, private pension plans, and other mechanisms to take care of the old. Again, the need for children declines.

In addition, rising incomes and urbanization mean greater access to educational opportunities for both men and women. Greater educational attainment is associated almost everywhere with higher labor force participation rates. In turn, higher labor force participation rates and higher incomes for both men and women mean that it is even more costly to raise children. If women or men stay home to provide childcare, the lost earnings from doing so are large. That is, the opportunity cost of raising children increases with higher incomes and higher labor force participation rates. Also, with more parental time spent working outside the home, more outside help is needed inside the home, the opportunity cost of parental work inside the home rises, and more pressure is placed on women (also on men if the home work is shared equally) to work two shifts—one inside and one outside the home. Hence, fertility rates decline. (These issues, including women and their second shift, and the costs of sexism are discussed in Chapter 8.)

In short, high or rising economic output is accompanied by processes that result in a decline in the fertility rate.

Conclusions

Malthusian pessimists and Smithian optimists agree that population is an important economic variable. Population is the denominator in the calculation of per capita income and output figures. Population size and a population's age and sex distributions affect the labor force and labor force participation rates. Population size influences aggregate demand and the demand for particular goods and services. Migration is important at the national and subnational level. People are the key actors in the modern economy's continuum of industrial means and consumer ends. But agreement ends there. The economic, environmental, and ecological implications of demographic change remain contentious. The future remains highly uncertain.

Neither the Malthusian pessimists nor the Smithian optimists are correct in their projections of continued population growth. In contrast, recognition of the importance of population, the complexity of demographic and economic interaction, and the inherent variability of critical demographic variables conditioned by cultural and economic factors leads to very different conclusions from those of the Malthusian pessimists or the Smithian optimists.

First, there is little reason to expect that rates of population growth or decline are inevitable or predetermined. The actual experience of different countries is diverse. Second, because demographic rates are at least in part determined by cultural and economic conditions, public policy is an important ingredient in the demographic equation. For example, public policy and other factors in China have pushed the Chinese birth rate down to the same level as that in the United States. Third, because demographic rates vary across time and place, there can be no single demographic public policy goal that is always appropriate. Those who advocate such a goal, such as proponents of zero population growth, simply ignore the obvious. Finally, a worldwide economy of abundance, though possible with a much larger population than today's, would probably result in slower world population growth, not faster.

A Digression on Measuring Demographic Rates

During our discussion of demographic variables, we refer to various statistical measures. These are not difficult measures to understand, but since they are not typically taught in economics courses, we offer this brief explanation of some of the most common measures.

A crude rate such as a CBR is defined as the number of births (or some other demographic event) per thousand persons. For example, in the United States at the beginning of the twenty-first century, the CBR was about eleven per thousand while the crude death rate was approximately eight per thousand. Crude rates provide useful summary measures of very complex demographic processes, but they hide many useful details.

Age-specific rates reflect the fact that demographic events are more likely to occur at some ages than others. Eighty-year-olds are more likely to die in a given year than twenty-year-olds. As with a crude rate, age-specific rates can be expressed as x per thousand, but also as x per 100,000 and sometimes in per person terms. Age-specific rates can be reported for single years of age or for groups. For example, the *Statistical Abstract of the United States* (U.S. Bureau of the Census 2003) reports an age-specific death rate for the U.S. male population 85 years old and older in 2000 as 6,863.3 deaths per 100,000.

Table 3.2

Example of Total Fertility Rate (TFR)

Age of woman	Age-specific fertility rate	Number of years in group	Contribution to TFR = Col B x Col C
12–14	0.0015	3	0.0045
15–19	0.0814	5	0.4070
20–24	0.1652	5	0.8260
25–29	0.1514	5	0.7570
30–34	0.1053	5	0.5263
35–39	0.0549	5	0.2745
40–44	0.0169	5	0.0845
45–49	0.0039	5	0.0195
Total			2.8993 = TFR

Source: 2000 Census of Mexico for the State of Chihuahua.

TFR is a hypothetical rate representing the total number of births that a woman would have if she were exposed to all the age-specific fertility rates during her lifetime. For example, in Table 3.2, from the 2000 Census of Mexico for the State of Chihuahua, the calculated TFR (2.8993) indicates that if a woman were exposed to each of the listed age-specific rates for the number of years indicated, she would have a total of 2.8993 children. The age-specific rates were calculated for a particular time (in this case, the year 2000), so no individual female will be exposed to exactly these rates. Hence, a TFR really is a hypothetical measure of fertility. It is significant, however, because a TFR of 2.08 indicates the replacement level: with a TFR greater than 2.08, the population will grow, while a TFR below 2.08 means that a population will eventually decline.

4

Resources and the Environment

We are environmentalists. We are concerned with the truly horrible things being done to the air that we breathe, the water that we drink, and the habitats of numerous species. We are very concerned about global warming. We also are concerned about the needless waste of resources associated with modern patterns of consumption. We are abundance economists. We strongly believe that abundance is possible for everyone, no matter where they live. The resources and technology necessary to achieve abundance for all are available now, have been available for a long time, and will be available for centuries to come. Nor is there any inherent conflict between achieving abundance and improving the environment. But a lot of nonsense about these issues has been written. In this chapter we hope to challenge your thinking on these issues. Give abundance a chance.

Although resource and environmental issues are related—especially in the popular press—we treat them separately. Our colleague and friend, James Swaney (2003) forcefully points out that serious environmental damage can occur without running out of resources. Swaney and others argue that damage to fragile ecosystems is a far greater threat to the way people live than the classic Malthusian resource constraint.

The environmental problem is not that people are running out of things. It is not that they are using up the environmental stuff they have. Rather, the problem is that they are causing harm to the fragile environmental systems in which they live. Swaney, like many others, is not optimistic that people will take the appropriate actions to curtail and reverse ecosystem damage. In any case, it is important to make a distinction between scarcity of resources and the environmental consequences of an unregulated industrial economy.

What Are Resources?

Scarcity is the key concept in modern economics. As we pointed out in Chapter 1, modern economics is often defined as the study of the allocation of scarce resources among competing wants. Most textbooks, however, spend little time defining the concept of resources and even less explaining what this concept might mean. There are reasons for this omission. Many economists, including textbook writers, assume that everyone knows that resources are scarce. More to the point, a serious discussion of the concept of resources would mean that much of what was written on the remaining pages of the textbook would be wrong, because a more sophisticated understanding of resources leads to a more sophisticated understanding of economics.

In what follows, we adopt Erich W. Zimmermann's functional concept of resources. As Zimmermann explains, the word *resource* "does not refer to a thing or a substance but to a function which the thing or substance may perform or to an operation in which it may take part." Zimmermann regards the physical universe—the planet earth—as "neutral stuff" from which resources are created when humans apply their knowledge to it (1951, 7). This is extremely important— what is and is not a resource changes over time with changes in technology, institutions, wants, and even prices.

A given thing or substance may be a resource at one time and not at another. In the late eighteenth century, uranium was not a resource. No one yet knew the physics of how to make uranium useful or dangerous. If people decide that uranium is too dangerous, it may again become "neutral stuff." Before World War II, natural rubber was an important resource used for making tires and other goods that needed flexibility. During the war, natural rubber, produced mainly in Brazil, was very difficult to obtain. Scientists soon discovered alternatives—nylon and rayon. During the war years, natural rubber ceased to be regarded as a resource. In recent years, modern industry has concluded that natural rubber has some properties that artificial substances do not have. Natural rubber is again a resource.

A couple of hundred years ago, even petroleum was not very useful and in an important sense was not a resource. Back then, the vast reserves of crude oil under Texas, Persia, and Arabia were worthless. Advances in the community's joint stock of knowledge—that is, its technology and institutions—changed the status of petroleum from "neutral stuff" to resource by the middle of the nineteenth century. Indeed, it was in 1859 that "Colonel" Edwin Drake (who was not a colonel) drilled the world's first commercial oil well in Titusville, Pennsylvania (Zimmermann 1951, 498).

What prompted Drake to drill for petroleum? Many changes had occurred in the community's joint stock of knowledge. Among other things, whale oil, which was in common use as a lubricant and as a source of fuel for lamps, was becoming more difficult to obtain and more expensive. And knowledge of how to distill petroleum into useful commodities such as kerosene made "black gold" a viable alternative to whale oil (Yergin 1992).

With the development of the internal combustion engine, petroleum became an even more valuable resource. Perhaps someday, petroleum will no longer be regarded as a resource. Jeremy Rifkin, for example, suggests that the next energy revolution will be based on hydrogen, an abundant substance that does not generate carbon dioxide as a pollutant (2002). Rifkin's optimistic assessment of advances in hydrogen-fueled mechanical devices may or may not be correct, but it demonstrates his recognition that resources are not static.

Mainstream scarcity economists also recognize that the useful amount of a resource found in nature depends on more than geology. Technology is important. The oil industry is now able to drill for oil in places that were too deep or too difficult to find a quarter of a century ago. Prices are important. Most so-called resource economists claim that there is more oil in the ground at $80 per barrel than there is at $10 per barrel. There is more to the concept of proven reserves than how much crude oil there is in the ground—the amount depends directly on current prices and current technology.

From this perspective, human wants, which may or may not be translated into what economists call demand, also have something to do with how much oil is in the ground. People demand petroleum products to run their SUVs, farms, and factories. But demand is a funny thing. Clearly, demand is powerfully influenced by the specific nature of the society people live in. Is the demand for an SUV a natural phenomenon that everyone is born with? The historical record indicates otherwise. The demand for SUVs has something to do with advertising, the attainment of status, and conspicuous consumption. As bad as many roads are, it is still not likely that people need four-wheel-drive SUVs merely for transportation.

Automobile manufacturers already know how to make vehicles that use much less fuel than an SUV. This requires no new technology. To a limited extent, such gas-efficient vehicles are already in production. Switching to fuel-efficient vehicles increases the amount of oil in the ground from the perspective of an economist. So, despite the allegedly high price of oil and the alleged possibility that the world is running out of oil, consider the possibility that the amount of oil in the ground is culturally and technologically determined. Transportation engineers also know how to make safe and fast mass transit systems that move people around with far less need for carbon emissions and even no need at all for oil.

Global warming may be the ultimate challenge, but pessimism is not warranted. The preponderance of evidence suggests that the people of the world need to take action on global warming now. Yet they do not need to abandon the quest for abundance. There are many alternatives to the carbon-based economy that do not depend on new technological innovations, as well as alternatives that will depend on technological breakthroughs.

Wind and solar power production are in their infancy, as is conservation of electrical power through more efficient lighting, cooling, and heating systems for homes, offices, factories, and warehouses. Renewable and sustainable power that does not add to global warming is the energy of the future.

Perhaps the future holds even more. We do not wish to speculate ourselves, but some experts argue that humanity is not constrained by the planet's finite resources because the technology exists to exploit resources found on the moon, asteroids, and even other planets. Dennis Wingo (2004) makes an eloquent case that humanity can indeed exploit useful resources on the moon and nearby asteroids. He essentially accepts the fact of limited resources on planet earth. He is particularly concerned with limited energy (hydrocarbon) resources, but offers two possibilities for solving the energy problem. He argues that improvements in fuel cell technology and the development of economical nuclear fusion (not fission) are well within sight. Both fuel cells and fusion would offer clean alternatives to dirty hydrocarbon-based technology. The immediate resource constraint on widespread use of fuel cell technology is the availability of platinum and other metals in the platinum metals group. The (not so) immediate resource constraint on fusion technology is the availability of helium-3. Wingo makes the case that both platinum and helium-3 are available in meaningful quantities on the moon and nearby asteroids. Further, he argues that platinum and helium-3 could be returned from the moon at reasonable costs. Wingo is not the first to suggest that one reason for space exploration is to obtain materials for use on earth, but his argument is very nicely presented. The main point is that perhaps—just perhaps—people are not limited to resources that can be found on earth.

None of this means that the geologists and physicists are wrong about the finite nature of the planet as humanity's physical home. There are only so many things here. None of this means that people should be wasteful or disrespectful to their own home. None of this means that they should be complacent or assume that technological change will always save them. What it does mean is that they should be very careful about claiming that they are running out of resources. They are not. Nor is the availability of resources a major obstacle to achieving abundance for all.

However, policy choices are needed today that will move toward elimination of global warming and other environmental degradation. Citizens and governments can make specific policy changes today that will help, and they have no excuses for failing to do so.

Then What Is a Shortage?

When most contemporary mainstream economists speak of a shortage, they have a particular technical definition in mind. The technical definition of a shortage emphasizes the importance of prices, not the physical limitations of a finite universe, in determining what is in short supply. In almost any introductory economics textbook, you can find a shortage defined in terms of supply and demand. According to the standard approach, a shortage occurs when the quantity demanded of a good or service exceeds the quantity supplied at some particular price (see Figure 4.1). If the price were higher (say, Pe rather than P1 in Figure 4.1), then the shortage would disappear. The higher price would eliminate the shortage that existed at the lower price because consumers at the higher price buy less while producers produce more. That is, a shortage has meaning to most economists only in relation to a given price.

To eliminate the shortage depicted in the Figure 4.1, the price needs to rise high enough to clear the market—up to the price where the two curves intersect. When a market clears, the quantity supplied that flows into the market is exactly equal to the quantity demanded that is removed

Figure 4.1 **Shortage**

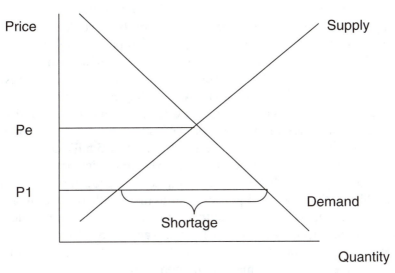

from the market. So, nothing is left behind in the market, no inventory held by frustrated sellers in search of a sale at the market price and no frustrated buyers in search of a purchase at the market price. Of course, even more than price is involved here. Government could also subsidize producers and shift the supply curve to the right by enough to eliminate the shortage at the old price. Government could even produce enough itself to satisfy the excess demand at the old price. For that matter, China could be allowed to produce the product by exploiting the unemployed peasants who are moving into its cities and sell it in the United States through manipulation of the exchange rate.

Both authors of this book live in the southwestern part of the United States, where water is often a critically important political and economic issue. Citizens of the Southwest are often told that water defies the laws of physics: water runs uphill toward money. In southern New Mexico, water for irrigation in 2005 sold for $37 per acre-foot. An acre-foot is approximately 327,000 gallons, enough to cover one acre a foot deep. This means that irrigation water sold for about 1/100th of a penny per gallon, or about 0.000001 cents per ounce. A bottle of drinking water purchased at a local convenience store in the same area at about the same time costs $1.20 for a twenty-ounce bottle, or about six cents per ounce. At six cents per ounce, a gallon of water cost $7.68, or $2.5 million per acre-foot—several thousand times the price of irrigation water. Is there a water shortage in New Mexico? You figure it out. Hint: there would be no shortage of bottled water if the authors of this book could sell it to all buyers in the area for the same price of $2.5 million per acre-foot. Your intrepid authors would solve the region's water problems by buying up all the irrigation water at $37 per acre-foot, purifying it for a few cents a gallon and then reselling it to everybody, including agricultural buyers, at $2.5 million per acre-foot. Even people who understand the economist's price-determined definition of a shortage sometimes forget to apply it. There is no shortage of water in the Southwest at $2.5 million per acre-foot. There may be a shortage of cheap water in particular places, for particular uses. Nevertheless water is still used to grow pecan trees in the middle of the desert and golf courses in the middle of cities in arid regions. Water is still used so that tourists can even visit huge artificial water fountains (purely decorative) in Las Vegas, Nevada.

Price is not always the best indicator of resource shortages. The price of water, like the price of many other commodities, is not always the market-determined price noted in the textbooks. Sometimes, as in the case of irrigation water in New Mexico, the price is an administered price. That is, the price of water is determined by people in a position of power—people with the authority to set the price.

Price has been at the center of the running-out-of-resources debate. Pessimists (a polite name for those who make their living predicting the imminent end of the world as we know it) emphasize the real or inflation-adjusted prices of various commodities. Any sign of an increase in commodity prices convinces the pessimists that the world cannot produce enough food or oil to sustain a growing population. Lester Brown, who founded the World Watch organization (www.worldwatch. org), has been predicting an imminent food shortage for more than thirty years. Of course, Malthus started predicting the same thing two centuries ago. Paul Ehrlich (1990) has been making similar predictions about both food and various minerals since the 1960s. A major problem with the predictions of Brown, Ehrlich, and other doomsday forecasters is that none of their major predictions (and very few of their minor predictions) have come to pass. Bjorn Lomborg (2001), a statistician at the University of Aarhus in Denmark, has conducted a careful assessment of the predictions of Brown, Ehrlich, and others. Examining long-run trends in the production of various food and mineral commodities, Lomborg concluded that the doomsday predictions were incorrect because they were based on weak assumptions and/or very short-run data to project long-run trends. His conclusions are surprising because he set out to show that Julian Simon's (1996) similar analysis of food and commodities was wrong.

Limits to Growth

Perhaps the most famous attempt to demonstrate that the world is running out of resources was the effort of a group known as the Club of Rome. The Club of Rome published a study called *The Limits to Growth* (LTG) in 1972 and continues to update it (Meadows et al. 1972, 2004). The Club of Rome study was highly controversial when it was first published and many economists immediately dismissed it as nonsense.

The Club of Rome study was based on a computer model that attempted to examine alternative scenarios of what the world might look like in the next thirty, fifty, or hundred years. While the various versions of the model incorporated a number of theoretical structures from economics and the natural sciences, the underlying structure of the model was based on the biological model of overshoot and collapse. The authors describe the overshoot and collapse model as their worldview. The basis of the overshoot and collapse model is an exponentially growing population combined with finite resources. The population might be yeast cells, rabbits, human beings, or even industrial production. The population will grow exponentially because of what the authors term a positive feedback loop. That is, the growth rate of the population depends on the current size of the population. The more people there are, the greater will be the annual additions to the population. Eventually, the growing population encounters resource constraints, resulting in either gradual decline or sudden collapse. Hence, the authors conclude that humanity must ultimately face a declining standard of living, a declining population, or some other resource-related catastrophe.

A basic problem with the overshoot and collapse model is that human beings are not yeast cells or rabbits. Humans can and do deliberately change their patterns of fertility and mortality. If humans can control their own growth rate, there is little reason to suppose that the ultimate Malthusian catastrophe is just around the corner. Worse still, the LTG authors are guilty of letting their preconceptions of the way the world works dictate their conclusions. If you start with a model of overshoot and collapse, you should not be surprised that the conclusion you reach is overshoot and collapse.

All the LTG scenarios involved a rapidly growing population facing limited resources. Not surprisingly, all the scenarios suggested that the world would run out of resources and that the only ways to avoid this fate were a dramatic decline in production or a dramatic decline in population. We invite readers to examine the limits-to-growth model and reach their own conclusions about its validity. Our assessment, like that of many other economists, is that the model was based on faulty assumptions and resulted in false predictions of doom. In the initial 1972 study, the Club of Rome group was even worried that the world would run out of critical resources and be unable to feed its growing population before the year 2000!

Limiting Growth on Spaceship Earth?

The LTG model suggests either that the world must limit growth (because resources are finite) or that growth will be limited—not by people's own choices, but by finite resources. The limits in the LTG model arrive very soon. There is a simplistic element of truth in the LTG claims that provides them with great popular appeal. Before the LTG model was published, Kenneth Boulding, a remarkably productive and imaginative economist, performed some simple calculations. As Boulding explained, "I've made a little calculation that, if we go on expanding the human population at the present rate, it only takes a little over seven or eight hundred years before we have standing room over the whole earth, . . . it takes only 8,000 years—this is strictly within historical time—before the whole astronomical universe, two billion light years across, is solid with humanity" (1961, 213). On the basis of his "little calculation" and his understanding of the laws of physics, Boulding concluded that people must limit economic growth before the great Malthusian catastrophe occurs and they are all forced to eat algae for dinner—a prospect, Boulding assured his audience, that only the British, with their infamous tolerance for bad food, might find appealing.

Boulding was one of the first major economists to jump on the we-should-limit-growth bandwagon. He expressed a great deal of uncertainty about when humanity would face the limits to growth, but he held no uncertainty about the ultimate outcome. Boulding argued that traditional macroeconomics, including growth theory, ignored the fact that people live in a larger system than the economy. Traditional macroeconomics, he noted, took it as given that the natural environment could provide people with all the resources they needed and could accept the growing amount of waste that the economy produced. Boulding used powerful imagery to make his point.

Imagine, Boulding stated, the "cowboy economy" in which economic agents obtained raw materials from the natural environment, converted them to useful stuff, and in the process created waste products (1966, 9). If the number of cowboys was small, there was nothing particularly wrong with the cowboy economy since little damage was done to the environment. But people can no longer act as if they had a cowboy economy. Instead, Boulding argued, they should act as if they had a spaceship economy—a closed system in which the only resources available for the journey were the ones people could take with them in a small spaceship. Everything, including human waste, would need to be recycled and reused. People must change their ways or perish.

Global Warming

Since the early 1980s, many environmental scientists have been convinced that emissions from fossil fuels, mainly carbon dioxide, are contributing to a phenomenon known as global warming. The debate over global warming has been conducted in an atmosphere of ill will and political controversy. The United Nations, judging global warming to be a serious threat, established the Intergovernmental Panel on Climate Change (IPCC) to examine the possibilities of global warming, its consequences, and what might be done to prevent it. One of the results of the IPCC was the 1997 Kyoto Protocol that, if approved, would require a drastic reduction in carbon dioxide emissions. Many nations have signed the Kyoto Protocol, and are trying to follow it. But the United States and many poor nations have not signed it and are not trying to follow it. Despite the U.S. rejection of the Kyoto Protocol, the U.S Environmental Protection Agency (EPA) also considers global warming a serious problem. The EPA Web site contains a great deal of information on greenhouse gases and their effects on global warming.

We will not pretend to solve the global warming issue, but we would like you to think about it seriously. Although the connection between global warming and the use of fossil fuel is often presented in the media as an established scientific fact, there are serious skeptics of this view (Beckerman 2003; Hollander 2003; Lomborg 2001).

As recently as thirty years ago, environmentalists and many scientists were worried about global cooling and the impending arrival of a new ice age. A *Newsweek* article titled "The Cooling World" reported, "The evidence in support of these predictions has now begun to accumulate so massively that meteorologists are hard-pressed to keep up with it" (*Newsweek* 1975). Sudden reversals in scientific knowledge are not common, and it should not be surprising that the shift in scientific thinking from global cooling to global warming was met with some skepticism.

Climate change is not a new phenomenon. Geologists say that the earth was much warmer at certain points in the distant past than it is now. There is ample evidence of periodic ice ages. The last major ice age was some 10,000 to 20,000 years ago, and other evidence points to a mini ice age between 1400 and 1800 AD. Nearly all observers agree that the earth has been warming since the early 1800s—well before fossil fuel use could have been a major cause of global warming.

Since the scientific consensus now seems to favor the global warming hypothesis (Gore 2006), it is important to point out that the reduction of greenhouse gas emissions does not conflict with an economy of abundance and equality. It does, however, conflict with the present economic system that is dependent on the production and conspicuous consumption of goods and services that generate high rates of greenhouse emissions. But that system can be changed. Here are a very few specific examples of policies that would promote equality, environmental protection, and abundance. Low-emission mass transit systems should replace SUVs. Production could be shifted away from serving the contrived needs of conspicuous consumers to serving the more urgent and more generic needs for health care, adequate nutrition, education, housing, and personal safety. People exposed to malarial mosquitoes need millions of additional mosquito nets to keep them safe. People who have to use the great outdoors as their toilets need millions of environmentally friendly latrines and thousands of new sewer systems. For that matter, thousands of old sewer systems need replacing or upgrading. Millions more doses of low-cost generic medicines are needed as are millions more visits to physicians, dentists, optometrists, and nurses. Children and the elderly need millions of new day-care centers. All these needs can be met without contributing to global warming.

Sustainable Development?

Sustainable development has become a hugely popular concept in recent years. The term originated with the World Commission on Environment and Development sponsored by the United Nations in 1987. The report of the World Commission is also known as the Brundtland report after the commission's chair, Gro H. Brundtland of Norway. The Brundtland report defined sustainable development in the following terms: "Humanity has the ability to make development sustainable to ensure that it meets the needs of the present without compromising the ability of future genera-tions to meet their own needs" (United Nations 1987, 24).

Unlike many fads, the UN has institutionalized the concept of sustain-able development by creating a Division of Sustainable Development, which has a number of ongoing programs designed to promote the idea. Other major international institutions have also endorsed the sustainable development concept. The World Bank, for example, actively promotes sustainable development—a major change in policy—and has devoted an issue of its influential annual report to the concept (World Bank 2003). Textbooks on economic development (e.g., Todaro and Smith 2005) also incorporate major discussions of sustainable development. The topic is often mentioned on the nightly news and in political debates.

We applaud those who have endorsed and promoted sustainable de-velopment, but we have some serious reservations about the concept. We applaud the promoters of sustainable development because it is probably a good idea to link issues of development and the environment in the minds of policy makers and the general public. Such issues should be widely discussed. The commission's discussion of sustainable develop-ment should also be applauded because it emphasizes that development is not a fixed end, but a process of change. The members of the Brundtland commission should also be applauded because, at various places in the report, they sound almost like abundance economists: "Technology and social organization can be managed and improved to make way for a new era of economic growth. The Commission believes that widespread poverty is no longer inevitable" (United Nations 1987, 25).

Nevertheless, the concept of sustainable development suffers from several conceptual and practical weaknesses. First, the definition of sustainable development is so broad that nearly anyone could endorse it—no matter what their specific views on critical environmental and economic issues. More specifically, both President George W. Bush (2002) and former vice president and presidential candidate Al Gore have endorsed the concept of sustainable development, even though their views on environmental issues are miles apart. After all, everyone has to agree that unsustainable trends will not be sustained.

Second, most discussions of sustainable development, including the

Brundtland report, place too much emphasis on limiting production and consumption, particularly in the high-income regions of the world. Inequality is a serious world problem and should be addressed, but endorsing limits on production and consumption is an antiabundance, zero-sum view of the world. Further, this view is politically inept, bound to arouse the typical citizen's response "Sure, I endorse sustainable development, but don't take away my SUV. Instead, build me and everybody else in the city a safer and more pleasant mass transit system that is good enough to lure me out of my SUV."

Third, proponents of sustainable development tend to ignore the heterogeneity of the world. In short, what may be unsustainable in Tokyo or New York may be very sustainable in Texas, Wyoming, or India. Expanded mass transit would be great in Tulsa, Oklahoma, a typical midsize city with deteriorating roads, large traffic jams, and nothing but carbon-spewing buses for mass transit. But expanded mass transit is hardly required in Hatch, New Mexico, a very small town where the need for a new stoplight is problematic, let alone the need for a mass transit system.

The Environmental Kuznets Curve

The environmental Kuznets curve (EKC) is a hypothetical relationship between environmental conditions and per capita income. The EKC suggests an inverted U relationship between environmental damage and income per person (see Figure 4.2). The basic idea behind the EKC is very simple. At very low levels of income per person, environmental damage is limited or nonexistent. People living in the Stone Age did no harm to the environment, unless you happened to be a woolly mammoth that humans loved to eat. In other words, primitive agrarian societies, represented by point A on Figure 4.2, are relatively clean from an environmental standard. As technology advances and income increases, so does people's ability to damage the environment; point B may represent an industrial society in which various forms of pollution are common. At higher and higher levels of income, the EKC hypothesis suggests that society becomes concerned about the environment and has the technological capability and political will to improve the environment, thus reaching point C on the EKC.

The EKC is based on the work of economist Simon Kuznets, who suggested in 1955 that there might be an inverted U relationship between

Figure 4.2 **An Environmental Kuznets Curve**

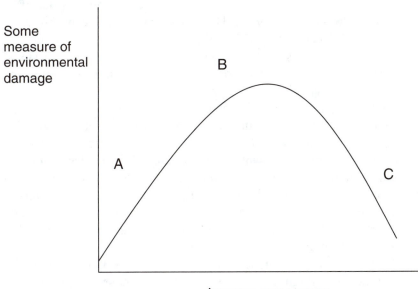

Source: Kuznets (1955).

the level of income and inequality in the distribution of income. The reasoning behind the original Kuznets curve was also very simple. At low levels of income (think Stone Age income levels), everyone is poor and there is little income inequality. As technology, institutions, and income increase, inequality becomes more pronounced. In the last stages of a Kuznets income curve, people can produce enough income to eliminate poverty, and income inequality would also be reduced.

Economists have spent a lot of time and effort examining the environmental and income inequality versions of the Kuznets curve. In both cases, the results of these efforts have been mixed. Some researchers report what they describe as strong evidence that the Kuznets curve exists, while others find little evidence to support the Kuznets hypothesis. There are a number of highly technical problems in evaluating the EKC hypothesis, but some of those problems can be described in straightforward terms.

A major problem with examining the EKC is that the data needed are often unavailable. Very few nations have collected data on environmental conditions for long periods of time. In the United States, for example, widespread concern about environmental issues simply did not exist before the 1960s or early 1970s. The Environmental Protection Agency was not established until 1970. So no one was collecting systematic data on such variables as carbon dioxide or sulfur dioxide emissions. The result is that it is simply not possible to reach definitive conclusions about the EKC hypothesis.

Another major problem with the EKC is that no one really knows the shape (what economists call the functional form) of the curve. Why, for example, should this curve be smooth? Would it not be reasonable to expect various ups and downs along the length of the curve? Perhaps the curve should be multidimensional instead of being drawn in two dimensions. Also, what variable should be placed on the vertical axis to represent environmental damage? Should this variable be carbon dioxide (the current villain of global warming)? Should it be some other variable or a combination of several variables?

There is also no agreement among EKC researchers about where the peak of the curve might be. That is, even among those researchers who find evidence of an EKC relationship, no one seems to know what the threshold level of per capita income is that, once reached, would lead to improving environmental conditions. Indeed, if such a threshold exists, it may be different for different types of pollutants.

It would be nice—even comforting—if there were a nice smooth EKC. The solution to environmental degradation would be obvious: higher incomes will automatically fix the problem. But that is not what the evidence, such as it is, suggests. Economists and environmental scientists agree that there is a great deal of uncertainty associated with the EKC. So why should we discuss this concept? There are two reasons. First, despite the uncertainty, some researchers do find that environmental conditions improve with income. Second, none of the EKC-related research suggests that rising incomes inevitably lead to more environmental damage. The second reason is more important than the first. At least so far, there is no evidence to suggest that an economy of abundance rules out a clean and safe environment.

The Hollander Hypothesis

Jack Hollander, a retired environmental scientist from the University of California at Berkeley, has taken the basic argument of the EKC one step further. He argues that the greatest danger to the environment is widespread poverty. Hollander's book "makes the case that poverty is also linked to violence against the environment and that a global transition from poverty to affluence is essential to bringing about an environmentally sustainable world" (2003, xi). For Hollander, the environmental problems of the poor are very different from those of the rich. Rich nations may worry about global warming or the ozone layer. In poor nations, environmental problems are always local and particularly brutal. The poor, Hollander asserts, suffer from an environment characterized by hunger, contaminated water supplies, rampant diseases, and extremes of inequality.

For Hollander, the core of the environmental debate is the relationship between affluence and the environment. He argues that there is no mystery about this relationship: "People of means have always sought to live amidst beautiful surroundings, regardless of the squalor that may have been nearby" (27). In other words, the affluent are naturally environmentalists. Hollander's solution for the world's complex, subtle, and difficult environmental problems is to make everyone affluent so that everyone will have a stake in solving them. Along the way, Hollander examines several major environmental issues, including population growth, food supply, and the availability of fresh water, fossil fuel use, and air quality. In each case, he concludes that the environment would be improved if poverty were eliminated. We agree with him. If abundance can be spread so that more people enjoy it, more people will be able to afford environmental improvement, including reduction of carbon emissions. Stopping growth and the spread of abundance, on the other hand, makes it harder for many people to afford environmental quality.

To sum up, environmental quality and resource availability do not form barriers to economic abundance. Instead, environmental quality cannot be sustained without economic abundance. Widespread poverty and inequality are inconsistent with environmental quality. More than that, environmental quality and economic abundance reinforce each other. In the long run, there is no tradeoff between them. In the long run, humanity must pursue them both simultaneously.

II

Inequality

Why Abundance Escapes Us

5

Inequality

Since we cannot blame the environment, natural resources, or excess population, this chapter will finally get down to explaining why communities fail to live up to their potential—why they suffer scarcity when they could enjoy abundance. Inequality prevents abundance. It does so by denying access to members of certain groups. Four major social inequalities are involved—classism, nationalism, sexism and racism.

Everybody knows about the vicious cycle of poverty. Poor, unhealthy, and uneducated parents are unable to provide the best health care and educational opportunities for their children. The children, like their parents, are then ill prepared to take full advantage of the community's joint stock of knowledge. The children of poor parents start their lives at a severe disadvantage. They start out behind and fall further and further behind. Their plight gets worse because they are caught up in a vicious cycle of cumulative causation spiraling them downward. Unless they are able to sustain heroic efforts to break out of the cycle, it continues pulling them further down.

But who starts their lives in poverty? How does society select the unfortunate one? Four systems of inequality are at work in modern society, pulling people in selected groups down. Sexism, racism, classism, and nationalism select those to be denied full access to the community's joint stock of knowledge and it is the operation of those social inequalities that snatch away the promise of abundance. Here, very briefly, is a preview of some of the ways social inequality prevents abundance: Labor force participation rates of women are lower than men. Unemployment rates for persons of color are higher than for other groups. Men are paid more than women. Children work long hours in sweat shops of poor countries producing athletic shoes for consumers in rich countries instead of spending their time learning. Even the economies of rich countries require a running margin of unemployed workers to maintain workplace discipline. Extreme nationalism results in international instability and war.

Inequality, in all its various forms, reduces the total output of the economy. Reducing inequality means everybody could have more goods and services available. In the following chapters, we will explain how reducing or eliminating the more serious systems of inequality will put abundance within reach. Even the mainstream of economics, though still fixated on scarcity, is showing an improved understanding of the relationships between inequalities and growth retardation (Alesina and Rodrik 1994; Benabou 2000).

Are we suggesting some sort of utopian society in which everyone has exactly the same income? No, we are not. Complete equality is a silly and unattainable idea. We do argue that the path to abundance is through greater equality and that genuine abundance and greater equality can only be achieved together.

Class, nation, sex, and race sort people into different groups. These are the "differentia specifica" for each system of grouping—the specific differences (real and imaginary) between people who benefit from the community's joint stock of knowledge and those who cannot fully participate. Sexual orientation and religion are also used, as well as other differentia specifica. Systems of inequality always involve some such system of grouping. The class system (classism) uses ownership of the means of production as the differentia specifica to sort people into the unequal groups. The race system uses race; the gender or sex system uses sex and the nation system uses nation. The sorting into unequal groups is the meaning of inequality.

Inequality is systematic. It affects the whole social system in which people participate. These systems of inequality are woven into the market system itself. The power exercised in each system of inequality is institutionalized in market rules and property rights (Dugger 2005). The rules and property rights produce a particular distribution of income and wealth. The more effective the top dogs are at institutionalizing property rights and rules that benefit them at the expense of the underdogs, the larger the share received by those on top and the smaller the share received by those on the bottom. But there are many mongrels—neither top dogs nor underdogs—in the inequality mix as well.

Inequality: The Illness

Inequality is a social illness, a collective disorder that divides people who are actually equals into superiors and inferiors. It is a social illness because it keeps people from achieving the abundant society. It benefits some groups at the expense of others. The complex and intertwined systems of inequality empower some people and disempowers others. To disempower means to strip away a person's ability to pursue an objective. To empower, of course, means to enable a person to pursue an objective. Empowerment, of course, also means access to the community's joint stock of knowledge.

The result of inequality is that those who are empowered use those who are disempowered. In sex or sexism, men use women. In race or racism, one race uses another. In nation or nationalism, strong nations use weak ones. (For further discussion of inequality, see Dugger 1996, 1998; for recent discussions of race, gender, and class, see Mills 2003, Wright 2005, and Zweig 2004).

Assume for just a moment that we are playing games, instead of really exploiting each other. The game assumption is not intended to trivialize exploitation, but to help us think more clearly about what is going on in classism, racism, sexism, and nationalism. These four inequalities are deadly, not trivial and the game assumption helps us understand them in order to combat them Let us consider three games—Russian roulette, poker, and room project. To play Russian roulette, the players take turns putting one bullet in a revolver, spinning the pistol's chamber, aiming at their head, and pulling the trigger. The game continues until everyone has had a turn or until someone blows his or her brains out. Bad game! To play poker, the players get together with lots of drinks and junk food and deal out the cards, betting their hard-earned cash on each hand. Some of them win; some lose. Good game for the winners; bad for the losers. To play room project, the players get the needed materials, hammers, saws, and screwdrivers and build a new table for their room. When the game is over, all the players have the use of a nice table—a bit rustic, perhaps, but they can all enjoy it and use it for playing poker or for catching their blown-out brains if they are so stupid.

The first game, Russian roulette, is known by economists as a negative-sum game. In Russian roulette, there is a terrible loss among the players. One dies. Adding up the positive value of the winnings (zero) and the negative value of the losings (immense) results in an immense negative sum. Avoid this game!

The second game, poker, is known by economists as a zero-sum game. In poker, the amount that the winners gain is the same amount that the losers lose. Subtracting what the losers lose from what the winners gain gives zero. The wins and the losses cancel each other out, resulting in a zero sum—not a bad game but not a good one, either. The third game, room project, is known as a positive-sum game. In room project, the players build something new for a room—a table, for example. Everyone can help and everyone can enjoy the table. There are no losers in this game. Summing up the winnings and subtracting the losings gives a positive sum. Wonderful game—build something today!

Inequality is such a pervasive feature of society that most people find it hard to see that it is a negative-sum game. As Theodore Roszak, a well-known historian and social critic, notes:

> This is the sort of insight our angriest dissenters tend to miss when, in the course of heroic confrontation, they open themselves to the most obvious kinds of police and military violence. They quickly draw the conclusion that the status quo is supported by nothing more than bayonets, overlooking the fact that these bayonets enjoy the support of a vast consensus that has been won by the status quo by means far more subtle and enduring than armed force. (1969, 267)

Many other social critics have seen through normality and explained how people fool themselves. We will confine our discussion to three of them: C. Wright Mills, Simone de Beauvoir, and William Ryan.

In an analysis of sociology textbooks and textbook writers in the United States, C. Wright Mills probes how intellectuals fool themselves and teach others how to do likewise. Published over sixty years ago, his essay, "The Professional Ideology of Social Pathologists," is still fresh and provocative (1943). Mills explains how textbook writers teach their readers to see people who are poor or marginalized by systematic inequality as being pathological rather than victimized by exploitation. Society is not sick. Only a few deviant individuals within it are sick. They are not social problems, just individual problems. Their plight is due to individual behavior, not social structure. If they are hurting, it is because they need to adapt to the norms of their society. Readers who are convinced by this argument are thus also convinced that society does not need to be changed. In the absence of disrupting social movements, wars, or other turmoil, the textbook writers encounter little resistance in selling their ideology of individual pathology. It is the path of least resistance in sociology. Scarcity is the path of least resistance in economics. It sells well, too.

To explain how easily people are fooled by the ideology of the elites,

Simone de Beauvoir relied on the concept of otherness in her classic book *The Second Sex*, published in France in 1949. Sexism distorts the way people understand themselves. As Beauvoir explained:

> Thus humanity is male and man defines woman not in herself but as relative to him; she is not regarded as an autonomous being. . . . She is defined and differentiated with reference to man and not he with reference to her; she is the incidental, the inessential as opposed to the essential. He is the Subject, he is the Absolute—she is the Other. (1989, xxii)

Beauvoir extended the concept of otherness to include all forms of inequality:

> Thus it is that no group ever sets itself up as the One without at once setting up the Other over against itself. . . . In small-town eyes all persons not belonging to the village are "strangers" and suspect; to the native of a country all who inhabit other countries are "foreigners"; Jews are "different" for the anti-Semite. Negroes are "inferior" for American racists, aborigines are "natives" for colonists, proletarians are the "lower class" for the privileged. (xxiii)

Unfortunately, it is easy for society to blame the victims of ill treatment for their sorry plight. Something is wrong with the ones who are hurting. The victims are to blame for deviating from educational, moral, or other norms. High school dropouts are lazy (never mind that many schools are inadequate). Unwed mothers are sluts (never mind that many girls are raped). The system is fine and does not need to be changed. It is the victims who need to be fixed, to be cured of their deviance. Obviously, if the victims are at fault, everyone else is free from blame. William Ryan discussed this particular fogging of the human brain in the context of the mythology of the great American middle class. Ryan's original concept of blaming the victim was a critique of those in the late 1960s who blamed the negro family for allegedly creating a self-defeating culture of poverty that generated poverty regardless of what white society did or did not do. Ryan showed that this claim of black family pathology was wrong because it confused cause (racial discrimination) and effect (high poverty among African-American families.) It blamed the victims of racism for the disintegrating effects racism has had on the black family and on other aspects of black life (Ryan 1976). Daniel Patrick Moynihan was prominent among those who claimed that the black family was pathological (1965). Moynihan argued that the black family was disintegrating due to an internal dynamic of its own and the result was an explosion of black poverty. It may not have been intended to do so, but the Moynihan argument provided those who wanted one with a ready to use excuse for doing little or nothing to help African Americans participate fully in the American economy.

Myths give us imaginary excuses regarding inequalities, enabling the inequity to continue. (Interesting treatments of myths are in DeMott 1990, 1995, and 2000.) One such myth, used to excuse the inequities involved in western imperialism, was the so-called white man's burden that Rudyard Kipling wrote about in a poem published in the February 1899 issue of *McClure's Magazine*. The title of the poem was "The White Man's Burden: The United States and the Philippine Islands." It was in support of U.S. imperialism and its buncombe provided an excellent rationalization of empire. The conquest and the violence were for the victim's own good and were a great burden to the conqueror, not at all to the conqueror's benefit.

The myth kept imperialists consciences clear by allowing them to claim that they were not exploiting the lesser breeds, but civilizing them instead (never mind that many peoples had a rich heritage of civilization long before the imperialists arrived). The consciences of men who exploit women are protected by the myth that the men are helping the "weaker" sex (never mind that they are often helping themselves to the "weaker" sex and that it is the "weaker" sex that feeds, clothes, and cleans up after them). The consciences of whites who exploit blacks are protected because the whites fool themselves into thinking that they are helping their "lesser" black brothers and sisters (never mind that the blacks do much of the hard work in the community). The consciences of capitalists who exploit workers are protected because the capitalists fool themselves into thinking that they are helping the profligate workers by accumulating capital for the workers' use (never mind that the workers build the machines, pipelines, and buildings; figure out how best to use them; and pay for them in inflated rent and consumer prices; while the capitalized value of the assets is then claimed by the owners when they sell their shares of stock on the stock market). Current mythology also emphasizes that the top dogs and the underdogs pursue their economic relations in the free market, which benefits everybody, as long as government is prevented from interfering with it (Friedman 1962; Friedman and Friedman 1980).

These myths are defense mechanisms that protect people from unpleasant realities about inequality. Two simple defense mechanisms are particularly powerful. One defense mechanism shields the top dogs from the truth; the other shields the underdogs (Dugger 2000). The conscience of the top dogs is protected when they are able to fool themselves into thinking that the game they are playing is really for the benefit of the underdogs. While their defense mechanism keeps the top dogs feeling good about themselves, the defense mechanism that works on the underdogs does the opposite to them. It does not defend them. It defends the status quo against them. This second defense mechanism makes the underdogs feel bad about themselves instead of angry about systematic forms of inequality. The victims of systematic inequality are taught to blame themselves for it. African-American and African-French schools, for example, can continue to be inadequate as long as their victims take personal blame for not getting the education they need. Only when they blame the systemized inequality instead of themselves does dissent occur.

Only by seeing through the myths can people realize that inequality is a negative-sum game. A true flash of insight is required to recognize that it is a bad game and should be avoided. Such recognition is neither easy nor painless.

Our little exploration of what is called game theory suggests an important characteristic of the systems of inequality—whether the system is based on class, nation, race, or sex. Systems of inequality involve a negative-sum game. They generate more losses than gains and prevent people from achieving abundance.

Calculating whether a system of inequality locks people into a negative-sum, relationship is straightforward. Let G equal the gains from maintaining a system of inequality. Let L equal the loss suffered from the system of inequality. Then the system of inequality's sum can be expressed as an equation:

$$SUM = G - L < 0$$

And when the sum is negative, as indicated, it is a negative-sum relationship. The real challenges come in constructing empirical estimates of G and L. In this book, we focus on L. We doubt that G (the gains from racism, sexism, classism, and nationalism) is greater than zero, but if you want to try to estimate G, go ahead.

Since the sum can be zero, positive, or negative, this simple equation divides the world of human relationships (games) into three basic types and makes it clear that negative-sum relationships should be avoided, positive-sum relationships enjoyed, and zero-sum ones played only with both eyes open. Avoid the drinks, silly.

Several rewarding hypotheses and empirical explorations could be built out of measuring the different gains and losses encountered when people participate in the systems of inequality. If the issues we have raised regarding nationalism, classism, sexism, and racism interest you, we urge you to turn your curiosity about inequality into a career in empirical research. In this book, we pursue our empirical curiosity primarily by looking at the costs of unemployment and lost work effort, but you could spend a whole career looking much further than we have.

The systems of inequality are not inevitable. They can be stopped. Short of that, their rules can be fundamentally altered. However, it is hard for the underdogs and mongrels, who lack power, to stop the games or alter the rules. Besides, the underdogs and mongrels are fooled into thinking they deserve their ill treatment. The top dogs have the power to stop the games or change the rules. However, they lack the will. Why should they make any changes? Their consciences are clear. They make out just fine, thank you very much.

Inequality in the United States: One Potbelly and Two Tables

Some empirical measurements of inequality are in order at this point. A frequently used empirical estimate of inequality is the Gini ratio, named after the Italian statistician Corrado Gini who developed it a century ago. It is also called the Gini coefficient and is extremely helpful because it can be used to measure any dimension of inequality that can be quantified—income or wealth most frequently. The Gini ratio makes a great illustration because its graph shows that a society becomes unequal by growing an unhealthy potbelly. The Gini ratio measures the size of society's potbelly when inequality grows or shrinks. The larger the potbelly, the more unequal and unhealthy the society.

For example, Figure 5.1 shows the Gini ratios for the households that make up a society and their incomes. The percentages of total income are on the vertical axis and percentages of households are on the horizontal axis. A society made up of households with equal incomes is depicted in the top chart. Each household falls on the diagonal line called the "line of perfect equality." In such a completely equal society, the Gini ratio would be 0. A society in which there is some inequality is depicted in the

Figure 5.1　**The Trim (Equal) Economy and the Potbelly (Unequal) Economy**

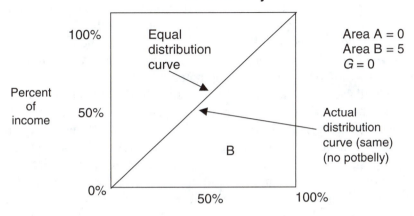

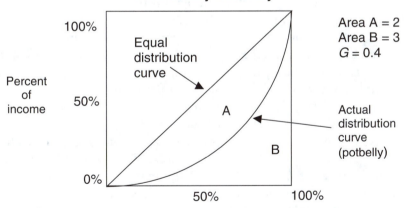

$$\text{Gini ratio } (G) = \frac{\text{area A}}{\text{areas A} + \text{B}}$$

bottom chart of Figure 5.1. This society has a Gini ratio of 0.4. Thus, the Gini ratio measures the size of the potbelly (area A) relative to the size of the lower triangle defined by the axes and the line of perfect equality.

If it were possible to have a completely unequal society where one household gets all the income, then that society's potbelly would take up the whole graphed area below the diagonal and would be measured as a Gini ratio of 1.0 (not depicted in the figure). So the ratio can range between 0 (no potbelly) and 1.0 (all potbelly).

We will use the Gini ratio here to measure the degree of inequality in the distribution of money income to households in the United States. In Table 5.1 we report the Gini ratio for U.S. households. We include in the table the distribution of income to the five quintiles of U.S. households plus the share of the top 5 percent of U.S. households. (A quintile is a fifth or 20 percent of the total. So the top quintile would be the top fifth or top 20 percent.) In Table 5.1, the trend toward greater household inequality since 1970 is clearly visible—a reversal of the trend from the 1940s to about 1970. The Gini ratio rose significantly during the period. The U.S. waistline sagged dangerously. The share of income going to the poorest fifth of the households fell during the period. The poor got poorer. The share going to the top fifth of households rose and the share going to the richest 5 percent of households rose even faster. The rich got richer and the very rich got richer even faster. The table contradicts the conventional view that economic conditions have improved for the underdogs relative to the top dogs in the United States. Economic conditions have gotten worse for the underdogs and the mongrels as well. (A more detailed view of an earlier period is in Clark 1996.)

Table 5.1 does not show the actual incomes received by different people in the United States; it just shows measures of how unequally the income was shared out. Table 5.2 shows actual median incomes for 2003. Hispanic women and black women fared the worst while white, non-Hispanic men fared the best. Subtracting black men's income from white, non-Hispanic men's income reveals a racial income gap of $10,396. Subtracting white, non-Hispanic women's income from white, non-Hispanic men's income shows a sex or gender gap of $14,030.

Global Inequality

We need to look internationally to complete our empirical survey of inequality. Table 5.3 shows the Gini ratios for the twenty most populous

Table 5.1

Quintile Household Shares and Gini Ratios for Aggregate Income in the United States, 1967–2001
(in percent, for shares)

Year	Gini	Poorest fifth	Second fifth	Third fifth	Fourth fifth	Richest fifth	Top 5 percent
2005	0.469	3.4	8.6	14.6	23.0	50.4	21.2
2000	0.462	3.6	8.9	14.8	23.0	49.8	22.1
1995	0.450	3.7	9.1	15.2	23.3	48.7	21.0
1990	0.428	3.9	9.6	15.9	24.0	46.6	18.6
1985	0.419	4.0	9.7	16.3	24.6	45.3	17.0
1980	0.403	4.3	10.3	16.9	24.9	43.7	15.8
1975	0.397	4.4	10.5	17.1	24.8	43.2	15.9
1970	0.394	4.1	10.8	17.4	24.5	43.3	16.6
1967	0.399	4.0	10.8	17.3	24.2	43.8	17.5

Sources: The Gini ratio is from the U.S. Census Bureau, Historical Income Tables-Income Equality, Table A-3, www.census.gov/hhes/www /income/histinc/p60no231 tablesa3.pdf.

The household shares of aggregate income are from the U.S. Census Bureau, Historical Income Tables-Income Equality, Table H-2, www .census.gov/hhes/www/income/histinc/h02AR.html.

Table 5.2

Median Income of People in the United States Fifteen Years Old and Older by Race, Sex, and Hispanic Origin, 2003

Male	
All races and origins	$33,196
White	$35,141
White, not Hispanic	$37,373
Black	$25,822
Hispanic, any race	$24,451

Female	
All races and origins	$20,922
White	$21,069
White, not Hispanic	$21,687
Black	$19,752
Hispanic, any race	$16,748

Source: U.S. Census Bureau, Historical Income Tables-People, Table P-2. www .census.gov/hhes/www/income/historic/p02.html September 17, 2008.

nations in the world. The table also shows the gross domestic product (GDP) per person and the growth rate of the GDP per person for the same twenty nations. The nations are also ranked in the table according to their Gini ratio, GDP per person, and growth rate. The last two— GDP per person and the growth rate of GDP per person—are measures of economic performance. As GDP per person and its growth rate rise, economic performance is said to rise. The Gini ratio, of course, is a measure of inequality. As inequality rises, the ratio rises.

Two diametrically opposed hypotheses can be examined with the table, an inequality and an equality argument. The inequality argument claims that economic performance is a positive function of inequality so the table should show a positive relation between inequality and performance. In contrast, the equality argument claims that economic performance is a positive function of equality so the table should show a positive relation between equality and performance. According to the inequality argument, more income and wealth for the privileged and the rich will improve economic performance because they will save more, invest more, and innovate more. Their responses to more for them will improve economic performance. Furthermore, if their income or wealth were redistributed to the poor, the resulting inefficiency would cause total output to fall (Okun 1975). This is the conventional wisdom that supports the trickle-down effect: benefits given to the top strata of society (capitalists) trickle down to the lower strata (workers). This conventional wisdom legitimates concentrated wealth and privilege (also, capitalism).

According to the equality argument, however, more income and wealth for the underprivileged and the poor will improve economic performance because they will work more, save more, invest more, and innovate more. Their responses to more for them will improve economic performance. This is the unconventional wisdom that supports the bubble-up effect: benefits given to the bottom strata of society bubble up to the rest of society. This unconventional wisdom is important to the economics of abundance.

If we support the inequality argument, we should expect the rankings in columns 3 and 4 of Table 5.3 to be ascending—to start low and then go up. If we support the equality argument, we should expect the rankings in columns 3 and 4 to be descending—to start high and then go down. However, columns 3 and 4 are neither ascending nor descending. Instead, the rankings in those columns jump around in an almost random manner. This observed behavior in Table 5.3 seems to indicate that economic performance, as measured by GDP per person and by growth rate in GDP per person, is not affected by the level of inequality in a nation, at least for the twenty most populous nations. At least, the table suggests that the conventional wisdom is wrong. We are not the only economists to come to this unconventional conclusion. Steven Pressman and others recently investigated the empirical relation between economic performance and equality or inequality. Pressman found a slightly positive relation between performance and equality. His finding supports the equality argument. Unfortunately, he also found that the relation was not statistically significant (Pressman 2005).

Communities do not have to give more privileges and wealth to the upper strata in order to improve economic performance, nor does giving more privileges and wealth to the lower strata have to cause economic performance to decline. But can communities improve their economic performance by giving more privileges and wealth to the lower strata? Table 5.4 probes into that question.

In Table 5.4, the Gini ratio, GDP per person, and growth rate are given for each of the Scandinavian countries—also for the United States and the world for comparison. Scandinavia is famous for its egalitarian poli-

Table 5.3

Gini Ratios for Top Twenty Most Populous Nations

Gini-ranked nations	Gini ratio	GDP per person		Growth rate	
		Rank	Amount	Rank	Rate
1. Brazil	59	5	4,642	15	0.8
2. Mexico	55	6	3,717	14	0.9
3. Nigeria	51	19	248	18	−0.7
4. Philippines	46	12	1,209	16	0.1
5. China	45	14	944	1	8.1
6. Iran	43	10	1,801	18	−0.7
7. Thailand	43	8	3,000	2	5.5
8. USA	41	3	31,891	11	2.0
9. Turkey	40	9	2,942	10	2.1
10. Viet Nam	37	17	413	3	4.8
11. Indonesia	34	13	1,060	4	4.4
12. Egypt	34	11	1,250	6	2.9
13. France	33	4	30,790	13	1.7
14. Pakistan	33	15	518	7	2.8
15. India	32	16	493	5	3.2
16. Bangladesh	32	18	396	9	2.2
17. Russia	31	7	3,257	19	−1.2
18. Ethiopia	30	20	124	17	−0.1
19. Germany	28	2	32,826	12	1.9
20. Japan	25	1	45,029	8	2.7

Source: United Nations Development Program, *Human Development Report,* various years.

Notes: The top twenty most populous countries are chosen according to their 2003 population as reported by the United Nations Development Program. The Gini ratio and the growth rate are in percent. The GDP per person is in U.S. 1995 dollars. The growth rate is for per person GDP for 1975–2000. William M. Dugger provided the rankings.

cies. The Gini ratios in Scandinavia are all very low, among the lowest in the world. The equality argument implies that economic performance in Scandinavia should therefore be very high, and indeed it is. The economic performance of the Scandinavian nations is among the highest in the world, comparing quite favorably to that of the United States. The two sides of the equality versus inequality debate may never agree, but Scandinavia presents strong empirical evidence that economic performance can be a positive function of equality.

Supporters of the conventional wisdom generally dismiss the Scandinavian experience by saying that it is too exceptional, that Scandinavia is too homogenous, that classism, nationalism, sexism, and racism are very

Table 5.4

Gini Ratios for Scandinavian Countries

Nation	Gini ratio	GDP per person	Growth rate
1. Denmark	25	39,332	2.8
2. Sweden	25	33,676	1.6
3. Norway	26	48,412	2.8
4. Finland	27	31,058	2.0
Average	26	38,120	2.3
5. World	N/A	5,801	1.4
USA (from Table 5.3)	41	31,891	2.0

Source: United Nations Development Program, *Human Development Report, 2005.*
Note: The Gini ratio is a percent. GDP per person is in US dollars in 2003. Growth rate is an annual percent for GDP per person, 1975–2003.

low there. However, we take the Scandinavian experience as making our point: the inequalities of classism, nationalism, sexism, and racism have been pushed to the very margins of Scandinavian society, allowing the full participation of all citizens to generate abundance.

Although neither one of us would call himself a social activist, we have studied the various forms of inequality and written and spoken against them since the 1960s. Our experiences and studies have led us to the conclusion that each inequality game should be stopped altogether. Changing the rules is not enough. Prayers, good intentions, and individual changes of mind are all wonderful, but not enough. Collective action is required to stop the games. Stopping the nation game will require a league of pacifist peoples with independent taxing and war-making powers. Ending the class game will take a powerful global labor movement. The sex game must be dealt with by a powerful league of nonsexist men and women. The race game must be stopped by a powerful league of nonracist men and women. All must work in concert and in peace.

Stopping the games will raise challenges aplenty for the coming generations and is clearly worthy of their best efforts. Without powerful collective responses to rein in the inequality games, they will continue to push humankind down the path of scarcity instead of abundance (Peach 1996).

Classism

Class is a social system that sorts people into groups with unequal access to power and the community's joint stock of knowledge. Class is the opposite of widely held beliefs in democracy and equality before the law. Class is largely ignored in economics textbooks, but widely discussed in the popular media.

At least one well-known TV commentator, Lou Dobbs of CNN, has devoted a good part of his career to an analysis of what he calls the disappearing middle class in America. What does the disappearing middle class consist of? According to Dobbs, members of the middle class are hardworking (for wages) households and families struggling to pay their bills. At the same time, members of the privileged upper class live well and receive high incomes by manipulating the system—for example, by manipulating the tax laws, exporting U.S. jobs, particularly manufacturing jobs, to other nations, and importing cheap labor in the form of undocumented workers. How do they do this? The upper class has access to political power that the "struggling middle class" does not. Dobbs, an inherently conservative fellow, even speaks openly of class warfare: the title of his book is *War on the Middle Class* (2006).

Whether you agree or disagree with Lou Dobbs is unimportant. What is important here is that Dobbs and many others speak openly of class. They do so because class is a meaningful concept. Nearly 100 years ago, Thorstein Veblen made the following remarks about class:

> The population of these civilized nations now falls into two main classes: Those who own wealth in large holdings and who thereby control the conditions of life for the rest; and those who do not own wealth in sufficiently large holdings, and whose conditions of life are therefore controlled by others. It is a division, not between those who

have nothing—as many socialists would be inclined to describe it—but between those who own wealth enough to make it count and those who do not. (1964, 160–161)

Veblen's emphasis on the distinction between "those who own enough wealth to make it count and those who do not" is important. Nearly everyone can tell a story about this difference. Some people have easy access to members of Congress; others do not. Even in a university environment, we suspect that a potential donor with a lot of money might have an easier time getting an appointment with the university president than an anonymous freshman struggling with the culture shock of being at a university for the first time. But it is not necessary to divide society into only two classes. Indeed there are many classes and several of them will be described in this chapter. It is not necessary to believe in conspiracy theories or to think that class warfare is imminent to find class a useful analytical device. Classism, like nationalism, racism, and sexism, is an obstacle to economic abundance. In this chapter we explain why.

A class is a group of people who get their living in the same way. Class is a larger grouping than occupation. There are more occupations than classes. Pipe fitters, carpenters, and bricklayers are all in different occupations, but in the same class—the working class. Bill Gates owns Microsoft and Donald Trump owns real estate, but they are in the same class—the upper class. The ranking of classes and the relations between them form the class system. There are several classes in a class system, and they vie for wealth, power, and status. Sometimes one class becomes the most powerful class and dominates one or more of the less powerful classes. Often, there is no single dominant class.

Class systems are negative-sum games, impediments to abundance. In all class systems, members of the most powerful classes claim to be the great benefactors of society and act as if they were the fountainhead of all progress. Of course, they are neither. Great social benefactors come from all classes and progress comes from growth in the community's joint stock of knowledge, not from a particular class.

A brief review of some class systems is a worthwhile endeavor. We begin with a look at slavery and feudalism, two of the most obvious class systems. We then take a look at classism in contemporary economies, including classism in market-oriented or so-called capitalist economies.

Slavery

Slavery was a vicious system involving rape, corporal punishment, and humiliation. Years after it was ended, the anger it created still burned deeply into the hearts of many former slaves. Here are some reflections of an anonymous American ex-slave, made many years after the Civil War ended slavery in the United States:

> I was riding on a streetcar, long after freedom, and I passed the cemetery where my (white) father was buried. I started cussing. "Let me off this damn car and go see where my goddamn father is buried so I can spit on his grave—a goddamn son of a bitch." I got no mercy on nobody who bring up their children like dogs. How could any father treat his child like that?—bring them up to be ignorant, like they did us. If I had my way with them all, I would like to have a chopping block and chop every one of their heads off. Of course, I don't hate them that is good. There are some good white folks. Mighty few, though. (Mellon 1988, 456–457; parenthesis in original)

Slavery is the most violent and vile of the class systems. It is a market-based system. Slaves can be bought and sold on the market like cattle. Remnants of slavery still exist in various parts of the world.

Slavery was the dark side of classical Greece and ancient Rome. It faded in the Western world after the fall of the Roman Empire, but returned with a vengeance during the European conquest of Africa and the Americas (Davis 1966). Native Americans did not want to work for the Europeans, and they made poor slaves because they could run away and find refuge and because contact with Europeans infected them with contagious diseases to which they had not built up immunities. Africans, though no more willing than Native Americans, found it much harder to run away and find refuge because their original communities were an ocean away. Furthermore, Africans had built up immunities to European-borne diseases through generations of contact. The African holocaust began when the Europeans' conquest of the New World ignited a demand for workers there. About 9.5 million Africans were taken by force from Africa and shipped to the Americas during the roughly four centuries of the Atlantic slave trade. Three different areas absorbed most of the imported slaves: Brazil, the Caribbean, and the southern English colonies (Curtin 1969; Low and Clift 1981, 8).

In the United States, slaves kidnapped in Africa or in the free states of the North could be sold on the slave market to the highest bidder. They and their descendants were forced to work their owners' land. Owners could whip or mistreat their slaves at will. Some owners raped their slaves or took them as concubines. Such practices were common (Gordon-Reed 1998). Some historians play down slavery's brutality (Fogel and Engerman 1974). Others play it up (Anderson 1995). The slave states enforced slavery through a series of legal codes. Slavery remained deeply entrenched in the southern slave states of the United States after the Revolutionary War.

Slavery was practiced in the New World from just before 1500 to about 1870, when it was ended in its last major stronghold—Brazil. However, it continues today in parts of Africa and in new forms in many other parts of the world. David Brion Davis says:

> While traditional chattel slavery is still widespread in such Saharan nations as Niger, Mauritania, Chad, and Sudan, it is immensely overshadowed by what modern antislavery groups describe as "new forms" of slavery—the men, women and children who are physically forced to work, often under guise of meaningless contracts, in sweatshops or in building roads and pipelines for multinational corporations. Along with the exploitive use of indebtedness as an excuse for forced labor, there is also an enormous international traffic, especially in eastern Europe and south Asia, in "sex slaves"—often girls or young women who have volunteered for decent-sounding jobs, only to find themselves coerced into prostitution. (2006, 330)

Feudalism

Feudalism, which replaced the slavery of the Roman Empire, although not completely, may be somewhat less vile than slavery. Feudalism was not a market-based system: it was based on violence, not exchange. It involved a kind of semiorganized political system of warlords vying against each other for power.

Without a slave market, the lower classes could not be treated like mere property—sold on the market for so many dollars by the upper class of the times. The barbarian invasions of Europe during the Dark Ages snuffed out a lot of things, including the lights at most of the slave markets of the old Roman world. The serfdom of feudalism largely replaced slavery. Serfs still were subject to some forms of involuntary servitude, but they could not be sold outright as could slaves.

Feudalism involved a network of lords who were only very loosely tied together into a political system by the monarchy to which they all owed their allegiance. The system was highly decentralized, with the king vainly trying to maintain a political center of gravity, as it were, and with the lords all pulling in their separate directions. Markets of any significance were impossible because of the resulting lack of law and order. Large cities, likewise, were virtually impossible. Life was lived in the countryside, where the people followed local customs. Feudal practices were highly localized and varied enormously from one place to another. Travel and exchange between localities were limited not just by a lack of roads and other means of transportation, but more effectively by the generalized lawlessness and violence. Local self-sufficiency was the rule; specialization and market exchange, the exception.

The feudal period for most of the old Roman Empire began around 600 AD and ended around 1200. Although the Roman Empire collapsed before the year 600, historians date the beginning of feudalism then because the collapse was followed by an unstable period in which warlords and invaders fought over the spoils of the old empire. The fighting and generalized mayhem evolved into a more organized and stabilized form of violence. That was feudalism. Feudalism began collapsing before 1200, but historians date its end about then because the great flowering of the Italian city-states was clearly under way by then. However, putting a single date on the end of feudalism is not strictly accurate. After all, the serfs were not freed in Russia until the time of the American Civil War.

The feudal lords (progeny of former warlords) settled down to take their living from large rural estates by having the serfs work their land for them. In return, the lords provided protection against the raids of other lords and gave the serfs small plots of land to work on their own. Serfs did not pay rent in money, but they did have to work a certain number of days for their lord or perform certain services for him. Sometimes the serf also paid the lord a portion of the crops raised. At least in theory, there was a degree of mutual responsibility between the lord and his serfs because the lord protected the serfs while the serfs worked the land for the lord. Each lord was the bogeyman to his neighbor's serfs, but he could be cruel enough to his own serfs as well. Some lords claimed the "first night privilege" with all new brides among their peasants. Some found countless ways of belittling and exploiting their own serfs while plotting raids against the domains of their neighbors. Continuous strife and violence were inherent features of feudalism. Historians Henri Pirenne and A.L.

Morton both provide excellent treatments of feudalism, although both pay more attention to the doings of kings and queens than such doings warrant (Pirenne 1937; Morton 1979, 15–152).

Feudalism eventually evolved into a system known as mercantilism. Mercantilism, which was well developed by the fifteenth or sixteenth century in Western Europe, was also a class system. Under mercantilism, the purpose of the economy was to add gold and silver to the monarchy's treasury. At the time, gold and silver, rather than a nation's ability to produce goods and services for its citizens, were regarded as the wealth of a nation.

Capitalism and the Mixed Economy

Adam Smith's *Inquiry into the Nature and Causes of the Wealth of Nations* (1776) was a devastating attack on mercantilism, its associated class system, and its restrictions on trade. Smith's advocacy of a market or capitalist system was an eloquent condemnation of the class system prevailing under mercantilism. Yet Smith, like other classical economists, recognized that classes would still exist under capitalism. He spoke openly of the working (or laboring) class, merchant classes, and the upper classes. It would be a serious mistake to conclude that capitalism is a "classless" system. Nonetheless, that serious mistake is made in most economics textbooks that rely exclusively on one school of economics—the neoclassical school. In neoclassical economics, not only is economics defined exclusively in terms of scarcity but also issues are analyzed exclusively in terms of isolated individuals living in classless economies. Class allegiances and class interests do not affect the hypothetical, isolated individuals who are the sole inhabitants of the neoclassical textbook world.

Although we use the term *capitalism* in our discussion of class systems, contemporary economies are better described as a mixed system in which the public sector (government) plays an important role and many of the most important questions concern the interaction of the public and private sectors. Even Smith, the great advocate of the benefits of a market system, devoted much of his book to a discussion of the appropriate role of the public sector.

Capitalism and the modern state have evolved together. Nation-states have, for the most part, pacified the everyday affairs of their citizens, even if the nation-states themselves have engaged in calamitous international wars. Nation-states imposed peace and order on the domestic relations of their citizens by creating an elaborate network of property rights, regulations, laws and courts, police and sheriffs. All these have combined to establish markets, promote specialization, and institutionalize a class system.

Capitalism, in all its modern variations, is a class system. Karl Marx earned his fame—or notoriety—largely on the basis of his analysis of class in a capitalist system. Marx argued that there were essentially two classes: the bourgeoisie (roughly those who own and control capital) and the industrial proletariat (the working class). For Marx, class conflict— perhaps violent conflict—was inevitable. As pointed out earlier, class can be a useful analytical concept even if there are more than two classes and class conflict takes more subtle forms than Marx envisioned. Veblen's distinction between "those who own enough wealth to make it count and those who do not" is a meaningful starting point.

In textbook theory, individual capitalists—those with "enough wealth to make it count"—provide the capital accumulation and technological innovation that generate sustained growth. In return, individual capitalists receive a profit, but only if they are successful and their revenues exceed their costs. Otherwise, their losses will force them out of business. Being an individual capitalist is quite risky, especially for small businesspersons and entrepreneurs who accumulate capital—their own and other people's—and invest it in new businesses that could easily fail. Theirs is a risky bet. Established capitalists know better. They hedge their bets.

In textbook theory, capitalism is a positive-sum game that has generated several centuries of economic growth for areas that quickly adopted it. Most economics textbooks and manuals emphasize the "great man" theory of history, portraying individual entrepreneurs, inventors, and business tycoons as the great drivers of the social provisioning process. In economic practice, however, it is not the capital accumulation and technological innovation of great individual capitalists applauded in the textbooks, but the cumulative technological progress of numerous communities, that drives an economic system forward. To get the real story, readers need to venture outside the economics manuals. The technological, scientific, historical, and class aspects of the communal process are explained by Ayres ([1944] 1962), Conner (2005), Zinn (2003), and Braverman (1974).

The economic significance of the community's joint stock of scientific and technological knowledge is illustrated by what happened in Japan and Germany after World War II. During the war, Allied bombing wiped out most of the accumulated capital of Germany and Japan. However, in less than a generation, both Germany and Japan used their communal knowledge of modern science and technology to completely rebuild their economies. It was their accumulated community knowledge, not their accumulated individual capital, which mattered. Austin Goolsbee (2006) provides an interesting article on capital destroyed by war and on the community rebuilding.

Minor Classes

A simplistic view is that class systems are characterized by two major classes, one dominant and one subservient. However, minor classes are important also. The two major classes of feudalism were the serfs and their lords, and they set the tone of the class struggles within feudalism. Nevertheless, other minor classes also played roles in feudalism. Craftsmen, merchants, mercenaries, priests, and others were important at different times and places. Capitalism and contemporary mixed economies contain a number of minor classes, including farmers, managers, and bankers. These minor classes deserve brief attention.

Farmers

During the period in U.S. history when most European-Americans were farmers, farmers made up a kind of minor class within the American political economy. Most of the work on the farm was done by family members; little hired labor was used. Their growing power vis-à-vis slave owners led to the passage in 1862 of the Homestead Act, which granted 160 acres of public land (formerly Indian land) to any European-American adult who would settle it and live on it for five years. To make good their claim under the new law, the family lived on the acreage farmed instead of in a small town or village. The family farm thus became the American ideal. The Homestead Act encouraged family farming by European-Americans throughout the American West and sealed the doom of the remaining Indians.

Along with the Homestead Act, Congress also passed the Morrill Act in 1862. This act, signed by President Lincoln, created land-grant universities in each state. The purpose of the land-grant universities was to provide education to the industrial classes—particularly farmers.

Later changes to the Morrill Act added the agricultural extension and research roles to the land-grant university mission. Nearly all observers agree that the land-grant universities contributed greatly to tremendous increases in agricultural productivity in the United States and around the world. The Morrill Act and its modifications were genuine contributions to abundance.

However, not everybody in the United States benefited from these new laws. After the Civil War and the Homestead Act, European-American land ownership and residence became widely dispersed throughout much of the American West. Spurred by generous subsidies, mainly federal land grants, railroads quickly spread across the West and the remaining Native Americans were cleared off the most desirable land, replaced by European-American farmers. The Indians were forced to move onto reservations. The result was not quite ethnic cleansing—more like ethnic reduction and concentration. Were the Indian reservations the first concentration camps?

Sitting Bull and the Sioux were some of the last Native Americans to effectively resist the spread of European farming and ranching. They were arguably the most fearless fighters in the history of America. Defending his hunting grounds in the Dakotas and Montana against all comers, Sitting Bull and his warriors defeated George Armstrong Custer and the U.S. Seventh Cavalry at the Battle of the Little Bighorn in 1876. After the battle, Sitting Bull took his people to Canada and safety. Then, in the continuation of an extraordinarily colorful life, he returned to the United States, was pardoned, played the role of Indian in a traveling Wild West Show, and finally returned a second time to his native land and people in the United States. His second return was a mistake. He was killed in his camp of Hunkpapa Sioux some miles away from Standing Rock Agency, South Dakota, in a gun battle with federal Indian agents in 1890 (Vestal [1932] 1957).

Historian Angie Debo, interesting in her own right, wrote widely about the American West, recounting both the European farmers' and the Indians' side of the story (Debo 1943, [1944] 1998, 1961). She chronicled the extraordinary transformation of the Great Plains from hunting ground to breadbasket to dust bowl and beyond. The account here draws on her body of work. Being a woman ahead of her time, she never held a tenure track position at any university, even though she was one of America's very best and most original historians and even though she needed and sought such a job. Her loss of the opportunity to teach her craft was also America's loss. Many college students lost the chance to be taught by one of the very best historians of the American West. There is an important lesson in that, which we will apply in a later chapter on universal employment.

Today, throughout Oklahoma, Montana, the Dakotas, and elsewhere in the former Indian territories, almost no trace of Sitting Bull and the other great war chiefs remains. But the peculiar settlement pattern characteristic of western U.S. states remains: towns are small and rare, but isolated houses and farm buildings, many now abandoned, dot the countryside. In Oklahoma there are Indian casinos. The slot machine has replaced the buffalo.

With the removal of the Native Americans, family farmers became very influential in state and federal government. In terms of political influence, they are referred to as the farm bloc, and they are still powerful enough to get many of the government programs they want. In particular, they are usually able to get the federal government either to keep farm commodity prices up by restricting production, buying up surplus production, or to grant generous subsidies for the production and consumption of farm products.

Modern communities are snatching scarcity out of the jaws of abundance, and such class conflict working through the government is one of the ways in which it is done. When the U.S. government removed the tribal people to reservations, the European-American farming class was clearly the beneficiary. Large government subsidies in the form of price supports and direct payments to farmers remains fundamental U.S. policy, justified as support for the family farm—even when the subsidies are paid to large corporations and not to the idealized version of the individual farmer. There can be no reasonable doubt, however, that, from the Homestead Act on, U.S. farm policies (along with technological change) contributed to tremendous increases in agricultural productivity. Without these policies, many more Americans would have occupations requiring them to look at the backside of a mule plowing a field.

Although the history of farmers in the two places is profoundly different, there is also a powerful farm bloc in India that is able to get the Indian government to take large amounts of grain off the market in order to keep prices up. A few years back, Amy Waldman reported in the *New York Times* that hunger is a serious problem in India. As of 1999, of all children under three years old, 18 percent were severely malnourished, another 29 percent were moderately malnourished, and 53 percent were not malnourished. However, stored Indian grain surpluses had grown throughout the 1990s and into the new millennium. Wheat and rice surpluses rose from 18.2 million metric tons in 1998 to 58.1 metric tons in 2002. Nevertheless, the price of wheat and the price of rice were kept up by the government to benefit wheat and rice farmers. (Waldman 2002)

Management

Management has become another minor class within the present capitalist system. In the theory of capitalism, capitalists own and manage their own companies. In today's capitalism, however, the owners are often distant shareholders of large corporations that are run for them by others. In industrialized economies, the power of individually owned proprietorships has been taken away by widely owned corporations. Wave after wave of merger activity has swept over modern economies, organizing the old proprietorships into huge vertically and horizontally integrated corporate giants. Continuing horizontal and vertical integration has been supplemented with conglomerate mergers, all of which have meant that the scale of operation of each corporation has grown larger and larger. The resulting corporations have become more powerful, but also more difficult to manage and control, outliving and outgrowing their original founders' personal ability to run them.

The separation of ownership and control has become wider and wider as the stockholder-capitalists who owned the corporations found that they had to hire more and more specialized managers to run the corporations for them. These managers were hired workers, but they were in possession of information and expertise that gave them wiggle room relative to the owners (shareholders). The managers found that they can pursue some of their own interests, even when those interests contradict those of shareholders. The managers can finance their own pet projects, give themselves big salaries and expense accounts, pay inflated prices to their own private companies, manipulate the corporate stock and its market value, and "cook the books." However, they can do so only to the extent that they do not awaken the wrath of the owners or attract the wrong kind of attention from the legal system. In other words, they can pursue their own interests, but only up to a point. Beyond that point, which shifts back and forth according to the relative strength of management versus ownership, they become a minor, not a major player in the system. Two recent treatments of this subject are Bebchuk and Fried (2004) and O'Sullivan (2000).

The Enron scandal in the United States was one of several extreme cases at the turn of the millennium in which management pursued its own interest with an audacity that still astonishes. Enron was a large energy corporation headquartered in Houston, Texas. Several Enron managers made fortunes for themselves at the expense of numerous customers, employees, pensioners, creditors, and shareholders. Kenneth Lay was the chief executive officer during the company's most infamous period in the 1990s. He held a PhD in economics from the University of Houston and had numerous political ties to national and state politicians and government officials. In addition to manipulating the price of electrical power, some company managers manipulated the accounting system to pump up the earnings of Enron and inflate the value of its stock in order to make their stock options more valuable. Some of them paid themselves huge salaries and bonuses. Some of them created off-the-books entities to pump up the earnings and the value of their bonuses and stock options, also to divert earnings more directly into their own pockets. Although convicted of six counts of securities and wire fraud. Ken Lay never went to prison for his actions or inactions. He died vacationing at a Colorado ranch, awaiting sentencing. According to one estimate, the Enron scandal cost its shareholders alone about $70 billion in equity value (Bryce 2002, 7).

The scandal at Enron was not due to just a few bad apples in the management barrel. It was due to a structural characteristic of managerial capitalism: the separation of corporate ownership and control (Berle and Means 1968). The shareholders, being absentee owners, have an agency problem. They have to give control of their corporation to the managers, who act as their agents, but then the owners have less than perfect control over their agents. Their agents can therefore pursue their own interests rather than the interests of the shareholders. That is exactly what some of the employees at Enron did. They acted as their own class and pursued their own managerial class interest.

Bankers

In addition to landlords, farmers, and corporate managers, bankers and many others in the financial sector form another minor class. They exert their influence through their own actions and through the country's central bank—the Federal Reserve System in the United States (Greider 1987). Central banks regulate interest rates and the banking industry. They are particularly influential in the European Union and in countries with independent central banks. An independent central bank is independent from the political power of the central government, and that freedom gives bankers opportunity to exercise their own influence on the central bank. Their weight is always exerted in an effort to keep up bank profits through the maintenance of high interest rates and other restrictive monetary policies—the set of policies favoring bankers could be called "hard" money. The policies are hard on people who are unemployed and on people who wish to borrow money, although bankers insist that such policies actually benefit everyone in the long run.

Central bankers (such as Alan Greenspan and Ben Bernanke, former and current chairs of the Federal Reserve) have a general tendency to think that inflation is a more serious problem than unemployment. It could be argued that central bankers are either born with or soon acquire an overwhelming fear of inflation—just as other people are afraid of heights, public speaking, or being confined in very small places. Inflation can indeed be a very serious problem and should be addressed by policy, particularly monetary policy. But central bankers have been known to keep interest rates high even though there are no significant signs of inflation.

A far greater threat than inflation to abundance is unemployment. Below, we provide estimates of the costs of unemployment. If central banks were as dedicated to reducing unemployment as they are to reducing inflation, the world would be a far more abundant place.

Like the central bank for the European Union, the Federal Reserve is an independent central bank in which bankers have considerable influence. In fact, the twelve district banks of the Federal Reserve System are "owned" by the member commercial banks in each district. Their objective, as a minor class, is the same as the goal of farmers—they wish to keep the price of their products up. When farmers are successful, their influence harms the poor the most because poor people must spend the largest part of their budget just to feed themselves. Nevertheless, in the United States and elsewhere, much emphasis is placed on keeping up agricultural prices to save the endangered family farm. High interest rates and hard money, however, are not justified as the means of saving endangered bankers. Instead, high rates and hard money are suffered in silence and the independence of the central bank is glorified, as if it were the very linchpin of democracy (Further discussion is in Forder [2005]).

When bankers are successful, their influence harms people who are in debt or who wish to borrow because they must pay high prices for bankers' products—the interest rates on loans. The bankers' influence also harms the economy as a whole because high interest rates and other restrictive monetary policies push up the rate of unemployment.

In the European Union, the independent central bank has been following a policy of hard money for nearly a generation. In France, the resulting high unemployment—the average unemployment rate was 10.7 percent for 1993–2003 (UNDP 2005, 288)—has been hardest for the French-born North Africans segregated in huge housing projects located outside of the prime urban areas of France. A *New York Times* article by Elaine Sciolino quotes a young man nicknamed Looping, the son of an Algerian immigrant, who lives in a tough project in the small town of La Courneuve, a few miles outside of Paris. Looping describes his plight in a vivid lament: "The sun never shines. The buildings are gray. The people are gray. Everything is gray. It's the same people and there is nothing to do, nothing to do. You wake up every morning looking for work. But why? There isn't any" (Sciolino 2005, 1).

To benefit themselves, minor classes can and do disrupt the workings of modern economies, often with the help of an arm of government. Nevertheless, the problem is not that the government interferes with the perfect market or the free market. There is no perfect market and there is no market free from government (Dugger 2005). The problem is that the interests of different classes interfere with the public interest and, when they can, the different classes will use government to take advantage of others. Government is the terrain over which and with which class conflict is waged. Laissez-faire is not the answer. Laissez-faire merely makes the existing order sacrosanct, when the existing order is a product of government action in the first place. Dictatorship is not the answer, either, since it merely replaces one arbitrary order with another. The answer is a government guided by a democratic process that is strong enough and honest enough to continually search for and fight for the public interest against the narrow class interests of those who would use government for themselves.

As historian Charles A. Beard states:

> In reviewing the history of government in Western Europe, from the disintegration of the Roman Empire to the opening years of the nineteenth century, we discover that wherever the simple sword-won despotism of

the war leader, prince or king, is supplemented or superseded by some form of representation, it is not the people, considered as abstract equal personalities, who are represented, but it is propertied groups, estates.

(1957, 44)

Such propertied groups, here called minor classes, reduce the community's ability to produce abundance by institutionalizing protections of their own self-interest at the expense of whoever is unlucky enough to suffer the consequences. (Economists refer to this activity as "rent-seeking." What is involved is trying to get something for nothing, whether it involves actual rent or not.) Landlords charge high rent and justify themselves by invoking sacred property rights. Bankers gouge customers with high interest rates and justify themselves by claiming to be fighting inflation. Farmers try to charge high prices for their crops and justify themselves with praise of the family farm. Managers use their powerful positions in corporations to enrich themselves and justify their actions by invoking the need for incentives. With or without the support of the state, these groups all help themselves at the expense of the community. Nevertheless, the major damage usually is done by the major classes, not by the minor ones.

Classism and Unemployment

How does the pursuit of class interest thwart the full use of the community's stock of knowledge and skill? One word answers the question: unemployment. Classism, when combined with sexism, racism, and nationalism—all discussed in subsequent chapters—contributes to unemployment and robs the community of abundance.

The cost of unemployment is the biggest cost of the class system. Unemployment—not scarce resources and not scarce capital—is the greatest obstacle to achieving abundance. The problem is not a lack of resources. The problem is that people do not use the resources they have.

To understand why, a brief field trip to explore the natural history of unemployment, so to speak, is required. We begin by charting the U.S. unemployment rate from 1890 to 2005 in Figure 6.1 and then dig deeper with Table 6.1. The data used to plot the chart comes from the table.

Many people probably believe that unemployment is due to laziness. The unemployed are just too lazy to work so their plight is a personal problem, not a public issue. Figure 6.1 shows a curious discrepancy with

Figure 6.1 **The Laziness Hypothesis**

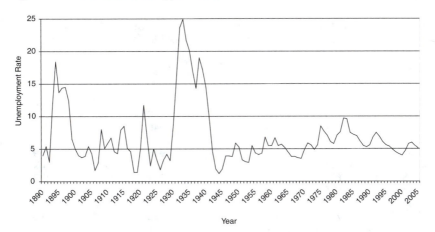

this laziness hypothesis. If unemployment is due to laziness, then the chart shows that laziness fluctuates up and down in an uneven cyclical motion and is occasionally punctuated with very large jumps, as occurred around the turn of the twentieth century, the early 1920s, the 1930s, and again in the early 1980s.

But no evidence exists that lazy Americans actually behave in such a jumpy, cyclical manner. No one we know of has ever presented an argument that laziness is a kind of viral social infection that cyclically swings through the population, occasionally breaking out into huge waves of contagious laziness like a flu epidemic. We must conclude that it is very unlikely that personal laziness can explain the behavior of the unemployment rate in the United States as demonstrated in the chart. The laziness hypothesis is therefore rejected.

The rate of unemployment for the five generations depicted in Table 6.1 averages slightly above 6.5 percent, but it ranges from a high of 24.9 percent at the depth of the Great Depression in 1933 to a low of 1.2 percent at the height of World War II in 1944. It was below 2 percent during seven of the 116 years and above 15 percent during nine of them. According to the unemployment data, the worst depressions occurred in 1893–1898 and 1930–1940. The data for the earlier period are not strictly comparable to the data for the later period because of significant changes in the nature of work and workers over the long period of time covered by the table. During the later period, people generally started working

110

Table 6.1

Five Generations of U.S. Unemployment, 1890–2005
(number in millions, rate in percent of civilian labor force)

Year	Number	Rate	Year	Number	Rate
2005	7.6	5.1			
2004	8.1	5.5	1947	2.3	3.9
2003	8.8	6.0	1946	2.3	3.9
2002	8.4	5.8	1945	1.0	1.9
2001	6.8	4.7	1944	0.7	1.2
2000	5.7	4.0	1943	1.1	1.9
1999	5.9	4.2	1942	2.7	4.7
1998	6.2	4.5	1941	5.6	9.9
1997	6.7	4.9	1940	8.1	14.6
1996	7.2	5.4	1939	9.5	17.2
1995	7.4	5.6	1938	10.4	19.0
1994	8.0	6.1	1937	7.7	14.3
1993	8.9	6.9	1936	9.0	16.9
1992	9.6	7.5	1935	10.6	20.1
1991	8.6	6.8	1934	11.3	21.7
1990	7.0	5.6	1933	12.8	24.9
1989	6.5	5.3	1932	12.1	23.6
1988	6.7	5.5	1931	8.0	15.9
1987	7.4	6.2	1930	4.3	8.7
1986	8.2	7.0	1929	1.6	3.2
1985	8.3	7.2	1928	2.0	4.2
1984	8.5	7.5	1927	1.5	3.3
1983	10.7	9.6	1926	0.8	1.8
1982	10.7	9.7	1925	1.5	3.2
1981	8.2	7.6	1924	2.2	5.0
1980	7.6	7.1	1923	1.0	2.4
1979	6.1	5.8	1922	2.9	6.7
1978	6.2	6.1	1921	4.9	11.7
1977	7.0	7.1	1920	2.1	5.2
1976	7.4	7.7	1919	0.5	1.4
1975	7.9	8.5	1918	0.5	1.4
1974	5.2	5.6	1917	1.8	4.6
1973	4.4	4.9	1916	2.0	5.1
1972	4.9	5.6	1915	3.4	8.5
1971	5.0	5.9	1914	3.1	7.9
1970	4.1	4.9	1913	1.7	4.3
1969	2.8	3.5	1912	1.8	4.6
1968	2.8	3.6	1911	2.5	6.7
1967	3.0	3.8	1910	2.2	5.9
1966	2.9	3.8	1909	1.8	5.1
1965	3.4	4.5	1908	2.8	8.0
1964	3.8	5.2	1907	0.9	2.8
1963	4.1	5.7	1906	0.6	1.7
1962	3.9	5.5	1905	1.4	4.3

(continued)

Table 6.1 *(continued)*

Year	Number	Rate		Year	Number	Rate
1961	4.7	6.7		1904	1.7	5.4
1960	3.9	5.5		1903	1.2	3.9
1959	3.7	5.5		1902	1.1	3.7
1958	4.6	6.8		1901	1.2	4.0
1957	2.9	4.3		1900	1.4	5.0
1956	2.8	4.1		1899	1.8	6.5
1955	2.9	4.4		1898	3.4	12.4
1954	3.5	5.5		1897	3.9	14.5
1953	1.8	2.9		1896	3.8	14.4
1952	1.9	3.0		1895	3.5	13.7
1951	2.1	3.3		1894	4.6	18.4
1950	3.3	5.3		1893	2.9	11.7
1949	3.6	5.9		1892	0.7	3.0
1948	2.3	3.8		1891	1.3	5.4
				1890	0.9	4.0

Sources: For 1890–1970, United States Bureau of the Census, *Historical Statistics of the United States: Colonial Times to 1970.* Washington, DC: U.S. Government Printing Office, 1975 (Series D85–86), p. 135. For 1971–2005, United States Bureau of Labor Statistics, bls.gov/pub/special.requests/lf/aatl.txt.

Note: For persons sixteen years old and over, except prior to 1947 the figures are for persons fourteen and over. Excludes Alaska and Hawaii prior to 1960.

at an older age than in the earlier period, because over time the need for education increased and kept people in school longer. Also, during the earlier period, more people were engaged in agriculture than in industry and services and more people were self-employed. Finally, more women worked outside the home during the later period.

Workers in the generations that entered the job market during the depressions of the 1890s and 1930s had a very hard time, indeed. Their timing was most unfortunate. Getting that first job was very difficult and holding onto a job was not easy, either. On the other hand, the generations that entered the job market in the boom times of 1901–1907, 1925–1929, 1942–1948, 1951–1953, 1965–1970, and 1995–2000 had a much better shot at landing a good job. Their timing was just about perfect, except that three out of the six boom times were also war times (World War II and after, 1942–1948; the Korean War, 1951–1953; the Vietnam War 1965–1970), so workers could have ended up in a combat zone instead of a good job.

The production and personnel needs of national war have always trumped the vested interests and class interests of economics. In war booms, a good shot at a job could have gotten a worker shot. The three boom times that were not also war times ended very abruptly in economic declines. The boom at the opening of the twentieth century (1901–1907) ended in the collapse known as the Rich Man's Panic. The Roaring Twenties ran straight into the Great Depression. The new millennium began with a recession.

The unemployment rate goes up and down in erratic waves throughout the whole period, with war booms and depressions superimposed upon the wavelike cycles. These movements are called the business cycle, which has been going on, we think, since capitalism began. Accurate measurements of such cyclical movements go back only a few generations, not much further than the 1850s (Sherman 1991; Kindleberger 1996).

The year 1946 was a watershed year—the first full "normal" year of peace after World War II. The U.S. Congress passed the Employment Act of 1946, which committed the federal government to the maintenance of economic stability. After 1946 the federal government began to continuously apply stabilization policy to the economy. The President's Council of Economic Advisers and the Joint Economic Committee of the House and Senate were established by the Employment Act of 1946. Many of the one-time policies that were used to fight the Great Depression evolved into sustained and institutionalized stabilization programs after 1946. We can measure what effect the evolution of continuous stabilization policy had on the unemployment rate after 1946. For one thing, the soaring highs and the diving lows were eliminated. The rate never rose above 15 percent after 1946, nor fell below 2 percent, either. Stabilization policy lopped off the peaks and filled in the valleys of the business cycle after 1946. The average unemployment rate for the fifty-six years before 1946 was 8.2 percent. The average for the first fifty-six years after 1946 was 5.3 percent, a difference of 2.9 percent. Aided by the Keynesian advance in economic knowledge, stabilization policy has made a big difference in the average rate of unemployment, lowering it by more than a third.

People have not become less lazy since 1946. They have become more skillful at stabilizing the economy. The economic knowledge they have gained is an addition to the modern community's joint stock, used to improve economic performance. Experience has proved that it can be done (Further discussion is in Lekachman [1966]). Although U.S. economic performance improved over the generations, the country can do better. During the period being analyzed, over half a billion worker-years of production were wasted. That is, if the unemployed had been employed, the United States could have had the output of goods and services produced by roughly half a billion people working for one full year. Imagine what they could have achieved. The lost output and the lost opportunity it entailed staggers the mind. Think of the houses, apartments, factories, warehouses, pipelines, railroads, subways, highways, wind farms, solar panels, schools, hospitals, homeless shelters, elder-care facilities, youth hostels, parks, wildlife refuges, research institutes, and vaccines that the nation does not have, but could have had. Think of the free school lunches that could have been served, the basketball teams that could have been coached, the research projects that could have been conducted, the discoveries that could have been made, the technology that could have been shared, the diseases that could have been cured, and the free prescriptions that could have been filled with those wasted half a billion worker-years. And this is the waste experienced by one of the most advanced economies on the planet. It does not include the wasted worker-years in other countries with far larger workforces, such as China and India. This lost output is why we claim that scarcity is not inevitable, that abundance could be within our grasp.

The facts are clear for all to see. The unemployed are not lazy. They are the promise of plenty. In theory, the capitalist class shoulders the financial burden of hiring the working class, and entrepreneurs accept the uncertainty of innovation—of building new businesses for trying out new products and new processes. They take the risks and shoulder the burdens in exchange for the chance to make a profit. They search through the economy for unemployed workers to employ in their new endeavors, not resting in their entrepreneurial quest till all available resources have been snapped up. Great theory! In practice, however, the economy has worked very differently. In practice the economy has wasted a vast pool of human talent. This profoundly important point is further emphasized by Table 6.2, which shows the wasted real gross domestic product (GDP) in the United States.

Table 6.2 focuses on an important detail for a shorter span of time than the table before it—the amount of waste experienced in the United States during the last quarter of the last century. During this span of time, economic statistics were far more accurate than during earlier spans. If everyone who was seeking a job had actually been employed in one, how much additional GDP could the United States have produced? Using data from the President's Council of Economic Advisers, we made

Table 6.2

U.S. Wasted Real Gross Domestic Product, 1975–1999

Year	Unemployed civilian workers (in millions)	Real GDP (in billions of 1996 dollars)	Real GDP per worker (in thousands of dollars)	Wasted Real GDP (in billions of dollars)
1975	7.9	4,084	47.6	376.1
1976	7.4	4,312	48.6	359.3
1977	7.0	4,512	49.0	343.3
1978	6.2	4,761	49.6	307.5
1979	6.1	4,912	49.7	303.3
1980	7.6	4,901	49.4	375.1
1981	8.3	5,021	50.0	415.1
1982	10.7	4,919	49.4	529.0
1983	10.7	5,132	50.9	544.8
1984	8.5	5,505	52.4	445.6
1985	8.3	5,717	53.3	442.6
1986	8.2	5,912	53.9	442.3
1987	7.4	6,113	54.4	402.5
1988	6.7	6,368	55.4	371.0
1989	6.5	6,592	56.2	365.3
1990	7.0	6,708	56.5	395.3
1991	8.6	6,676	56.7	487.8
1992	9.6	6,880	58.1	557.4
1993	8.9	7,063	58.7	522.5
1994	8.0	7,348	59.7	477.5
1995	7.4	7,544	60.4	447.0
1996	7.2	7,813	61.7	444.0
1997	6.7	8,160	63.0	421.9
1998	6.2	8,509	64.7	401.2
1999	5.9	8,857	66.3	391.4
Total				10,568.6

Source: The Council of Economic Advisers, *Economic Report of the President,* various years, and the authors' calculations. Washington, DC: U.S. Government Printing Office.

the following calculations for the last quarter of the last century. First, we divided the GDP for each year by the number of workers it took to produce it. That gave us the GDP per worker. Then we multiplied the GDP per worker by the number of unemployed workers each year. That gave us the wasted GDP. Last, we summed the wasted GDP for the twenty-five years and got a total waste for the period of $10,568.6 billion or about $10.6 trillion. The United States thus wasted about $10.6 trillion in output in the closing quarter of the last century. The nation threw abundance out, along with the unemployed, but preserved the class system (Further discussion of class and class systems is found in Roemer [1982] and Wright [1985]).

The accumulated knowledge of the community demands that we frame some pointed questions. We know that the United States can reduce the unemployment rate through collective action and the magic of modern fiscal and monetary policies. Indeed, the nation has already done so, as indicated by the decline in unemployment engineered after 1946 and the reduced frequency and intensity of recessions in the post–World War II era. Unemployed resources produce waste, not abundance. Should unemployment be allowed to continue, or should it be eliminated? Can unemployment be eliminated without serious changes to the class system?

7

Nationalism

This chapter is not so much about nationalism as it is about nationalism run amok. The chapter is short and anything but sweet. Nationalism can mean pride in one's national community and the desire to pursue its common good—admirable sentiments to be sure. Unfortunately, there is also the perversion of nationalism, which is chauvinism. Chauvinism, the dark side of nationalism, refers to the zealous, belligerent pursuit of patriotism—the attitude expressed by the phrase "my country right or wrong." Chauvinism, like classism, racism, and sexism, is another thief of abundance. Mikhail Gorbachev, former leader of the Soviet Union, was a Soviet nationalist but an antichauvinist. He had something of interest to say about the difference between nationalism and chauvinism: "People must learn to distinguish between true national interests and their nationalistic perversion. Any claims to national exclusiveness are intolerable and insulting, and this also goes for the nation in whose name they are voiced. . . . one should first of all combat one's 'own' nationalism and chauvinism, and this should be done primarily by members of the nationality concerned" (Gorbachev 1987, 286–287).

Nationalism prevents abundance in three main ways: (1) the direct and indirect costs of war, including the arms race, (2) the costs of inadequate worldwide access to the community's joint stock of knowledge, and (3) the ill-conceived and badly implemented policy choices that keep people from drastically reducing the costs of nationalism. We will have something to say about each of these unfortunate aspects of nationalism, but it is the second item (limiting access to the joint stock of knowledge) that is most powerful in constraining the path toward abundance. We begin with some rough numeric estimates of the costs of nationalism.

The Direct and Indirect Costs of War and
Military Expenditures

Although the costs of war (human and economic) are enormous, there are
no reliable estimates of these costs for all wars during, for example, the
last century. Oddly, it is even difficult to define exactly what war is and
what expenditures should be counted as costs of war. Some wars, such
as World War II, are relatively easy to define. But was the undeclared
Vietnam War a war? What about the U.S. military actions in Panama and
Grenada? What about the current war in Iraq? What about the dozens of
armed conflicts that occur somewhere in the world each year? The truth
is that we cannot provide good estimates of the worldwide costs of war.
We can provide some data (uncertain at best) of the costs of the largest
and most destructive war to date: World War II.

The costs of World War II are at best rough estimates. The figures
cited here are commonly cited in the literature (Ziemke 2007). The human death toll of the war has been estimated to be 55 million persons,
including roughly 6 million Jews killed during the Holocaust. No one
can estimate the number of nonfatal injuries due to the war, but surely
the figure is several times the 55 million who died. But this is not the
only human cost of the war. Tens of millions of school-age children had
their educations disrupted (Ichino and Winter-Ebmer 2001). Add in also
the costs of involuntary migration, family disruption, and a long list of
other "costs" and the human toll of World War II is staggering.

The direct economic costs of World War II include at least three
categories of costs: (1) military expenditures by all sides, totaling about
$1 trillion in 1940s dollars, which is about $10 trillion in 2000 dollars,
(2) the unknown costs of destruction of economic infrastructure such
as buildings, roads, and industrial capacity, and (3) reduced economic
output, meaning lost gross domestic product (GDP), in many nations for
many years. There are other costs, of course, but we think this is enough
to give an idea of the cost of one war. Of course, there have been many
other wars.

We do not discount the real technological advances that are sometimes
made under the duress of war needs. World War II produced startling
advances in technology, including the development of radar, the jet air-
plane (by the Germans), rayon (as a replacement for rubber), and yes,
even the atom bomb and the more benign forms of nuclear reaction.
Nevertheless, many of these breakthroughs would have occurred with

or without the war, and speeding up technological change seems to be less than an admirable reason for war.

What do military expenditures cost today? Worldwide military expenditures are very difficult to estimate, although several organizations attempt to do so. A well-respected and comprehensive estimate is provided each year by the Stockholm International Peace Research Institute (SIPRI), accessible at www.sipri.org/. SIPRI estimates that world military expenditures in 2006 were slightly over $1.2 trillion (reported in 2005 dollars) and that this figure had increased by 37 percent over a ten-year period. Between 1996 and 2006, SIPRI estimates that total world military expenditures were $10.4 trillion dollars. SIPRI also reports that fifteen nations accounted for 83 percent of all military expenditures, with the United States alone accounting for 46 percent of the total.

What could the world have done with $10 trillion over the last decade if it had not been spent on military expenditures? The world could have spent a lot of it on health care, education, and other measures that are known to result in increased output. According to SIPRI, however, "A comparison of government spending priorities between samples of countries in different per capita income groups shows that the lower the income group, the higher the priority given to military spending in relation to social spending."

Direct military expenditures by the United States are displayed in Table 7.1. The first thing to notice in Table 7.1 is that U.S. defense expenditures are very large. From 1940 to 2006, the United States spent $10.2 trillion on defense in current dollar terms and $19.1 trillion in real (2000) dollars. The figures in the table are from the budget of the U.S. federal government and define national defense spending quite narrowly. The figures do not include many of the costs of national defense that show up in other parts of the government budget or that do not show up in the budget at all. The costs of the Veterans Administration and defense-related activities such as the Central Intelligence Agency and the National Aeronautics and Space Administration are also not included in the table. The cost of the deaths caused by the practice of nationalism is not included, nor is the debt cost of financing most wars. (Refer to the discussion of costs in Chapter 3.)

Economist Bruce S. Jansson, using a different approach to nationalism and national defense, estimates the cost of excess military spending and excess interest paid on the national debt of the United States at just under 7 trillion 1992 dollars for the period from 1931 to 2004 (2001,

Table 7.1

Military Expenditures in the United States

	Nominal GDP	Real GDP (in 2000 dollars)	GDP price deflator	National defense expenditures (billions of current dollars)	Defense expenditures (in 2000 dollars)
1940	101.4	1,034.1	9.81	1.7	17.3
1941	126.7	1,211.1	10.46	6.4	61.2
1942	161.9	1,435.4	11.28	25.7	227.9
1943	198.6	1,670.9	11.89	66.7	561.2
1944	219.8	1,806.5	12.17	79.1	650.1
1945	223.1	1,786.3	12.49	83.0	664.6
1946	222.3	1,589.4	13.99	42.7	305.3
1947	244.2	1,574.5	15.51	12.8	82.5
1948	269.2	1,643.2	16.38	9.1	55.5
1949	267.3	1,634.6	16.35	13.2	80.7
1950	293.8	1,777.3	16.53	13.7	82.9
1951	339.3	1,915.0	17.72	23.6	133.2
1952	358.3	1,988.3	18.02	46.1	255.8
1953	379.4	2,079.5	18.24	52.8	289.4
1954	380.4	2,065.4	18.42	49.3	267.7
1955	414.8	2,212.8	18.75	42.7	227.8
1956	437.5	2,255.8	19.39	42.5	219.1
1957	461.1	2,301.1	20.04	45.4	226.6
1958	467.2	2,279.2	20.50	46.8	228.3
1959	506.6	2,441.3	20.75	49.0	236.1
1960	526.4	2,501.8	21.04	48.1	228.6
1961	544.7	2,560.0	21.28	49.6	233.1
1962	585.6	2,715.2	21.57	52.3	242.5
1963	617.7	2,834.0	21.80	53.4	245.0
1964	663.6	2,998.6	22.13	54.8	247.6
1965	719.1	3,191.1	22.53	50.6	224.5
1966	787.8	3,399.1	23.18	58.1	250.7
1967	832.6	3,484.6	23.89	71.4	298.8
1968	910.0	3,652.7	24.91	81.9	328.7
1969	984.6	3,765.4	26.15	82.5	315.5
1970	1,038.5	3,771.9	27.53	81.7	296.7
1971	1,127.1	3,898.6	28.91	78.9	272.9
1972	1,238.3	4,105.0	30.17	79.2	262.6
1973	1,382.7	4,341.5	31.85	76.7	240.8
1974	1,500.0	4,319.6	34.73	79.3	228.4
1975	1,638.3	4,311.2	38.00	86.5	227.6
1976	1,825.3	4,540.9	40.20	89.6	222.9
Transition quarter			40.20	22.3	55.5
1977	2,030.9	4,750.5	42.75	97.2	227.4
1978	2,294.7	5,015.0	45.76	104.5	228.4
1979	2,563.3	5,173.4	49.55	116.3	234.7

(continued)

Table 7.1 *(continued)*

	Nominal GDP	Real GDP (in 2000 dollars)	GDP price deflator	National defense expenditures (billions of current dollars)	Defense expenditures (in 2000 dollars)
1980	2,789.5	5,161.7	54.04	134.0	248.0
1981	3,128.4	5,291.7	59.12	157.5	266.4
1982	3,255.0	5,189.3	62.73	185.3	295.4
1983	3,536.7	5,423.8	65.21	209.9	321.9
1984	3,933.2	5,813.6	67.66	227.4	336.1
1985	4,220.3	6,053.7	69.71	252.7	362.5
1986	4,462.8	6,263.6	71.25	273.4	383.7
1987	4,739.5	6,475.1	73.20	282.0	385.3
1988	5,103.8	6,742.7	75.69	290.4	383.7
1989	5,484.4	6,981.4	78.56	303.6	386.5
1990	5,803.1	7,112.5	81.59	299.3	366.8
1991	5,995.9	7,100.5	84.44	273.3	323.6
1992	6,337.7	7,336.6	86.38	298.4	345.4
1993	6,657.4	7,532.7	88.38	291.1	329.4
1994	7,072.2	7,835.5	90.26	281.6	312.0
1995	7,397.7	8,031.7	92.11	272.1	295.4
1996	7,816.9	8,328.9	93.85	265.8	283.2
1997	8,304.3	8,703.5	95.41	270.5	283.5
1998	8,747.0	9,066.9	96.47	268.2	278.0
1999	9,268.4	9,470.3	97.87	274.8	280.8
2000	9,817.0	9,817.0	100.00	294.4	294.4
2001	10,128.0	9,890.7	102.40	304.8	297.7
2002	10,469.6	10,048.8	104.19	348.5	334.5
2003	10,960.8	10,301.0	106.41	404.8	380.4
2004	11,685.9	10,675.8	109.46	455.8	416.4
2005	12,433.9	11,003.4	113.00	495.3	438.3
2006	13,194.7	11,319.4	116.57	521.8	447.6
Totals				10,203.9	19,063.1

Source: Defense expenditures from *Economic Report of the President, 2007*, Table B-80. GDP and real GDP from U.S. Department of Commerce, Bureau of Economic Analysis, www.bea.gov. Final column: authors' computations.

Note: Through fiscal year 1976, the fiscal year ran from July 1 to June 30. Beginning October 1976 (fiscal year 1977), the fiscal year runs from October 1 to September 30. The 3-month period from July 1, 1976, through September 30, 1976, is a separate fiscal period known as the transition quarter.

355). No matter how the costs of war are calculated, the taxpayers have paid dearly.

Not all the expenditures described above were directly for war. A large percentage of the U.S. military budget was spent on the arms race with the former Soviet Union. An arms race involves two or more competing nations trying to surpass each other in the quantity and quality of offensive and defensive weaponry they accumulate. Arms races sometimes evolve into a form of war as well—either a cold war in which violent conflict is not conducted openly or a hot war in which it is.

While many nations have engaged in arms races, the most famous and dangerous arms race was between the United States and the Soviet Union. That arms race included a cold war as well. It began soon after World War II. In a curious twist, the two nations had been allies in the struggle against Nazi Germany and Imperial Japan. Their alliance quickly reversed itself, and the resulting arms race and cold war nearly destroyed the world as it was known at that time. World War II has been called a good war, but the cold war that followed was not. The cold war's threat to world survival ended with the dissolution of the Soviet Union beginning in 1989.

Most people who experienced it believed that the arms race between the United States and the Soviet Union would result in a nuclear exchange between the two that would destroy the world. Your intrepid authors were school children back then. In spite of what our teachers taught us to do when the atom bombs fell, we feared that hiding under our desks at school with our hands clutched over our heads would not save us. Instead, we believed that we and all our friends and families would be incinerated by the nuclear bombs that the communists planned to drop on us. In a recent history, John Lewis Gaddis provides the U.S. view of the conflict (2005). Mikhail Gorbachev gives a Soviet view (1987). Alva Myrdal gives the view from outside the two racing countries (1976).

In addition to federal expenditures, U.S. citizen-soldiers also have paid dearly. Battle deaths claimed 53,000 of them in World War I, 292,000 in World War II, 34,000 in the Korean conflict, and 47,000 in the Vietnam War—a total of 426,000 (U.S. Bureau of the Census 2005, 333). The totals are not in for the wars in Afghanistan and Iraq. These deaths were almost exclusively of young people in the prime of life with decades of productive activity ahead of them. Disability also cut a wide swath through the ranks. In round numbers, at least 2.1 million veterans were so disabled in the 1990s that they received compensation for their disabilities. In 2003, the number had risen to 2.5 million (338). In addition to the disabled veterans, military personnel on active duty numbered 1.4 million in 2003 (331). In recent years, then, active duty and disability knocked between 3 million and 4 million prime workers out of the U.S. civilian workforce annually.

There is no reason to believe that nationalism will stop running amok by itself and cause any less death and disability in this century than it did in the last. The dynamic of nationalist arms racing in the twenty-first century promises to continue building until war breaks out between belligerent nation-states or until something happens to break the nationalist dynamic of death. Pax Britannica, the peace imposed on much of the world by the might of the British Empire, could not stop it. Instead, Pax Britannica ushered in the carnival of death that was the twentieth century. Pax Americana, the peace imposed on much of the world by the United States after the end of the Cold War offers little hope of being different. This long-term perspective is discussed by Kennedy (1989).

We are not denying the possibility that there could be a reasonable amount of defense spending within the clear context of a reasonable global system of nation-states. Nor are we denying the possibility that there could be a just war aimed at ending injustice. However, we are insisting that our nation-state system is unreasonable and unjust and that wars within its context are almost sure to be unjust, unreasonable, and downright bloody awful. Furthermore, we insist that stopping such wars would contribute significantly to abundance and equality.

The Costs of Limiting Worldwide Access to the Joint Stock of Knowledge

The direct and indirect costs of military expenditures are not the only costs of nationalism. World production of goods and services is lower than it could be because nationalism means that not all people have the same access to the world community's joint stock of knowledge. The costs of lower output are far greater than the direct money costs of military expenditures. In this section, we provide rough estimates of those costs.

We begin with a simple arithmetic exercise. The world's 6.5 billion people produced and consumed more than $44 trillion worth of goods and services in 2006 (World Bank 2007). This includes 57 million metric tons of apples, 64 million metric tons of oranges, 597 million metric tons of rice, and 573 million metric tons of wheat (FAOSTAT 2003). World production of oil in 2002 was 66.8 million barrels a day; world coffee production in 2001 was 125 million 60-kilogram bags; world production of butter was 5.6 million metric tons; and the world produced 847 million metric tons of iron and steel (Commodity Research Bureau 2003).

In the United States, GDP per person as of 2006 was about $44,000 per year. This is not the highest GDP per person in the world, but it is high enough for the United States to produce about 30 percent of the world's total economic output. (In 2005 U.S. GDP was $12.7 trillion and world GDP was about $44 trillion.) In the European Union (EU), as of 2005 GDP per person was over $31,000 per year. The EU nations produced $9.98 trillion worth of goods and services in 2005, or about 22 percent of world GDP. Japan with a 2005 GDP per capita of $35,000 produced another $4.5 trillion worth of goods and services, or about 10 percent of world GDP.

In short, the United States, the EU, and Japan produce about 62 percent of total world output. The rest of the world has a GDP per capita of only $3,100 per year—and this includes some nations such as Australia and New Zealand with relatively high per capita GDP. If the 5.5 billion people not living in the United States, the EU, or Japan produced as much per person as the United States, world GDP would have been about $236 trillion in 2005—about $191 trillion more than the actual figure. That is, the increase in world output would be nearly five times as large as current world GDP! If we had used per capita GDP in the EU ($31,000) instead of in the United States for the example, world GDP would have been about $166 trillion, or about four times as large as the current figure. Using a different set of assumptions to calculate potential world GDP would give similar results. Almost any set of assumptions leads to a huge increase in world output.

The figures just calculated are, of course, hypothetical. Is it possible to increase output per person in the rest of the world to the current U.S. level? Yes, of course it is. What this requires is access to the world community's joint stock of knowledge; and it requires the political will to accomplish this task.

Consider the increases in GDP that were possible during World War II in the United States (and elsewhere). In the United States, GDP increased by 50 percent between 1940 and 1944. In 1939 the United States produced 800 warplanes. In 1944 the United States produced 50,000 warplanes. Similar increases in output occurred with other products. Although the country was coming out of the Great Depression and had a lot of people unemployed, similar increases in output could still be accomplished now. The computer industry could produce 50 percent more computers in a year or two, without reducing the production of other goods and services. Carmakers could easily produce more cars and trucks, since the automobile industry faces worldwide excess capacity. More wheat, rice, corn, and ice cream could be produced without reducing the production of other goods and services.

Producing enough to achieve abundance for everyone will not happen automatically. Strangely, many traditional economists, particularly growth theorists, write about the possibility (and sometimes the inevitability) of income convergence, the alleged tendency of per capita incomes among nations to converge over time. Waiting for such convergence to occur could take a very long time. Consider, for example, the possibility of income convergence between the United States and Mexico. According to the World Bank, Mexico's GDP per person in 2005 was $6,172 (measured in year 2000 dollars), while the same figure for the United States was $37,267. These figures, of course, depend on the exchange rate between Mexico and the United States, which has varied greatly over the last two decades. Nevertheless, we can use these figures to illustrate the time it might take for Mexico to catch up to the U.S. level of per capita GDP.

Assume for the moment that U.S. GDP per person does not change for several decades. This possibility is highly unlikely because the average U.S. GDP per capita increased at about 2 percent per year throughout the twentieth century. Let us also assume that Mexico's GDP per person increases by 2 percent per year. In approximately thirty-six years, Mexico's GDP per person would have doubled to $12,344, or about one-third of U.S. GDP per capita. In another thirty-six years, Mexico's GDP per person would again double to about $24,688. Another twenty years and Mexico's GDP per person would be about the same as in the United States. In other words, using these assumptions, it would take Mexico nearly a century (ninety-two years) to achieve income convergence with the United States.

However, this is not a likely scenario. Over the last twenty years, Mexico's GDP has grown slowly and erratically; and because Mexico exports nearly one-third of its GDP to the United States, the growth of Mexico's GDP is tied closely to growth in the United States. If the U.S. economy does not grow, then neither will Mexico's. Since we do not want to engage in fortunetelling (economic forecasting) in this exercise, we have produced Table 7.2 illustrating the time it would take for Mexico to achieve per capita GDP convergence with the United States under differing assumptions. Given current conditions, U.S.-Mexico convergence is not going to happen anytime soon.

Is Mexico's case unique? No, it is not. Consider how long it would

Table 7.2

**Hypothetical Convergence Times of Per Capita Income Between the
United States and Mexico**

	Mexico 1 percent	Mexico 2 percent	Mexico 3 percent
United States 0 percent	194 years	92 years	58 years
United States 1 percent	n/a	194 years	92 years
United States 2 percent	n/a	n/a	194 years

take Bangladesh, with a per capita GDP in 2005 of $432 (measured in 2000 dollars), to converge to U.S. levels. For Bangladesh and other nations with very low incomes to converge to U.S. levels would take many, many centuries. There are no guarantees in the growth game.

Even in the so-called industrialized or high-income nations, growth is not what it could be. Economists calculate on a regular basis what they refer to as potential GDP. Oddly, many economists worry when the actual rate of GDP growth is above the potential rate of GDP growth. What these fearful economists fear is inflation. What we fear is that the world's people are producing far less than they could in a noninflationary environment. For example, Sato provides an interesting discussion of the loss of output in Japan in recent years (2001). But this is hardly the end of the story.

World Output Is a Policy Choice

Perhaps you do not agree with our particular set of estimates of how much the world could produce in the absence of nationalism. We admit that these are rough estimates and you are welcome to calculate alternative (even more sophisticated) estimates. The general concept, however, should be obvious. The world economy (or economies) is capable of producing far more than it is currently producing. The constraints to doing so are not technological, environmental, or insufficient resources. These constraints are imaginary. The real constraints on increasing world output and achieving abundance are related to nationalism, classism, racism, and sexism. The constraints imposed by nationalism are deliberate policy constraints. People have chosen not to produce as much as they could.

The policies related to nationalism that impose real constraints on the ability to achieve worldwide abundance are, however, resource allocation constraints. Too many nations spend too much on military expenditures and war rather than on education, health care, decent and environmentally sound transportation systems, and a long list of other productivity-enhancing programs.

Education is a critical variable in individual and national productivity. People who do not complete high school as well as those who do not complete primary school are simply ill equipped to find adequate employment in a highly technological and globalized world economy. The evidence on the link between education and productivity per worker is very strong. People who have an education, on average, do much better in the modern workplace than those who do not.

Table 7.3 displays selected measures of educational attainment and per capita income (in 2000 dollars) for ten selected nations. (Figures for more than 200 nations are available from the World Bank [2007].) The implications of this table are obvious. The nations with low educational attainment also have low per capita GDP, while those with higher educational attainment figures have higher GDP. Of course, some lucky person without much education may win the lottery; an occasional high-school dropout may earn more than a graduate of a medical school, but these are the exceptions, not the rule.

What does education have to do with nationalism? If nations use their resources on military expenditures and other forms of nationalistic behavior, educational expenditures suffer. There are no good reasons why everyone, no matter where they might live, should not receive a decent education. The nations of the world can afford it.

The education problem is closely related to the health problem. It is exceedingly difficult to obtain a good education if you are constantly or frequently sick. At a minimum, being healthy requires some minimal form of shelter, an adequate diet, access to clean water and sewage services, and occasional intervention from a doctor. Can the world afford a healthy population? Of course it can. Many of these requirements are not very expensive. Treating the consequences of malnutrition, unsanitary waste disposal, and undrinkable water costs much more. Given the increasingly mobile population of the world, the wealthy nations should regard clean water, good food, and other health-related items in Ethiopia or Bangladesh as critical to their own health as a domestic problem. Diseases do not respect international boundaries.

What does health care around the world have to do with nationalism?

The answer is the same as for education. All nations around the world, poor nations as well as wealthy ones, choose to spend their resources on building armies rather than providing health care.

There are other policy choices that contribute to the world's failure to achieve abundance for all. Trade policies, migration policies, patent and copyright policies (also known as intellectual property rights), and regressive income tax policies are merely some of the examples.

We are not naive. We do understand that eliminating the costs of nationalism so that everyone might enjoy abundance is a bit more complex and difficult than described above. For many people and governments, economic development and abundance are dangerous and subversive ideas. The concept of abundance threatens long established political, social, and cultural power structures. Resistance to fundamental structural change is to be expected, but this does not mean that the ideas presented here are impossibly utopian.

The United Nations (UN), for example, has adopted what it calls millennium goals aimed at eliminating the worst examples of absolute poverty. Specifically, the UN's aim is to bring the nearly 2 billion people who live on less than two dollars per day (measured in 1993 dollars) above this absolute poverty line by the year 2015. The UN thinks this goal is possible. We think the UN goals are not ambitious enough. The UN millennium goals, which can be found at www.un.org/millenniumgoals/, are as follows:

- Eradicate extreme hunger and poverty.
- Achieve universal primary education.
- Promote gender equality and empower women.
- Reduce child mortality.
- Improve maternal health.
- Combat HIV/AIDS, malaria, and other diseases.
- Ensure environmental sustainability.
- Develop a global partnership for development.

The complete report assessing the progress of the UN in achieving the millennium goals can be accessed at their Web site. The current (2007) assessment is that the results are "mixed" but that the effort to eradicate the worst forms of poverty can still be achieved by 2015. We are not so optimistic as the UN analysts in the short run, but we are more ambitious for the long run. The world community can do better than the UN goals, which are only a first step along the long-run path to abundance.

Table 7.3

Education in Selected Nations

Nation	Primary completion rate	Progression to secondary school (percent)	School enrollment secondary net (percent)	School enrollment tertiary (percent gross)	2005 GDP per capita ($U.S.)
Bangladesh	76.6	86.0	42.7	6.5	423
Chad	31.6	51.3	10.8	1.2	561
Denmark	99.4	100.0	91.7	73.9	47,769
Ethiopia	55.0	84.2	27.9	2.7	157
France	98.7	98.9	93.4	56.0	34,936
Mozambique	42.0	53.2	7.1	1.2	335
Pakistan	63.2	69.0	21.0	4.6	711
Senegal	52.2	60.8	20.9	5.4	707
Switzerland	96.9	99.9	83.1	47.0	49,351
Uganda	57.1	36.2	13.0	3.4	303

Source: World Bank, World Development Indicators, www.wdi.org.

Notes: Primary completion rate is the percentage of students completing the last year of primary school. It is calculated by taking the total number of students in the last grade of primary school, minus the number of repeaters in that grade, divided by the total number of children of official graduation age.

Progression to secondary school refers to the number of new entrants to the first grade of secondary school in a given year as a percentage of the number of students enrolled in the final grade of primary school in the previous year.

Net enrollment ratio is the ratio of children of official school age based on the International Standard Classification of Education 1997 who are enrolled in school to the population of the corresponding official school age. Secondary education completes the provision of basic education that began at the primary level, and aims at laying the foundations for lifelong learning and human development, by offering more subject- or skill-oriented instruction using more specialized teachers.

School enrollment, tertiary (percent gross): Gross enrollment ratio is the ratio of total enrollment, regardless of age, to the population of the age group that officially corresponds to the level of education shown. Tertiary education, whether or not to an advanced research qualification, normally requires, as a minimum condition of admission, the successful completion of education at the secondary level.

8

Sexism

Being men, we think it wise to open this chapter with a cautionary note: "To listen to most men dilating authoritatively on the subject of women is to suffer a positive increase in one's ignorance" (Montagu 1974, 49).

Because we take this warning seriously, we will keep this chapter short to minimize the probability of sounding like two ignorant men. With a few exceptions—Ashley Montagu being the major one—we also will rely mainly on the work of women as our definitive sources. Montagu, although male, seems sound enough, since he comes to the conclusion that women are naturally superior to men.

What is sexism? The more polite term *gender discrimination* often is used instead, but they both mean the same thing. Since there is nothing polite about it, we will use the more frank term *sexism*. Although women could dominate men, in our time sexism involves men dominating women. It is a system of inequality, a negative-sum game using sex or gender as the *differentia specifica*—the characteristic used to separate people into the top and bottom groups. Today, women are designated the underdogs and men the top dogs. This division harms the women and benefits the men. Along with the other harmful practices discussed in this primer to economic abundance, sexism helps communities to snatch scarcity out of the teeth of abundance. Defined very simply, sexism today is a system of male supremacy in which men acquire power over women and use it to take advantage of them. Sexism involves men shirking housework and childcare, stereotyping, violence, and workplace discrimination. When related to the family, the system of male supremacy is called patriarchy—male rule of the family.

In patriarchy, the men, the patriarchs, are supposed to be tender and protective toward women, watching out for their welfare. Chivalry toward women may be the sexist ideal, but it is not always the practice. In fact, sexism can be very violent. A World Bank study found that more than one in five women in many countries had been subjected to physical violence in their relationships (Heise, Pitanguy, and Germain 1994, 6–9). Apparently a significant number of men have a perverse need to lord it over women, not just verbally and not just in terms of prestige or status, but physically. This sad fact regarding the exercise of male superiority is a warning that something is dreadfully wrong in the relations between men and women. Ashley Montagu reflects, "The truly superior person doesn't need to lord it over anyone; it is only the inferior person who, in order to feel that he is superior, must have someone to look down on. The genuinely superior person looks neither up nor down; he looks straight at you" (1974, 10).

Sexism and the Space Age

Are men really superior to women? Quite frankly, out of the thousands of college men we have taught in the last thirty-five years, the majority probably believed so. This is not a scientific sample, but we think it significant, nonetheless. We also think that belief in male superiority is incorrect. Let us examine the most obvious case supporting male superiority. Table 8.1 shows world records set by men and by women in selected track and field events. It shows that men can run faster, jump higher and farther, and throw things farther than women can. This information could be useful if the community needed someone to run ahead and warn that a saber-toothed tiger was coming or to throw a rock or a spear at the cat. But modern hunters do not need to do any of those things. Modern hunters have cell phones and rifles. Besides, saber-toothed tigers are extinct.

The last column of the table shows that the difference between men and women in most of the athletic events is not remarkable A woman of superior ability can beat a man of average or even above-average ability at any event except, maybe, javelin. Since we no longer fight saber-toothed tigers with rocks and sticks, the differences between men and women in jumping, running, and throwing are of little modern significance outside the rarefied world of high-performance athletics. As more girls are given the opportunity and the encouragement to participate seriously in athletics, we strongly suspect that the differences between the peak performances of male and female athletes will decline. We predict that, given the same training and encouragement, men and women of similar size will perform almost the same in track and field events.

Table 8.1

World Records in Track and Field

Event	Men	Women	Difference in percent
100-yard ash	9.77 seconds	10.49 seconds	7
Mile run	223.13 seconds	252.56 seconds	13
Marathon	7.495 seconds	8.125 seconds	8
High jump	2.45 meters	2.09 meters	15
Long jump	8.95 meters	7.52 meters	16
Shot put	23.12 meters	22.63 meters	2
Javelin	98.48 meters	71.70 meters	27

Source: www.trackandfieldnews.com.

In the real world, challenges are different than those in athletics. There is one life-threatening physical feat of enormous community significance and individual difficulty that women can do and men cannot do at all. Women can give birth. The annual birth rate among females of childbearing age in the United States is 68.4 per thousand. For males it is 0.0 (U.S. Bureau of the Census 2005, 61). There is also one physical feat that women can do better than men—live longer. In 2001 for white people in the United States, life expectancy at birth was 75 years for males and 80 for females (73). As the proud, old ones say, "Old age is not for sissies." Neither is childbirth.

The male is believed to be smarter than the female, particularly by the former. But the reality does not reflect the myth. Generalizing from an analysis of the test scores and performances of many boys and girls, Montagu concludes, "In short, the age-old myth that women are of inferior intelligence to men has, so far as the scientific evidence goes, not a leg to stand upon. Indeed, by present tests and standards of measurement girls, on the whole, do better than boys" (1974, 150).

To sum up our brief exploration of male superiority: the belief that men are superior to women in some way that is meaningful to modern times does not have a leg to stand on.

Stereotyping Women

The differences between the athletic abilities of men and women are small and not important in the modern world. Women are superior in physical abilities that really count. Women may even be smarter than men. Why, then, does the belief in male superiority persist, particularly among men?

Only a few generations ago, women faced many legal disabilities imposed on them by the state. The legal restrictions were often promoted (by men) as protection for the so-called weaker sex. However, the result was often to hold women down while men took advantage of them. Married women usually were restricted in their ownership of property. Women's conditions of employment outside the home were restricted as well. Their access to birth control and abortion often was limited by law, not just by a lack of scientific advance. They were not allowed to vote (Miles 1989). Many of those legal disabilities have been removed in developed countries; but many restrictions still remain in poor countries. Even in developed countries, the removal of sexist laws from the books has not eliminated sexism, but has changed it from primarily de jure to de facto. Now stereotypes instead of laws hold women down so men can take advantage of them.

The exploitation of women within the family is facilitated by the stereotyping of women as inferior to men, who delegate all the hard work within the home to women, to keep them busy and out of trouble. Men also restrict the inheritance of property to themselves, insist on managing their own property and whatever property the wife brings to the marriage, and demand the right to allocate the family income, congratulating themselves when they "give" to their wives and children. Men justify this dominance because women, according to the stereotype, cannot allocate the available resources as well as men; women are not good with numbers and do not make good decisions under pressure. So depriving them of their right to decide is, again according to the stereotype, saving them and their family from their own incompetence.

The lack of scientific knowledge also used to limit women, particularly in their control of their own bodies. It no longer does, at least in many countries. Extraordinary advances have often crept into people's lives on cat paws, unassuming and unannounced:

> When in 1955 an American researcher at the Worcester Institute for Chemical Biology, Massachusetts, announced that he had isolated a group of chemical steroids of the progestagen type, the average woman neither knew of it nor cared. But Gregory Pincus had in fact discovered

the philosopher's stone of genetic science, the element with the power to
turn centuries of wishful dreaming into reality. For progestagens, Pincus
had discovered, had the power to prevent ovulation when taken orally.
Without fanfare, then, "the Pill" was born, an insignificant compound of
naturally occurring chemicals, yet in its impact due to change as many
lives as any other of this century's revolutions. (Miles 1989, 231)

Legal reform and scientific advance have both lifted age-old limitations on women. Now, understanding stereotypes is more important than
ever. A stereotype is a rigid mental image of the central characteristics of
a particular group. A stereotype is a prejudice. It comes from the fearful
beliefs of others, not from a person's own experience. A stereotype is
thus distinguished from a guiding mental image.

In order to achieve a working grasp of the world, everybody forms
mental images of the characteristics of different groups. For example,
after being attacked on several occasions by pit bull dogs that bite you
on the leg, you are correct to form a certain mental image of the salient
characteristic of attacking pit bulls. They bite! Then you behave according to that image when you meet another pit bull that attacks you. That
kind of working mental image is not necessarily a stereotype because it
has been formulated and reformulated through actual experience with
the group in question. It helps you avoid getting bitten. In contrast, a true
stereotype is not subject to formulation and reformulation through experience. Furthermore, being a form of prejudice, stereotypes are learned
from other prejudiced people, not from actual experience with the group
being stereotyped. A stereotype is rigid in the face of experience. It does
not change. It is a fixed prejudgment, not a flexible, practical guide. It
is a myth that is related to reality in the same way that the tooth fairy is
related to dentistry. A guiding mental image is experiential; it changes
with experience. A stereotype is ideological; it does not change with experience. In the face of contradictory experience, a stereotype demands
the reinterpretation of experience.

We must draw an important distinction between guiding mental image
and stereotype. One guides; the other misguides. A guiding mental image
is changed by contradictory experience into an amended image. A stereotype, however, changes contradictory experience into a confirmation
of the stereotype. Suppose you have formed a mental image from your
previous experience with attacking pit bulls that "all pit bulls bite." Then
you happen to walk by a pit bull that looks at you and just yawns. This

new experience changes your mental image: "attacking pit bulls bite, but other ones may just yawn." Now you have a more useful mental image to guide you in future encounters with pit bulls. However, suppose you learned from your parents, who hate pit bulls, the stereotype that "all pit bulls are vicious biters." Then you encounter the yawning pit bull. Misguided by the stereotype, you hit the dog on the head with a rock to warn it away from its clever ruse of lulling you into complacency with a fake yawn so it can viciously bite you when you are least expecting it. Moral of the story: Identify and discard your stereotypes. They hurt others and may get you bitten.

Stereotypes or myths are false, but they are not just false. The stereotype or myth of woman—"the Eternal Feminine," Simone de Beauvoir called it—substitutes itself for the reality of women. She explains what we are trying to get at better than we can. The stereotype or myth, Beauvoir states,

> substitutes a transcendental Idea, timeless, unchangeable, necessary. This idea is indisputable because it is beyond the given: it is endowed with absolute truth. Thus, as against the dispersed, contingent, and multiple existences of actual women, mythical thought opposes the Eternal Feminine, unique and changeless. If the definition provided for this concept is contradicted by the behavior of flesh-and-blood women, it is the latter who are wrong: we are told not that Femininity is a false entity, but that the women concerned are not feminine. The contrary facts of experience are impotent against the myth. ([1952] 1989, 253)

In societies suffering from deeply entrenched sexism, the prejudiced older men and even some of the women go to great lengths to teach the younger men and women that women are inferior and to teach each group its proper gendered role. This teaching takes place in the home, the school, the church or synagogue or mosque or temple, the literature, the art, and the mass media of a sexist society. In short, it is everywhere. If the sexes are segregated, allowing young people little direct experience with each other, such biased teachings meet little resistance. While they are growing up, segregated young people encounter little that contradicts their indoctrination.

Great difficulties are encountered in sexist societies when children grow up and some wish to marry. The sexist segregation and indoctrination have to be overcome in order to get young men and women together in a social space that is at least partly cleared of stereotypes so that it bears some resemblance to reality. Elaborate dating rituals, chaperoning, and marriage brokering are among the practices that have evolved in sexist societies as ways of introducing young men and women to each other. If they avoid hurting each other when they collide, it is not because their elders prepared them for companionship and mutually fulfilling sexual relations with another person. It is because they have drawn on the human ability to overcome, to transform themselves into something better or, at least, something different.

If they get married, young people usually carry the stereotypes reinforced by their segregated lives into marriage. To build a happy family, they need to integrate their lives—at least a significant part of their lives. In spite of all the stereotyping and other obstacles, some couples actually succeed in building a life together. Their pets do not turn out to be attacking pit bulls. Most of their kids, if they have any, do not turn out to be serial killers. Many other couples, however, continue to relate to each other as stereotypes and pursue separate lives, whether they live in the same house and sleep in the same bed or not. And their situation can get much worse.

Violence and Abuse

Marriage is celebrated everywhere as a wonderful event. Nevertheless, marriage can be a nightmare for women, particularly in societies where the families are strictly patriarchal. A strictly patriarchal family is one in which the male, the patriarch husband, is supreme and the females, the mother and the daughter, are far below him. His status and authority are far higher than any woman's. What he says is the law for the family. Women obey. In extreme Hindu patriarchy, for example, a man's widow was expected to throw herself on his funeral pyre and die with him. Some even did it. This should not be taken as a Eurocentric, pro-Christian remark, one that puts non-European, non-Christian women down even lower than European women (Olson 1994). After all, women are not allowed, even today, into the Roman Catholic priesthood. When patriarchal families, whether European and Christian or not, exercise considerable influence or coercion over young people's marriage choices, such "choices" can turn out very badly for the young wife, resulting in mental abuse, physical abuse, and in extreme cases even death. Despite the popular lauding of "family values," marriage can be a very troubled institution. Louise Laurence explains the depth of the domestic abuse problem: "The costs of domestic abuse have a reach far beyond what

one would ordinarily consider. It is known that battered women flood
hospitals and mental health facilities; crowd courts, shelters, and drug
treatment centres; burden child welfare offices; and cost businesses millions in lost workdays and decreased productivity" (1999, 124).

Physical/domestic abuse of women is not the only way men hurt
women. Men hurt women's psyches as well as their bodies. By denying
them equal status in their relationship, many men hurt the self-esteem of
the women who are their wives and lovers. Many men psychologically
abuse their wives and lovers, causing them despair and depression. Many
men do not value women as full partners in the relationship and tell them
so in words and deeds. Women are supposed to be happy in their relationships with men, but many are not and the psychological abuse from
men they love is the cause. This was the conclusion of a large survey
of American women conducted by Shere Hite, a Pulitzer Prize winner
(1987). Susan Faludi reported that, even though the survey responses
supported her, the backlash against Hite was bitter and personal (1991).
Nevertheless, Faludi concluded her own book on the woman's struggle
and the backlash against it as follows: "Whatever new obstacles are
mounted against the future march toward equality, whatever new myths
invented, penalties levied, opportunities rescinded, or degradations imposed, no one can ever take from the American woman the justness of
her cause" (1991, 460).

Job Discrimination

Job discrimination begins long before women enter the labor market
looking for a job. It begins with the stereotype that the only proper job
for women is to be a mother and stay at home, never entering the labor
market in the first place. In strict patriarchy, stereotypes of masculin-
ity and femininity determine choices more than individual talents and
interests. Men must work outside the home. Women must stay inside.
If women have talents for work outside the home, such as athletics or
dentistry, those talents are not considered appropriate and are wasted.
If men have talents for work inside the home, such as childcare or
cooking, those talents are considered inappropriate and are wasted,
likewise. Such wastes add to the costs generated by classism and other
negative-sum games.

In recent decades, more women have disregarded the stereotypes
holding them back and moved out of the confines of the family and into

the labor market. Table 8.2 focuses on the recent movement of women into the U.S. job market, but similar movements are taking place or have already taken place in countries all over the globe.

The participation rate simply measures the percentage of men or women who could enter the labor market who actually do enter it. Table 8.2 brings out four significant characteristics of participation rates in the U.S. labor market. First, the participation rate for men is higher than for women but has been declining very slowly for about half a century. Had men shared equally with women the household and childcare activities of the family, the participation rate for women would have been much closer to the men's rate. But that is the point of gender inequality—the "superior" man pushes the burdens off onto the "inferior" woman and then sits back and enjoys his leisure at home. Inequality may result in many benefits for men around the house, but it also results in the inability of many women to contribute their talents to the labor market. The stereotypes of women generated by sexism keep them in their stereotyped role as female homemaker and discourage them from entering the labor market as workers.

Second, the participation rate for women jumped during U.S. participation in World War II (1941–45) and then fell in 1946. However, the female participation rate has never returned to its low prewar rates. Rosie the Riveter was not just a wartime stereotype of the woman worker in defense plants, helping her man win the war. Women entered the workforce in droves during the war and then many stayed. The war experience helped many women break into the labor market. They could break through stereotypes and other barriers because it was the patriotic thing to do.

Third, except for the blip after the war, the participation rate for women increased for over half a century, with the increase continuing dramatically during the women's liberation movement in the 1960s and 1970s. During the 1960s and 1970s, those daughters of Rosie the Riveter drove sexism out of their lives and then pushed into the labor market in even greater numbers.

Perhaps a fourth characteristic of the female participation rate is just becoming visible. Female participation may have reached a peak in 1999. The gradual rise that had been going on for over half a century seems to have hesitated slightly after that year. Sexism seems to be on the march once again, with rising stereotyping once again restraining women in their move into the labor market.

Table 8.2

Labor Force Participation Rates in the United States by Sex, 1940–2006
(in percent)

Year	Male	Female	Year	Male	Female
1940	82.5	27.9	1974	78.7	45.7
1941	83.8	28.5	1975	77.9	46.3
1942	85.1	30.9	1976	77.5	47.3
1943	87.4	35.7	1977	77.7	48.4
1944	88.2	36.3	1978	77.9	50.0
1945	87.6	35.8	1979	77.8	50.9
1946	81.1	30.8	1980	77.4	51.5
1947	86.8	31.8	1981	77.0	52.1
1948	87.0	32.7	1982	76.6	52.6
1949	86.9	33.2	1983	76.4	52.9
1950	86.8	33.9	1984	76.4	53.6
1951	87.3	34.7	1985	76.3	54.5
1952	87.2	34.8	1986	76.3	55.3
1953	86.9	34.5	1987	76.2	56.0
1954	86.4	34.6	1988	76.2	56.6
1955	85.4	35.7	1989	76.4	57.4
1956	85.5	36.9	1990	76.4	57.5
1957	84.8	36.9	1991	75.8	57.4
1958	84.2	37.1	1992	75.8	57.8
1959	83.7	37.1	1993	75.4	57.9
1960	83.3	37.7	1994	75.1	58.8
1961	82.9	38.1	1995	75.0	58.9
1962	82.0	37.9	1996	74.9	59.3
1963	81.4	38.3	1997	75.0	59.8
1964	81.0	38.7	1998	74.9	59.8
1965	80.7	39.3	1999	74.7	60.0
1966	80.4	40.3	2000	74.8	59.9
1967	80.4	41.1	2001	74.4	59.8
1968	80.1	41.6	2002	74.1	59.6
1969	79.8	42.7	2003	73.5	59.5
1970	79.7	43.3	2004	73.3	59.2
1971	79.1	43.4	2005	73.3	59.3
1972	78.9	43.9	2006	73.5	59.4
1973	78.8	44.7			

Sources: For 1940–54, U.S. Bureau of the Census, *Historical Statistics of the United States: Colonial Times to 1970.* Washington, DC: U.S. Government Printing Office, 1975, p. 132. For 1955–2006, U.S. Council of Economic Advisors, *Economic Report of the President, 2007.* Washington, DC: U.S. Government Printing Office, 2007, Table B-39.

Note: Data for the periods 1940–54 and 1955–2001 are not strictly comparable. They come from different sources. The participation rate is for the civilian noninstitutionalized population sixteen years of age and older during recent years and fourteen years of age and older before 1947.

Clarification: The participation rate is a simple concept. The first number in the table for the year 1940 means that 82.5% of all civilian (non-military) men over 14 who were not institutionalized were in the workforce in 1940.

Some Simple Arithmetic

One of the things that women's increased participation made possible in peacetime was a rising rate of retirement among older men. The increasing number of women in the workforce outside the home has done more for the United States than that. We see that war trumps sexism. But not only does the hard work of women help win wars; it also makes the peace more productive. Had more women stayed in the labor market and at work after World War II, U.S. output could have remained that much higher. How much is output lowered by the stereotypes of sexism?

Table 8.3 presents an annual estimate of how much output has been lost each year since 1980 due to the sexist stereotyping that keeps women out of the labor market. First, in a worksheet supporting Table 8.3, we calculated how many women are kept from getting a job in the labor market by assuming that the unemployment and participation rates for women would be the same as for men if there were no sexist stereotypes. We looked up the rates for men and applied them to the data for women to calculate the numbers of women who would be working if there were no sexist stereotypes. Then we looked up the numbers of females working even with the sexist stereotypes and found the difference between them and the numbers of females who would be working without the sexist stereotypes. This difference gave us the figures in the second column of Table 8.3. Then we multiplied the difference by the gross domestic product (GDP) produced per worker (figures we looked up and put in the third column) and got the annual estimate we wanted—the annual amounts of GDP lost to sexism (figures in the fourth column). We used a simple Excel worksheet and downloaded the rates and numbers we needed from the online *Economic Report of the President* (2007).

The estimated lost GDP was at least $1 trillion per year measured by the purchasing power of the dollar in the year 2000. The total for the period covered by the table was almost $28 trillion—a tidy sum to lose.

Sexism is extraordinarily costly; and sexism is not necessary. The experience depicted in Table 8.2 proves that a significant rise in the female participation rate can take place: during the twenty-seven–year period from 1980 to 2006, the rate went up from 51.5 to 59.4 percent. Nevertheless, it should have started higher and risen faster. Because it did not, the country missed the abundance it could have had during the entire 1940–2006 period by a cumulative $28 trillion.

During the last fifty years, the U.S. economy has exhibited remark-

Table 8.3

Lost GDP in the United States Due to Sexism, 1980–2006

Year	Number of females excluded from work by sexism (in thousands)	Lost GDP per excluded female (in thousands of 2000 dollars)	Lost GDP (in trillions of 2000 dollars)
1980	21,529	51,979	1.12
1981	20,906	52,708	1.10
1982	19,403	52,140	1.01
1983	19,069	53,789	1.03
1984	19,696	55,365	1.09
1985	19,208	56,497	1.09
1986	18,621	57,151	1.06
1987	18,152	57,587	1.05
1988	17,949	58,648	1.05
1989	17,672	59,496	1.05
1990	17,515	59,873	1.05
1991	16,576	60,318	1.00
1992	16,173	61,916	1.00
1993	16,143	62,637	1.01
1994	15,558	63,672	0.99
1995	15,734	64,305	1.01
1996	15,410	65,733	1.01
1997	15,310	67,178	1.03
1998	15,521	68,969	1.07
1999	15,393	70,945	1.09
2000	15,981	71,714	1.15
2001	15,440	72,230	1.12
2002	15,228	73,626	1.12
2003	14,619	74,788	1.09
2004	15,246	76,864	1.17
2005	15,521	77,955	1.21
2006	15,910	79,234	1.26
Total			27.91

Source: Council of Economic Advisers, *Economic Report of the President, 2007.* Washington, DC: U.S. Government Printing Office, 2007, Table B-2, p. 230 (Real GDP), Table B-36, p. 234 (Employment), and Table B38, p. 276 (Unemployment Rates); and authors' calculations.

able growth. Between 1955 and 2005, for example, real GDP (in 2000 dollars) increased from $2.2 trillion to $11 trillion—a fivefold increase. This increase in real GDP could not have taken place without the dramatic increase in the labor force participation rates of women. Between 1955 and 2005, employment in the United States increased from 62.2 million to 141.7 million workers—an increase of 79.5 million workers. During those years, the labor force participation rate of women increased from

35.7 percent to 59.3 percent. Women accounted for 60.9 percent of the increase in U.S. employment between 1955 and 2005. If women in the United States in 2005 had the same labor force participation rate as in 1955, the U.S. economy would have had 25 million fewer workers and real GDP would have been much smaller than $11 trillion.

We must be careful, of course, in assessing these hypothetical computations. First, GDP in 2005 includes a lot of output that was not counted in 1955. For example, to the extent that household work performed by women in 1955 (not counted in GDP) has been replaced by paid work, the GDP figures are not comparable. An example of this phenomenon is childcare. Childcare performed by a nonworking woman in 1955 was not counted in GDP. Childcare provided at a day care center in 2005 is counted in GDP. Although this and many other possible examples demand caution in their interpretation, the basic computations in the previous paragraph are still meaningful. U.S. GDP in 2005 would have been considerably less if the labor force participation rates of women had not increased over the 1955 figure.

There is also an international dimension to the labor force participation rate (LFPR). Female LFPRs in many nations have been increasing over the last two or three decades, but in some nations remain extremely low by twenty-first–century standards. Table 8.4 exhibits female LFPRs for the nations and areas with the lowest female LFPRs reported by the World Bank (2005). Unfortunately, these may not be the actual lowest female LFPRs because many nations do not even collect such data.

Even if women escape the stereotypes of the patriarchal family and seek their freedom by themselves in the job market, they will find job discrimination greatly limiting their job choices, pay, and career advancement. Job discrimination hurts women in many ways. They are crowded into traditional occupations where the large supply of female job seekers—elementary school teachers, nurses, and day-care workers—pushes wages and salaries down. Their potential employers fear that they will leave their jobs to have children, so they are devalued as permanent workers. Their advancing career reaches the barrier of the "glass ceiling" encountered in many managerial and professional job ladders. Also they are, plain and simple, exploited (Figart 1997). Women who are the head of their own household (with no man present) have a harder time supporting their household than men. Since women are paid less than men, they have to work a regular job plus a part-time one in order to earn the same income as men. Table 8.5 gives a glimpse into the world of the woman heading her own household. She has done slightly better since 1980 and 1990, with her income rising

Table 8.4

Female Labor Force Participation Rates in Selected Nations and Areas, 2005

Country/area	2005 rate
West Bank and Gaza	10.9
Saudi Arabia	18.5
Egypt, Arab Republic	21.6
Oman	23.6
Sudan	24.2
Turkey	27.2
Morocco	28.7
Jordan	28.9
Bahrain	30.7
Yemen, Republic	30.8
Tunisia	31.1
Middle East and North Africa	31.1
Sao Tome and Principe	31.7
Swaziland	32.9
Pakistan	33.7
Libya	33.9
Guatemala	35.2
Lebanon	35.7
India	36.0

Source: World Bank, World Development Indicators, WDI online, August 14, 2007, https://publications.worldbank.org/WDI/

from about 60 to about 70 percent of her male counterpart. Nevertheless, a sizable gap between the two remains—30 percent in recent years. The figures in the table compare households headed by a male with no wife present to households headed by a female with no husband present.

Who Keeps House and Raises the Children?

The different participation rates and income levels for men and women lead to another issue—who does the housework and raises the children? This is the second shift issue. While Table 8.4 above showcased the financial plight of women heading households without husbands, the second shift issue is faced even by women with husbands present. When men and women share a household (unless they spend their life in a full-service hotel), they have to divide both the labor of earning income by working outside the household and the labor of all the housework that needs doing when the paying job is finished. That work is done on the second shift, and it takes much longer

Table 8.5

Incomes of Male and Female Heads of Household in the United States
(income in current dollars)

Year	Male	Female	Female as a percent of male (in percent)
1980	17,519	10,406	59
1990	29,046	16,932	58
2000	37,727	25,716	68
2001	36,590	25,745	70
2002	37,739	26,423	70

Source: U.S. Bureau of the Census, *Statistical Abstract of the United States, 2004–2005,* 124th ed. Washington, DC: U.S. Government Printing Office, Table 674, p. 448.

when the couple has children. Children require endless rounds of cooking, feeding, bathing, laundering, and nurturing. They get sick and need taking to the doctor. They get cavities and need taking to the dentist. They need schooling and all sorts of lessons and help with homework. They thrive on emotional support, guidance, and reading at bedtime; they do not thrive without all this parenting. How much do men really support the entrance of women into the labor market by doing housework and childcare? How much of the second shift is done by men?

The second shift issue was first addressed by Arlie Russell Hochschild in the 1980s. She found that many men enjoyed playing with their kids more than their fathers did. Beyond that pleasant chore, though, most women who enter the workforce outside the home have to do most of the second shift themselves. According to Hochschild, "Though many couples now believe in sharing, at this point in history few actually do share" (2003, 210). The practical result of their second shift burden is that women work a full month of twenty-four-hour days every year that men do not (2003, 4).

The problem really lies with the participation of men, not women, or, rather, the lack of men's participation in the second shift. As women have moved into the labor market and out of the home, men have failed to pick up the slack left by the women's absence. As a result, women now work two shifts instead of just one. What is required is to get men to share the second shift. There is a problem of laziness that contributes to the failure to achieve abundance, but it is not laziness in women or the unemployed. It is laziness in men who do not do their share of housework and childcare. And that is the point of patriarchy all along—to get the women to do the work.

9

Racism

Race Is a Social Fiction

Racism is ugly, nasty, and unjustifiable. Superficially, racism is easy to define: it involves acting on the belief that one race (usually one's own race) is superior to some other race. The problems start when people try to define and identify different races, drawing boundaries around them to keep people in their assigned racial places. Without the boundaries, members of the allegedly inferior race may cross into the allegedly superior one, avoiding the racial stigma altogether. And what good is racism without the stigma? However, there are no defensible boundaries between races because there are no biologically distinct and completely separate groups of human beings. "Race" is thus a very vague biological category.

Crossing the color line is often referred to as "passing" when it is done more or less permanently and "shuttling" when it is done frequently over the course of a lifetime. Passing and shuttling are easiest when done by a person who does not resemble the stereotyped image of the allegedly inferior racial group or who resembles one of the stereotypes only slightly (Cox [1948] 2000, 122–123).

There are various indistinct groups of people sharing observable characteristics—fat ones, thin ones, short ones, tall ones, old ones and young ones, dark ones and light ones. Even colonized and colonizer groups sometimes appear different, at least to each other (Memmi [1967] 1991). But each group gradually merges into its opposite, with one naturally passing into the other. For example, let us consider the fat versus thin groups. People in the fat group can be classified as the truly immense, weighing over 600 pounds. Next come the exceptionally large, in the 500-pound range. The merely large folks in the 400-pound range come next and then the big people in the 300-pound range. Finally, people in the 200-pound range could still be classified as fat, allowing them also to look down on thin people with contempt. However, in the 200-pound class a few people can be found who might be considered thin, particularly those over seven feet tall. Should they be allowed to stay in the select group of people entitled to call themselves fat and entitled to look down on the woefully thin? The point of this example is that boundaries between groups of people are arbitrary. In any grouping, the differences between individual group members can easily overwhelm the differences between the groups. There are no truly natural groups of homogeneous people, only sets of arbitrary distinctions that can easily become stereotypes.

Individuals whose ancestors came from areas near the equator often have more skin pigment than other individuals whose ancestors came from areas near the poles. Nevertheless, skin color is very hard to use as an operational category determining a person's race as either black or white. That is, it is not possible to sort every human on earth into one of the alleged races, unless it is done arbitrarily. Human skin color runs through a very wide range, in the same fashion as human weight. There is no real or natural dividing line between "black" and "white" skin color, even though much has been made of black and white races in the United States and elsewhere. Besides, human skin color is never actually black and it is never actually white. It is a complex mixture of browns and reds and yellows. Race is not so much a distinct and separate biological category naturally occurring in the world around us as it is a cultural and ethnic category artificially implanted into the human head. Human groups genetically intersect and overlap in numerous ways, forming an astonishing amalgamation of diversity, not a set of readily identifiable distinct and separate groups. People do have different outward features, but they are generally insignificant in terms of behavior. People may or may not pass these traits on to their children. Along with Albert Memmi, we suggest ignoring insignificant human differences, instead taking an instrumental approach to understanding humans and their activities: "Science is neither Western nor Eastern, any more than it is bourgeois or proletarian [or white or black]. There are only two ways of pouring concrete—the right way and the wrong way" ([1967], 1991, 152). We quote Memmi because he was a remarkably cosmopolitan man. He was born in Tunisia while it was a colony. There he learned Arabic, his mother tongue. He was also Jewish. He moved to France where he studied at the

Sorbonne in Paris. He became a writer and shared his wisdom about how it was to live at the intersection of three different cultures.

Racists, however, make a big deal out of insignificant human differences. Racists believe that all people can be readily placed in separate, distinct biological groups that do not intersect or overlap. Furthermore, racists believe that membership in such a (make-believe) racial group determines the nature of the individual person. Racists—such as Adolf Hitler—also believe that their own race is superior to other racial groups and deserves more rights, powers, and privileges than lesser breeds. And that is the point of racism. Racism does not involve a biological classification based on the actual observation of meaningful differences between human groups; instead, it involves a series of stereotypes that serves as justification for some people to take advantage of others. These stereotypes are not susceptible to contradiction by the evidence. That makes racism a social fiction. Racism is taught to people by other racists. For further discussion of racism and prejudice in general, see Allport (1958).

Race, religion, and ethnic background can get all mixed up in the minds of the deeply prejudiced. The resulting mental concoction can be fatal. Adolf Hitler, for example, believed that Jews constituted a race inferior to what he considered the superior Germanic or Aryan race. Of course, Jews really are a group of people who share a religion, not a biologically distinct group of folks that form a race. Nevertheless, that fact did not stop Hitler from instigating the mass murder of millions of Jews. That fact had not stopped the Spanish Inquisition, which had opened for business in 1492, or the Portuguese Inquisition, which began in 1536. More than four centuries before the Nazis, the Iberian inquisitors hunted down and killed Jews and "New Christians"—that is, Jews or Muslims who had converted to Christianity under varying degrees of coercion or whose ancestors had done so. According to the racism of the Iberian inquisitors, the blood of the New Christians was impure. (Blood types are different from alleged racial types, by the way. Furthermore, inheritance passes through genes, not blood.) The Iberian inquisitors burnt their victims. The Nazis, adding a modern twist, gassed theirs. In both eras, the murderers then confiscated their victims' wealth and property. The slaughter of the innocents did not lack a coldly rational economic motive (Gitlitz 1996; Shirer 1959).

Racism can drag humans down to the very depth of depravity. It does not matter what group is being victimized and it does not matter that

Table 9.1

The Geographical Distribution of the Human Population, 2000
(in millions)

World	Africa	N. America	S. America	Asia	Europe	Oceana
6,085	803	487	348	3,686	730	31
100%	13.2%	8.0%	5.7%	60.6%	12.0%	0.5%

Source: U.S. Bureau of the Census, *Statistical Abstract of the United States, 2004–2005,* 124th ed. Washington, DC: U.S. Government Printing Office, Table 1319, p. 840.

race is a social fiction; racism is the enemy of humanity everywhere and in every time.

Racism is resistant but not impervious to some perspective. Table 9.1 provides a geographical perspective by showing the geographical distribution of the human population in 2000. The table shows that the principal groupings of human beings are not determined by the color line that has separated and disturbed America for over 300 years. Folks usually classified as "white" hail largely from Europe and North America, while those usually classified as "black" hail largely from Africa. The table indicates that most people are neither. In fact, from the global point of view, both whites and blacks are minorities. Asians are by far the most numerous humans.

Although the U.S. Census Bureau does its best to report counts of the population by race, ethnicity, and even ancestry, the agency recognizes the difficulty of defining these illusive concepts and the fuzzy nature of the categories it reports. All racial, ethnic, and ancestry reporting in the U.S. census is done by self-identification because there is no scientific or objective definition that can be used.

The Census Bureau recognizes six separate racial categories:

• White alone
• Black or African-American alone
• American Indian and Alaska Native alone
• Asian alone
• Native Hawaiian and Other Pacific Islander alone
• Some other race alone

In addition, Americans participating in the census may identify themselves by listing multiple racial categories—even all six—in combination.

This bewildering array of racial choices results in fifty-seven different and unique combinations of "race." But census data can be even more confusing because the racial data in the 2000 census are not comparable to the data in the 1990 census. As the Census Bureau notes, "the Census 2000 data on race are not directly comparable with data from the 1990 census or earlier censuses. Caution must be used when interpreting changes in the racial composition of the U.S. population over time" (U.S. Bureau of the Census 2001). The reason is that the 2000 census was the first in which multiple racial categories were permitted. Therein lies the source of the confusion. Yet the confusion merely reflects the mixed-up racial composition of the U.S. population that has resulted from hundreds of years of intermixing.

In addition to race, the Census Bureau recognizes two ethnic categories: Hispanic (or Latino) and non-Hispanic. Since a person of Hispanic origin can be a member of any of the six racial groups defined by the Census Bureau, we now have 114 race and ethnic categories (2 x 57). And again, the 2000 census data on ethnicity (Hispanic or non-Hispanic origin) are not compatible with earlier censuses. For the 2000 census, the order in which race and ethnicity questions were asked was altered, resulting in very different responses to the ethnicity question. In the 2000 Census, the ethnicity (Hispanic) question appeared first. In previous censuses, the ethnicity question appeared after the race question. In the earlier censuses many Hispanics checked the "other" race category creating great confusion in the data. The Census Bureau began collecting data on Hispanics only in 1950, using the label "Spanish origin." However, there was no self-identification in the 1950 census. Indeed, there was no question to identify the Spanish origin population. Instead, the Census Bureau compared citizens' names to a list of allegedly Spanish origin names—a dubious procedure at best.

If race and ethnicity are confusing, so is another census classification: ancestry. Here is what the Census Bureau says about ancestry: "Ancestry refers to a person's ethnic origin or descent, 'roots,' or heritage; or the place of birth of the person, the person's parents, or ancestors before their arrival in the United States. Some ethnic identities, such as 'Egyptian' or 'Polish,' can be traced to geographic areas outside the United States, while other ethnicities such as 'Pennsylvania German' or 'Cajun' evolved in the United States" (U.S. Bureau of the Census 2006, 29). Confused? We are and so, apparently, is the Census Bureau: "The intent of the ancestry question was not to measure the degree of attachment the respondent had to a particular ethnicity. For example, a response of 'Irish' might reflect total involvement in an Irish community or only a memory of ancestors several generations removed from the individual" (29). The Census Bureau ancestry data result in about 1,000 ancestry categories. Naturally, multiple combinations are possible and we hesitate to count the total number of such categories. The ancestry category "American" was allowed. The authors wonder about Texan or Okie as an ancestry category and will lobby the Census Bureau to include these terms in future data collection efforts.

Our point here is that the government agency that should know most (and probably does know most) about collecting race, ethnicity, and ancestry data does not really know how to do it and has been changing its methods for at least fifty years.

In his monumental study, the Swedish economist Gunnar Myrdal provides some logical perspective on racism, U.S. style. Myrdal's book is dynamite. He explains that while "white" people in the United States were egalitarian and humanitarian, they also denied African-Americans their fundamental rights and treated them grossly unequally and cruelly. This was a profound logical contradiction, and the only way European-Americans could justify it was to deny the basic humanity of their victims—that is, to become racists. Whites thus moved beyond rational discourse into a "magical sphere" of their own minds: "In this magical sphere of the white man's mind, the Negro is inferior, totally independent of rational proofs or disproofs. And he is inferior in a deep and mystical sense" (1944, 100). To understand this mental contradiction, Myrdal continues,

> we have to work as a detective reconstructing the solution of a crime from scattered evidence. For both the student of popular beliefs on the Negro and the detective, the guide to the explanation is given in the question: To Whose Good? Beliefs are opportune; they are in the service of interests. It is these general and specific rationalization needs which give the beliefs their pertinacity. They give to the stereotypes their emotional load, and their "value" to the people who hold to them. (108)

Racism Is Real and Costly

How has racism—along with classism, nationalism, and sexism—contributed to humanity's failure to achieve abundance? By now, a pattern should be clear. Racism and all the other forms of unfair advantage

Table 9.2

**Black Versus White Unemployment Rates in the United States,
1972–2007** (in percent of the civilian labor force for that group)

Year	White	Black	Year	White	Black
1972	5.1	10.4	1990	4.8	11.4
1973	4.3	9.4	1991	6.1	12.5
1974	5.0	10.5	1992	6.6	14.2
1975	7.8	14.8	1993	6.1	13.0
1976	7.0	14.0	1994	5.3	11.5
1977	6.2	14.0	1995	4.9	10.4
1978	5.2	12.8	1996	4.7	10.5
1979	5.1	12.3	1997	4.2	10.0
1980	6.3	14.3	1998	3.9	8.9
1981	6.7	15.6	1999	3.7	8.0
1982	8.6	18.9	2000	3.5	7.6
1983	8.4	19.5	2001	4.2	8.6
1984	6.5	15.9	2002	5.1	10.2
1985	6.2	15.1	2003	5.2	10.8
1986	6.0	14.5	2004	4.8	10.4
1987	5.3	13.0	2005	4.4	10.0
1988	4.7	11.7	2006	4.0	8.9
1989	4.5	11.4	2007	4.1	8.3

Source: Council of Economic Advisers, *Economic Report of the President, 2006.*
Washington, DC: U.S. Government Printing Office, 2008, Table B-42, p. 276.

reduce access to and use of the joint stock of knowledge. As a result, the community has scarcity when it could have abundance. It also has stereotypes and irrationality. The top dogs benefit and are better off than they would be if they were stopped from taking advantage. The underdogs mongrels are harmed by the advantages taken. Furthermore, the rest of the community is harmed by the lost production of goods and services and confused by the rationalizations given.

Nationalism, classism, sexism, and racism are all negative-sum games. One readily measured indicator of the extent of harm done is the extent of unemployment of the exploited group. Table 9.2 provides some needed historical background on the unemployment costs of racism. Using such a table does not imply acceptance of the existence of biologically distinct races of white people and black people, but it does clarify one effect of racist beliefs.

The data on black unemployment prior to 1972 are not readily available, but the table still gives data for thirty-four years of recent experience. Both white and black unemployment rates rose and fell with the upswings and downswings of the business cycle. However, the black unemployment rate was twice the white rate for the entire period and the gap between the two shows no improving trend. The black unemployment rate reached truly alarming levels in recessions: 14.8 percent in 1975, 19.5 percent in 1983, and 14.2 percent in 1992. During the period covered by the table, the black unemployment rate was below double digits only five times. For most of the period, the black community struggled under unemployment conditions experienced by the white community only during the depths of the Great Depression in the 1930s. That, by itself, is an astonishing fact. Discrimination against black workers has thwarted the black community's full participation in the economy for the last 400 years and in the labor market for at least the last thirty-four years. The black unemployment rate continues to be twice the white rate. Judging by this unemployment experience and contrary to public opinion held by a wide swath of the complacent white community, racism has not been stamped out in the United States—certainly not in the labor market. It is alive and still serving some white folks quite well while it still deprives everybody else of the goods that could have been produced and the services that could have been performed by those excluded. You can make your own estimate of the costs of racism, and we encourage you to do so. Our estimate of the unemployment costs for the United States in recent years is presented in Table 9.3.

The calculations that went into Table 9.3 require a brief explanation. First, we calculated real gross domestic product (GDP) per worker by dividing real GDP by the number of employed civilian workers for each year. Real GDP per worker was then used as the estimate of how much each excluded black worker could have produced that year if not kept unemployed by racial discrimination in the labor market. Second, we calculated the number of wasted black workers by first finding the difference between the black and white unemployment rates each year and then multiplying that difference by the black labor force for that year. For example, in 2005 the black unemployment rate was 10.0 percent and the white unemployment rate was 4.4 percent, then the difference between the two would be 5.6 percent. That 5.6 percent is the excess unemployment rate for blacks caused by racial discrimination. Then we multiplied the black labor force for 2005, which was 17 million, by their excess unemployment rate of 5.6 percent. That gives us 0.95 mil-

152

Table 9.3

Real GDP Lost Due to Racism in the United States, 1972–2007

Year	Real GDP per worker (thousands of 2000 dollars)	Wasted Black workers (millions)	Lost GDP (billions of 2000 dollars)
1972	49.97	0.462	23.1
1973	51.04	0.459	23.4
1974	49.77	0.505	25.2
1975	50.22	0.648	32.5
1976	51.16	0.667	34.1
1977	51.63	0.776	40.1
1978	52.21	0.790	41.2
1979	52.35	0.772	40.4
1980	51.98	0.869	45.2
1981	52.71	0.988	52.1
1982	52.14	1.167	60.9
1983	53.79	1.293	69.6
1984	55.36	1.132	62.6
1985	56.50	1.099	62.1
1986	57.15	1.079	61.6
1987	57.59	0.997	57.4
1988	58.65	0.926	54.3
1989	59.50	0.935	55.6
1990	59.87	0.906	54.2
1991	60.32	0.882	53.2
1992	61.92	1.076	66.6
1993	62.64	0.979	61.3
1994	63.67	0.898	57.2
1995	64.31	0.813	52.3
1996	65.73	0.879	57.8
1997	67.18	0.905	60.8
1998	68.97	0.801	55.3
1999	70.94	0.704	49.9
2000	71.71	0.669	48.0
2001	72.23	0.724	52.3
2002	73.63	0.847	62.3
2003	74.79	0.927	69.3
2004	76.86	0.931	71.6
2005	77.96	0.952	74.2
2006	78.20	0.848	66.4
2007	78.90	0.735	58.0

Source: Council of Economic Advisers, *Economic Report of the President, 2008.* Washington, DC: U.S. Government Printing Office, Tables B-2, p. 226, B-35, p. 269, Table B-37, p. 271.

Table 9.4

Median Weekly Earnings of White and Black Wage and Salary Workers, 2000–2007 (in dollars)

Year	White	Black	Black as a percent of White	White-Black gap
2000	590	474	80	116
2001	610	491	80	119
2002	623	498	80	125
2003	636	514	81	122
2004	657	525	80	132
2005	672	520	77	152
2006	690	554	80	136
2007	716	569	80	147

Source: U.S. Department of Labor, Bureau of Labor Statistics. "Weekly and Hourly Earnings Data from the Current Population Survey," http://data.bls.gov/PDQ/servlet /SurveyOutputServlet;jsessionid=f030e2147b37$3F$3F$0, September 16, 2008.

lion wasted black workers for 2005. Lost or wasted real GDP for 2005 is the 0.95 million wasted black workers multiplied by the real GDP per worker in 2005, which was $77,960. The total lost real GDP for 2005 was $74.2 billion.

For the thirty-six-year period covered by Table 9.3, the total lost GDP was $1,912.1 billion—an immense sum of waste. No wonder abundance was elusive. The average annual loss for the period was $53.1 billion. Imagine what kind of health program could be financed with $53.1 billion a year.

Not only is the unemployment rate for blacks much higher than for whites, but blacks get paid less, too. Table 9.4 shows a remarkably stable ratio of black to white pay. Blacks were paid 80 percent of white pay for most of the period covered, with one year's proportion falling to 77 percent and another year's proportion rising to 81 percent. However, the gap in absolute dollars widened from $116 to $147 per week.

Table 9.4 compared the weekly earnings of white and black workers over a recent seven-year period. Table 9.5 compares the money income of white and black families over a twenty-seven-year period. During the entire period, the money income of black families was always less than two-thirds the money income of white families. This is a large gap that results in a large difference in the standard of living of white and black families. In absolute dollars of constant purchasing power, the gap widened between 1980 and 2007 from $22,113 to $24,284. In terms of

Table 9.5

Median Money Income of Families by Race, 1980–2007
(in constant 2007 dollars)

Year	White income	Black income	Black income as a percent of White income
1980	52,477	30,364	58
1985	53,571	30,847	58
1990	56,771	32,946	58
1995	57,612	35,084	61
2000	63,849	40,547	64
2005	63,000	37,666	60
2007	64,427	40,143	62

Source: U.S. Bureau of the Census. "Historical Income Tables—Families." Current Population Survey, Table F-7, www.census.gov/hhes/www/income/historic/f04.html, September 16, 2008.

percentages, the black family rate stayed constant during the 1980s, rose in the 1990s, and seems to be falling again in the first years of the twenty-first century. As indicated by these tables, discrimination against black workers has not declined and the standard of living for black families remains depressed below that for white families.

Racism, of course, is more than a black and white issue. Tables 9.6 and 9.7, based on data from the U.S. Census Bureau's *American Community Survey* (2006), suggest that Hispanics, Native Americans, Hawaiians and other Pacific Islanders, those of some other race, and those who report more than one race also suffer from racism in both labor market characteristics and income. While little explanation of these tables is necessary, a few points are worth noting. First, blacks have the highest unemployment rate (12.9 percent) of any group in Table 9.6, but are followed closely by American Indians and Alaska Natives (12.3 percent) and those who report two or more races (10.4 percent). Hispanics, who in 2006 numbered more than 30 million persons, had an unemployment rate of 7.6 percent compared to their white non-Hispanic counterparts' unemployment rate of 5.4 percent.

Second, as shown in Table 9.7, several measures of income and poverty by race have a pattern similar to the unemployment rate. The highest percentages of persons below the poverty level occur among blacks (25.3 percent) and American Indians and Alaska Natives (26.6 percent). Hispanics, with a poverty rate of 21.5 percent, are more than twice as likely to fall below the poverty level as their white non-Hispanic counterparts, with a poverty rate of 9.3 percent. In a similar fashion, blacks have a per capita income of $16,559 that is only 56.3 percent of the white, non-Hispanic group's. Hispanics' per capita income of $14,736 is only 50.1 percent of the white-non-Hispanic group's. People listing two or more races have the lowest per capita income, $13,889 (47.2 percent of white non-Hispanics' income). The general picture does not change when we examine either household income or family income. A family contains two or more related individuals. A household contains one or more persons. Household is the broader category and includes all so-called "family households." The effects of race and ethnicity are obvious no matter what income variable we examine.

While we have concentrated in this chapter on racism and the social and economic consequences of racism in the United States, these are not uniquely American phenomenon. Racism and its economic consequences occur throughout the world. The extreme case of a belief in Aryan superiority in Germany before and during World War II has already been discussed. Other examples are, unfortunately, all too numerous and they are geographically widespread. Apartheid in South Africa was, until recently, a tragic example of racism that resulted in untold economic losses and human indignities. Racism or the effects of latent racism can be found in almost any nation.

The New Racism

We have made and supported with historical evidence claims that run strongly against the conventional wisdom in the United States. The conventional wisdom in the complacent white community is that the civil rights movement of the 1960s resulted in the elimination of racism and racial discrimination in the United States. According to this view, blacks and other racial groups are now on equal terms with whites. Therefore, affirmative action programs, set-aside programs, mandated integration of schools, and all other public policies that favor blacks over whites should be eliminated because they have become a new form of discrimination—reverse discrimination against whites.

This conventional wisdom is simply wrong. If whites really were suffering from reverse discrimination, the evidence would have shown up in our tables; but it did not. Instead, large gaps remain between the economic conditions of the white and the black communities. In the United States, the conventional wisdom is a new form of racism. It allows

156

Table 9.6

Selected Labor Market Characteristics by Race in the United States, 2006

Race	Number of persons sixteen years old and older	In labor force	Labor force participation rate (in percent)	Unemployment rate (in percent)
White	177,338,338	115,201,319	65.0	5.3
Black	27,452,330	17,268,746	62.9	12.9
American Indian and Alaska Native	1,779,262	1,060,390	59.6	12.3
Asian	10,517,576	6,914,632	65.7	5.3
Native Hawaiian and other Pacific Islander	323,418	222,735	68.9	8.2
Some other race	13,402,839	9,275,281	69.2	7.8
Two or more races	3,430,200	2,250,111	65.6	10.4
White Non-Hispanic	161,158,494	104,298,931	64.7	5.4
Hispanic	30,741,044	20,938,642	68.1	7.6

Source: U.S. Bureau of the Census, American Community Survey (2006), Tables C23002A through C23002I, http://factfinder.census.gov /servlet/DTGeoSearchByListServlet?ds_name=ACS_2006_EST_G00_&_lang=en&_ts=212510172020.

Table 9.7

Selected Income Characteristics by Race in the United States, 2006

Race	Poverty status in last 12 months (percent below poverty level)	Per capita income	Median household income	Median family income
White	10.5	$27,951	$51,429	$62,712
Black	25.3	$16,559	$32,372	$38,385
American Indian and Alaska Native	26.6	$15,736	$33,762	$38,800
Asian	10.7	$27,884	$63,642	$72,305
Native Hawaiian and other Pacific Islander	16.1	$18,689	$49,361	$52,104
Some other race	22.0	$14,183	$38,272	$39,156
Two or more races	16.8	$13,889	$42,213	$50,089
White Non-Hispanic	9.3	$29,406	$52,375	$65,180
Hispanic	21.5	$14,736	$38,747	$40,074

Source: U.S. Bureau of the Census, American Community Survey (2006), Tables S1701, S1902, S1903, and S19113A through S19113I, http://factfinder.census.gov /servlet/DTGeoSearchByListServlet?ds.

some whites to continue to take advantage of blacks by providing the needed legalistic supports (reverse discrimination suits) and the needed psychological rationalizations. It allows the negative-sum game of racism, along with classism, nationalism, and sexism, to continue robbing the nation of abundance.

10

A Summing Up

Universal Employment: A Different Objective and Its Context

We propose pursuing a different objective—universal employment—aimed at continuously increasing participation in productive economic activity. The object is to drive the economy's unemployment rate down closer and closer to absolute zero through collective and individual action. We introduce universal employment in this chapter in the context of inequality. Then we discuss universal employment at length in the next chapter.

In general universal employment is not part of the vocabulary of most economists, but we are not the first to suggest policies designed to eliminate unemployment. John Dewey, a famous American philosopher, did so in 1919. Dewey (1939 [1919], 420) wrote: "The first great demand of a better social order, I should say, then, is the guarantee of the right, to every individual who is capable of doing it, to work. . ." Our teacher, Wendell C. Gordon—to whom this book is dedicated—wrote frequently and passionately about what he termed the job guarantee from the early 1970s to the late 1990s. Gordon (1973, 328), argued that the job guarantee must be an important part of any poverty reduction program. Randy Wray (1997, 2007), an economist at the University of Missouri Kansas City, has written extensively on a policy of an employer of last resort. We have no objections to an employer of last resort, but we suggest other ways of achieving universal employment in the next chapter.

The most striking fact of the current economic condition is the huge pool of people across the globe that is not working with space-age skills and tools. Bringing them into full participation would not impose a cost on the global economy, but would produce an enormous benefit instead. People's thinking on this point has become confused in recent years: in today's conventional wisdom, the unemployed and underemployed are viewed as a collective burden, as hungry mouths that everybody else must feed. Properly understood in terms of universal employment, those hungry mouths would become productive hands instead. Thomas Malthus, emphasizing scarcity, was wrong. The one who was right was Harry Hopkins.

Harry Hopkins, one of the most important innovators of the twentieth century, was appointed by President Franklin Delano Roosevelt to head up the Works Progress Administration (WPA) in the early 1930s. While most economists thought government only interfered in economic affairs, Hopkins insisted that government could put the unemployed to work making badly needed goods and performing important services. When Roosevelt gave Hopkins the chance to test his idea, he proved that he was right and the others were wrong. He put millions of men and women on the WPA payroll and their output of goods and services was prodigious. They built schools, roads, bridges, courthouses, libraries, dams, airports, and animal shelters all over the country. Nick Taylor, American historian and author, gives some statistics on the WPA's accomplishments: the agency built

> 650,000 miles of roads, 78,000 bridges, 125,000 civilian and military buildings, 800 airports built, improved, or enlarged, 700 miles of airport runways. It served almost 900 million hot lunches to schoolchildren and operated 1,500 nursery schools. It presented 225,000 concerts to audiences totaling 150 million, performed plays, vaudeville acts, puppet shows, and circuses before 30 million people, and produced almost 475,000 works of art and at least 276 full-length books and 701 pamphlets.
>
> (2008, 523–524)

Hopkins laid out his plans once to an audience of farmers in Iowa City, Iowa. Somebody in the audience asked him who was going to pay for all this. And he said, "You are." Then he explained how that could be done, enlisting all the resources of the richest country in the world. He was right. That is how it was all paid for, and easily (183). The same thing could be done again, only this time on a global scale.

Another important context of universal employment needs to be discussed. In the Great Depression, when unemployment rose to nearly 25 percent of the workforce, it was not very hard to see who could do all the work that needed to be done—the unemployed could. But today the unemployment rate in the United States is far below the level reached in the Great Depression. Today, who will do the work? Is not the country at full employment? Quite frankly, economists cannot agree what the full employment rate of unemployment really is. Small wonder, for the phrase "full employment rate of unemployment" is as oxymoronic as they come. The answer given regarding the full employment rate of unemployment for the United States usually ranges from 3 to 7 percent. When pushed, most economists today refer to the non-accelerating inflation rate of unemployment (NAIRU), which is the unemployment rate at which the rate of inflation is stable. Unfortunately, economists cannot agree on what the NAIRU is either (Devine 2004). That still leaves the question: "Today, who will do the work needed to bring everyone within the grasp of abundance?"

For the answer, a number of unemployment rates and analogous pools of employable workers need to be discussed. Where should we look for people among the unemployed who can do the work needed to generate abundance? The aggregate unemployment rate can be defined as the sum of frictional, structural, and cyclical rates of unemployment, although economists have a hard time drawing a dividing line between the three. The frictionally unemployed are defined as workers who are simply moving from one job to another. Many economists argue that perhaps they could be helped to move faster by cutting their unemployment benefits. We regard this solution as a bit harsh and tightfisted. Instead, why not replace the guarantee of an income floor provided by unemployment benefits with the guarantee of a good job at a good wage? What is needed for abundance is not to bring back the welfare state, exemplified by Aid to Families with Dependent Children (AFDC), a large welfare program eliminated during the Clinton administration, but to bring back the WPA. The structurally unemployed are workers, whose structure of employment has collapsed around them, leaving them geographically isolated and possessed of outmoded job skills. These are prime candidates for getting back into productive participation. Cyclical unemployment is what Harry Hopkins was dealing with during the Great Depression. At that time the high unemployment rate was due to the very large business cycle that depressed the economy in the 1930s. The cyclically unemployed, if they can be brought back to work by reducing the cyclical instability of the economy, also can bring the nation closer to abundance.

Besides these three groups of unemployed workers, additional workers can be found among those kept from participating by race and gender discrimination. The textbooks seldom discuss what part of the aggregate unemployment rate is due to racial discrimination or why the female participation rate is still so much lower than the male rate. Women and African-Americans are two large pools of potential workers who can contribute to abundance.

More workers are also to be found in low-income countries. But bringing into active employment the unemployed and the farmers leaving the land in Africa, Latin America, and Asia while also bringing in the unemployed and underemployed of the developed countries will require concerted action in all of the countries involved. Clearly the industrialized countries will not absorb all the unemployed of the nonindustrialized. Just as clearly, rapid economic expansion of the industrialized countries will draw in both more immigrants and more imports.

By now it should be obvious that universal employment and abundance are incompatible with inequality resulting from classism, nationalism, sexism, and racism. Before explaining universal employment and related policies in more detail, we must address some previously neglected aspects of the inequality nexus.

Threads in the Tapestry of Social and Economic Inequality

If society is seen as a huge social fabric of human interaction, then classism, nationalism, sexism, and racism are threads woven into the huge tapestry. The threads weave in and out, overlap, intersect, and collide. The threads are woven together, sometimes reinforcing and sometimes conflicting with each other. Universal employment is a positive-sum game intended to move society toward abundance through greater participation in the productive economy. Classism, nationalism, sexism, and racism are negative-sum games of inequality that create scarcity. Along with a few lesser negative-sum games, they are the threads that weave inequality through the social fabric of society. Examples will clarify how these threads give structure to society, assigning people unequal roles and rewards and turning social provisioning processes into an economy of scarcity.

Sexism and classism collide, conflict, and reinforce each other. In the labor market, sexism means that women suffer from lower labor force participation rates, higher unemployment rates, and lower wage rates than men. At home, women often work a double shift, one shift for their employer and his profit and the second shift for their husband and his offspring (Hochschild with Machung 2003). Further, black women suffer the additional burdens of racism, experiencing even higher unemployment rates and lower wages than their white women counterparts. In a meaningful sense, black women suffer from triple exploitation. But when women learn that their difficult situations are political, they may be able to obtain concessions from both the exploiting employer and exploiting spouse. What women earn in the labor market helps them resist the exploitation of the patriarch at home. Alliance with patriarchs gives leverage to women trying to pry workplace concessions from employers. The patriarch and the employer each may inadvertently provide women with leverage against the ravages of the other. But no one should reach the erroneous conclusion that classism and sexism are on the verge of extinction.

Racism and nationalism can also collide, conflict, and reinforce each other. The U.S. military has significantly reduced racist practices in order to gain full participation of blacks and other minorities. Indeed, in the 1950s and 1960s, the military was far ahead of other major U.S. institutions in removing the worst aspects of racial discrimination. In this case, nationalism weakened racism. Nevertheless, blacks and other minorities have been over-represented in the military when compared to their proportions of the population as a whole. Discrimination in civilian labor markets, resulting in higher unemployment rates and lower wage rates for minorities, contributes to the over-representation of minorities in the military. In this case, racism reinforces nationalism. Racism and nationalism can reinforce each other in other obvious ways. Racism in Nazi Germany was used in propaganda for the homeland to support its wars against the "lower races." The principal form of Nazi racism was anti-Semitism, which led to the Holocaust. Leading German nationalists also used anti-Semitism after World War I to blame the German loss of the war on Jews.

Classism and nationalism collide, conflict, and reinforce each other. They reinforce each other when business and government push together for more spending on corporate-produced arms. This business-government-military combination is what President Eisenhower termed the "military Industrial complex." Eisenhower warned the nation that "we must not fail to comprehend its grave implications." Nearly fifty years after Eisenhower's warning, the military industrial complex is alive and well. A united front of business and government can even include large unions as junior partners when the war spending is used not only to generate profits, but also to generate union jobs in defense industries. This sophisticated grand coalition held together in the United States throughout the cold war. But after the cold war and the rise of outsourcing, unions have been dropped from the coalition. Now the national state and the transnational corporation reinforce each other (Cypher 2007). They are strong enough under current conditions, apparently, not to need union support.

When nationalism and classism conflict in the United States, national allegiance usually trumps class allegiance. U.S. labor leaders who opposed nationalistic wars in the name of class solidarity paid dearly. Eugene Debs and Bill Haywood, for example, both ended up in prison as a result of their opposition to U.S. participation in World War I (Haywood [1929] 1966; Salvatore 1982). Apparently organized U.S. labor learned a lesson from the experience of Debs and Haywood, since it played a largely cooperative role in World War II (Terkel 1984), Korea, Vietnam, and the cold war in general. Although clearly a junior partner during those wars, organized labor did enjoy an informal accord with the national government. The accord ensured the legitimacy of collective bargaining and a growing pool of jobs in defense industries. Organized labor continues playing the same supportive, junior role during the wars of the Middle East, but without the legitimacy and job pool provided by the original accord (Cypher 2007).

Does national war always trump class war? Does nation always trump race, sex, and class? More often than not, it does. Nevertheless, the answer is strongly affected by the time, place, and context. As the Vietnam War dragged on and on, for example, the nationalist trump card increasingly lost its power. When the national government loses credibility, as it did during the Vietnam War and as it is doing during the wars of the Middle East, the power of its nationalist trump card will fade. As any bridge player knows, you can run out of trump if you play it too often.

Faulty Social Valuation Processes: Emulation and Scapegoating

Regardless of whether class allegiance trumps national allegiance or sexism trumps nationalism, all forms of inequality are strengthened by social valuation processes that assign high value to top dogs and low value to underdogs. Principal among these social valuation processes are emulation and scapegoating. Emulation assigns admiration and high status to the top dogs. Scapegoating assigns contempt and low status to the underdogs. Emulating directs credit for good things upward, while scapegoating deflects blame for bad things downward. When something good happens, emulation assigns credit for it to the top dogs. When something bad happens, scapegoating assigns fault for it to the underdogs. When scapegoating and emulation work perfectly, top dogs are encouraged to feel good about themselves, even if their behavior is immoral and dysfunctional, and underdogs are encouraged to feel bad about themselves, even if their behavior is moral and productive.

Emulation

Taught to emulate their "superiors," the underdogs admire and mimic the top dogs. Instead of struggling against the exploitation of the top dogs, the emulating underdog wants to become a top dog. Emulation is a powerful social valuation process because it turns anger into admiration. Under the influence of emulation, underdogs who might become angry enough to protest or resist injustice instead become fawning rabble eager to get a glimpse of their idols and daydreaming about becoming one of them. Emulation is really quite marvelous, a kind of magical lens that turns night into day, down into up, and wrong into right. When viewed through the magical lens of emulation, a feudal lord appears to be a kindly protector and benefactor instead of a violent bully and reckless usurper. A Southern slave owner appears to be a concerned old master leading his dark charges with a firm hand instead of a greedy slave driver treating human beings like property. An extravagant, free-spending chief executive appears to be a high-tech genius and accumulator of capital instead of a corporate pirate and stock bonus profligate. When invading foreign countries, a warmongering president appears to be defending the homeland instead of pursuing personal glory. When relying on the reverse discrimination myth to support their decision against school desegregation, Supreme Court justices appear to be defenders of equality instead of racist bigots.

When something good happens, the top dogs pat themselves on the back and graciously accept the thanks and the rewards from emulating underlings for a job well done, whether or not they actually did it themselves. Two examples are worth mentioning. Thomas Edison is admired for inventing the light bulb even though all the elements that went into it were already known when, aided by a large and able laboratory staff, he (actually his staff) came upon them. Henry Ford is admired for inventing the automobile, even though several other people were driving theirs around before Ford. Both Edison and Ford were fine industrialists and knew their away around machinery very well, but neither put together his invention out of elements from his own head. Just like other inventors and entrepreneurs, they relied on large staffs of technical experts and combined and recombined concepts and elements that had already been invented. They used the joint stock of their community and added their own twist to it. Nevertheless, they were able to get individual credit for their inventions, and that is what mattered to their reputations and their pocketbooks.

Perhaps another example of emulation would be useful. General Douglas MacArthur is not remembered for having abandoned the Philippines and most of his troops when he fled the advance of conquering Japanese forces in 1942. Instead, he is celebrated for liberating the Philippines in 1944. Most Americans alive in the 1940s can remember seeing newsreels of MacArthur triumphantly stepping ashore in the Philippine Islands in 1944, but few remember newsreels of his fleeing the same in 1942. Because of emulation, generals are remembered for winning battles, not losing them. Similarly, patriarchs are remembered for family leadership, not wife abuse; CEOs for entrepreneurship, not gambling with the stockholders' money; presidents and prime ministers for defending the homelands, not reckless warmongering. Leaders and top dogs get credit for success and good fortune. People look up to them in gratitude for all their achievements, whether they really achieved anything or not. In doing so, their admirers are confused.

Our explanation of emulation draws from insights first provided by Thorstein Veblen. For him, studying a society of unequals, emulation was related to envy. People engaged in invidious personal comparisons between themselves and others. What was important in emulation was how a person stacked up against everyone else, not how the person's performance measured against objective standards. Conspicuous consumption and conspicuous leisure were the objects of envy. Veblen understood the power exerted by the rat race. Caught up in this social and economic competition, people feared being excluded from "decent" society. So they constantly struggled to waste more goods and efforts, conspicuously. As Veblen put it, "the decent requirements of waste absorb the surplus energy of the population in an invidious struggle and leave no margin for the non-invidious expression of life" ([1899] 1975, 362).

While Veblen emphasized the role of emulation in causing waste, we emphasize the role of emulation in causing confusion. We agree that emulation causes waste. But we pair emulation with scapegoating and emphasize emulation as a social valuation process that results in faulty evaluations. That is, Veblen argued that emulation caused waste because it resulted in conspicuous consumption, not capital accumulation, and in conspicuous leisure, not productive work. However, we go further and argue that emulation also causes confusion. Emulation leads people to make incorrect decisions based on faulty assignment of credit for socially beneficial things and equally faulty assignment of blame for socially detrimental ones. They credit the top dogs for the good and blame the underdogs for the bad. They do so because they are confused.

Scapegoating

While the magic of the emulation lens makes praise run uphill to the benefit of the top dogs, the magic of the scapegoating lens makes blame flow downhill to the detriment of the underdogs. Scapegoating is another astonishing, powerful social valuation process that turns social injustice into personal inadequacy. Instead of feeling angry at the top dogs for taking advantage of them or at the leaders for failing them, the underdogs feel guilty for causing their own problems. The righteous indignation that could be the emotional fuel needed to power reform and change is turned into self-loathing and self-doubt. Women who are beaten by their husbands often blame themselves for upsetting the men. Even victims of rape often blame themselves for allegedly provoking their attackers. Scapegoating means that shame replaces indignation; silence replaces the cry for justice. Scapegoating is not just the strong blaming the weak for being victimized; more important for maintaining inequality in society, scapegoating is also the weak blaming themselves for being inadequate or for provoking the strong.

Two powerful social flows are established in inegalitarian societies with emulation and scapegoating. Wealth and respect flow up; poverty and shame flow down. For underdogs who want to claw their way to the top of the social dung heap, the key to individual success is to work the flows to their own advantage: "Kiss up and kick down." These upward and downward flows put enormous pressure on those few underdogs who manage to push their way into the ranks of the top dogs. To maintain their new position, the former underdogs are compelled to put down the underdogs who never made it out of that group and to ridicule their claims of injustice while supporting the legitimacy of the top dogs and supporting their claims to privilege. These flows also perpetuate inequality by justifying the strong taking advantage of the weak. These flows impute productive contribution to the top dogs and unproductive incompetence to the underdogs. That is, people who are unusually well-to-do must be unusually productive. They must deserve their wealth. And people who are unusually poor must be unusually unproductive. They, too, must deserve their poverty. People cannot think otherwise and be comfortable in their stations in life, when the stations involve significant inequalities.

The Neglect of Negative-Sum Games

Because of the strength of emulation and scapegoating, perhaps we should go easy on academic economists who do not frankly discuss nationalism, classism, sexism, and racism. Most economists treat these inequalities superficially as deviations from the rationality and optimality of the free market. Even though the inequities and inefficiencies generated by these negative-sum games have not disappeared and show no tendency to do so, orthodox economists can always insist that in long-run general equilibrium these deviations will disappear. Orthodox economists are wrong. Inequality and scarcity are more than deviations from the natural harmony of the free market in long-run equilibrium. These negative-sum games are central problems of actual economies.

Exceptions exist in the wide world of economics. Heterodox economists do write frankly about exploitation and inequality. Some journals in which frank academic treatments are found are *Journal of Economic Issues*, *Review of Radical Political Economics*, and *Review of Social Economy*. Such journals are in the distinct minority. We recommend them. (Conflict of interest: we also research and write for them.)

When they do look squarely at inequality, most orthodox economists see it as necessary, even socially beneficial. They believe that it increases the society's pool of income. The larger the pool, the more it actually benefits the poor. Arthur M. Okun of the Brookings Institution wrote an outstanding statement of this position (1975). He used a leaky bucket analogy in which he compared egalitarian income redistribution to the carrying of water in buckets from one group of people to another. However, the buckets leaked. Water was wasted by carrying water in them from the rich to the poor. The more water you carried, the more you wasted. So there was a trade-off between equality and efficiency. More equality meant less efficiency. And the opposite would also hold: more inequality meant more efficiency (Dugger 1984, 34–36).

Most orthodox economists, including Okun, claim that inequality makes capital accumulation possible by directing large flows of income to the rich, who can afford to save it. If it were not for the high personal incomes of the rich, there would be no personal saving to finance investment. And that, so the argument goes, would reduce the rate of capital accumulation and the rate of growth. So inequality increases saving. The argument is faulty: saving out of personal income does not provide the major source of finance for investment. Corporate retained earnings do, and corporations do not require rich individual consumers to save anything out of their personal income. In fact, the significance of personal saving has been declining for years. A look at recent U.S. experience shows what we mean.

The Table 10.1 is very simple when considered as representing the following equation:

$$S = P + C - A,$$

where S is total private saving (net), P is the saving of persons, C is the saving of corporations, and A is an accounting adjustment for wage accruals less disbursements. The equation and the table say that saving in the private sector is equal to the saving of persons plus the saving of corporations. An accounting adjustment has to be made for wage accruals less disbursements. In 1990 persons saved 71 percent and corporations 29 percent of the total. But personal saving fell sporadically until actually turning negative in 2005. If the inequality-fuels-saving argument were true, then we should see a decline in inequality over the period covered by the table. One can always argue that other factors intervened. Nevertheless, we do not see such a decline in inequality. It actually increased. In 1990 the top fifth of people received 41.1 percent of all income and the bottom fifth received 5.3 percent. In 2004, the latest year the data are available, the top fifth's share had risen to 47.9 percent while the bottom fifth's share fell to 4.0 percent (U.S. Bureau of the Census 2007, 450). The rising inequality did not fuel more personal saving. The rich received more income, but the aggregate saving of persons actually declined.

Table 10.1

Private Saving in the United States, 1990–2006 (in billions of dollars)

Year	Total private saving (net)	Personal saving	Undistributed corporate profits	Wage accruals less disbursements
1990	422.7	299.4	123.3	0.0
1991	456.1	324.2	131.9	0.0
1992	493.0	366.0	142.7	−15.8
1993	458.6	284.0	168.1	6.4
1994	438.9	249.5	171.8	17.6
1995	491.1	250.9	223.8	16.4
1996	489.0	228.4	256.9	3.6
1997	503.3	218.3	287.9	−2.9
1998	477.8	276.8	201.7	−0.7
1999	419.0	158.6	255.3	5.2
2000	343.3	168.5	174.8	0.0
2001	324.6	132.3	192.3	0.0
2002	479.2	184.7	294.5	0.0
2003	515.0	174.9	325.1	15.0
2004	551.1	181.7	384.4	−15.0
2005	428.2	−44.6	378.6	5.0
2006	447.2	38.8	400.9	7.5

Source: Council of Economic Advisers, *Economic Report of the President, 2008.* Washington, DC: U.S. Government Printing Office, 2008, Table B-32, p. 264.

Many academic economists are simply unaware of these empirical matters. They avoid deep treatment of classism, nationalism, sexism, and racism because such topics require attention to "noneconomic factors." Studying noneconomic factors would require the economist to stray into sociology and other disciplines, but pure economists do not want to tarnish their reputations with other economists by associating with sociologists. So most orthodox economics has little meaningful to say about the noneconomic relations that keep abundance just out of reach. Instead, orthodox economics is the narrow study of scarcity. In the study of scarcity, abundance is impossible. Of course, a lively heterodox economics flourishes in the underground of the discipline (Dugger 1992).

Abundance needs to be included in economics. Economists should stop assuming that scarcity is inevitable and that abundance is impossible. Neither proposition is true. Society is held in scarcity and robbed of abundance by identifiable social practices. These practices are the result of human choices, not natural limitations.

Conclusion: Empirical Challenges

Nationalism, classism, sexism, and racism are usually excluded from the narrow discipline of economics as the study of scarcity. We have included them. We have concentrated on measuring only the costs of unemployment (classism, sexism, racism) and some of the obvious costs of war (nationalism). Even the unemployment costs alone are very large and make the study of these inequalities and their curtailment very important parts of economic science.

We urge you to make your own empirical estimates of the various sums involved in these inequalities that retard abundance. If you are so inclined, take our obviously preliminary work and go much further with the needed estimates of additional costs. Or, if you are inclined differently, attack us directly. We made quantitative empirical statements. To be specific, we claimed that the systems of inequality known as classism, nationalism, racism, and sexism are negative-sum games. They reduce production. Prove us wrong empirically, if you can, by demonstrating that these inequalities increase production. We believe that it cannot be demonstrated because it is not true. No torturing the data permitted.

III

Policies Promoting Abundance

11

Universal Employment

Focus on Full Participation

In this chapter, we continue our discussion of full participation. In particular, we propose the goal of universal employment. Pursuit of universal employment will raise participation through work and restrain the negative-sum games we have criticized throughout this book.

Getting the Price of Labor Right

First, society needs to get the price of labor right. That means removing payroll taxes on labor and setting an appropriate minimum wage. As of September 2008, the minimum wage in the United States was $6.55 an hour, as set by the federal government. By July 24, 2009, it will be $7.25. Some individual states have set higher minimum wage rates. Payroll taxes on labor in 2005 amounted to a total of $2.15 an hour, calculated by the Bureau of Labor Statistics as shown in Table 11.1.

The first thing to be done to get the price of labor right is eliminate the $2.15 an hour total of payroll taxes. The reason is simple. If lawmakers want to discourage an activity, such as smoking, they tax cigarettes—at $2.15 per cigarette, smokers certainly will be discouraged. Taxes designed to discourage unwanted behavior are known as sin taxes. Working is not sinful. Rather if lawmakers want to encourage an activity, such as employment, they do not tax it at $2.15 an hour. So the government needs to remove taxes on hiring labor. To replace the lost tax revenue, if it really needs to be replaced with new tax receipts, other forms of taxes should be raised.

Another step in getting the taxes right is to get the quasi-taxes right. A quasi-tax is an almost tax, something that has virtually the same practi-

Table 11.1

Estimating the Tax Burden on Wages

Category	Estimated amount per hour
Social Security	$1.19
Medicare	$0.30
Federal unemployment	$0.03
State unemployment	$0.15
Workers Compensation	$0.48
Total	$2.15

Source: U.S. Bureau of the Census, *Statistical Abstract of the United States, 2007,* 126th ed. Washington, DC: U.S. Government Printing Office, Table 635, p. 418.

cal effect as a tax. In this case, the quasi-tax is the payment for health insurance made by many employers and shared by many employees, depending on the particulars of each employment contract. Even though this is not a mandatory payment to the government, these insurance premiums are another tax on employing labor. They have the same effect as a tax on labor—they discourage the use of labor. They should be eliminated and replaced by a government insurance plan that provides universal coverage.

The lost revenue raised by this quasi-tax should be replaced by general revenue sources. This would not only reduce the tax burden on payrolls, but also eliminate a horrible mess that passes as the financial arm of our health care system. Some employers do not provide health insurance coverage so their employees frequently fail to pay for expensive hospital care and physician care or they suffer the consequences—death or declining health. When they fail to pay or when they fail to get the care they need, there is usually a sizable tab that somebody has to pick up. Either the unpaid physicians or hospitals pass as much of the tab onto their insured or wealthy patients as they can, or they absorb the loss themselves. Also, if possible, the unrecovered losses are pushed off onto the public in the form of higher Medicare and Medicaid costs. Clearly, the government needs to be more responsible and up-front about these costs and socialize them. Universal health insurance administered and financed by the federal government should replace the quasi-tax levied on payrolls and the shell game played with the cost of care for the uninsured.

Once the taxes and quasi-taxes are adjusted, the minimum wage for workers in the United States should start at $10 an hour, pegged to the

annual rate of inflation plus the annual rate of growth in labor productivity thereafter. Working at that wage for forty hours a week and fifty
weeks a year will earn the very poorest worker in this country $20,000
a year. Since a year has fifty-two weeks, workers would be allowed the
extra two weeks a year for slack—time off without pay, moving between
jobs, and miscellaneous work interruptions. Similar calculations for the
appropriate minimum wage should be made in other countries and the
appropriate enforcement programs should be established.

Why $10 an hour? Because it is just about enough to provide every
worker and family an earned income sufficient to pay for full participation as consumers in this society. The latest figures available at time of
writing are for 2005. According to the U.S. Census Bureau, the weighted
average poverty threshold that year was $15,557 a year for a family of
three and $19,971 for a family of four. U.S. families with income below
the threshold for their family size were living in official poverty. If the
$10 minimum wage had started in 2005, the minimum wage income level
of $20,000 a year would have been just about enough to keep a family of
four out of poverty, with a little slack. Appropriate adjustments upward
can be made for the year in which the federal government actually implements the higher minimum. The amount of slack will depend on the size
of the family and on the earner's working more than fifty weeks a year
or more than forty hours per week at time-and-a-half for overtime.

Many economists generally oppose raising the minimum wage. They
argue that the government should not provide a minimum wage in the
first place because it causes unemployment. However, this argument
involves a logical error loosely included under the rubric of the fallacy
of composition (Cohn 2007, 68–71). Orthodox economists commit this
fallacy when they do not allow for the minimum wage's effect on the composition of the labor market. In particular, the minimum wage increases
the demand for labor. An increase in the minimum wage increases the
income of workers who receive it and reduces the income of employers
who pay it. The shift in income toward lower-paid workers increases
the aggregate demand for goods and services in the economy since the
lower-paid folks will spend so much of their additional income. Higher
minimum wage rates increase consumer spending. Since the demand for
labor is derived from the demand for the goods and services it produces,
when the demand for goods and services increases, so does the demand
for labor. (In 2005, according to U.S. Bureau of Labor Statistics estimates, 1.9 million workers were paid the minimum wage or less. When

that many people get a big raise, the demand for labor curve is definitely affected.) A higher minimum wage also boosts wages near the minimum, pushing them up in the whole profile of wages paid to various kinds of workers (Levin-Waldman and Whalen 2007).

When the impact of the minimum wage on the demand for labor is included, the effect on employment of an increase in the minimum wage is indeterminate. Employment could go either up or down. In practice, an increase in the minimum wage has had no systematic effect on the unemployment rate. This is shown in Table 11.2.

The two sides of the argument can be summarized easily. One side holds that the demand for labor does not change when a minimum wage is imposed so a minimum wage causes unemployment. The other side holds that the demand for labor shifts up when the minimum wage is imposed (or raised). This shift up in demand could partially or wholly offset the effect of the minimum wage, leaving the resulting employment change indeterminate. Bowles provides a thorough analysis of the labor market, both orthodox and unorthodox (2004, 267–298).

Data on the minimum wage and unemployment are given in Table 11.2. The table casts considerable doubt on the empirical argument that the minimum wage causes unemployment. For almost half a century, there has been no stable empirical relation between the unemployment rate and the minimum wage rate.

Over the period covered by the table, the minimum wage rate was increased a total of fifteen times. In the years it was increased, the unemployment rate fell six times, rose eight times, and stayed the same once. Therefore, the empirical data show no clear relation between the unemployment rate and the minimum wage rate, although some negative effects may exist if we were to disaggregate the data. Perhaps the minimum wage does affect unemployment among teenagers.

Really determined econometricians can go much further than disaggregation, of course. They can torture the data until the data confess. The most effective way to do this is to subject the data to the feared variable lag "adjustment." This torture warrants our close attention because using it can always bring forth the desired confession from the data. Using our empirical data from Table 11.2, we will show how the adjustment is done so as to make the empirical data confess that a rise in the minimum wage rate always causes a rise in the unemployment rate.

First we insist that there is a variable lag between changes in the minimum wage and changes in the unemployment rate. Then we note that the

Table 11.2

Unemployment Rate and Minimum Wage Rate in the United States, 1959–2006

Year	Unemployment rate	Minimum wage
1959	5.5	1.00
1960	5.5	1.00
1961	6.7	1.15
1962	5.5	1.15
1963	5.7	1.25
1964	5.2	1.25
1965	4.5	1.25
1966	3.8	1.25
1967	3.8	1.40
1968	3.6	1.60
1969	3.5	1.60
1970	4.9	1.60
1971	5.9	1.60
1972	5.6	1.60
1973	4.9	1.60
1974	5.6	2.00
1975	8.5	2.10
1976	7.7	2.30
1977	7.1	2.30
1978	6.1	2.65
1979	5.8	2.90
1980	7.1	3.10
1981	7.6	3.35
1982	9.7	3.35
1983	9.6	3.35
1984	7.5	3.35
1985	7.2	3.35
1986	7.0	3.35
1987	6.2	3.35
1988	5.5	3.35
1989	5.3	3.35
1990	5.6	3.80
1991	6.8	4.25
1992	7.5	4.25
1993	6.9	4.25
1994	6.1	4.25
1995	5.6	4.25
1996	5.4	4.75
1997	4.9	5.15
1998	4.5	5.15
1999	4.2	5.15
2000	4.0	5.15
2001	4.7	5.15
2002	5.8	5.15
2003	6.0	5.15
2004	5.5	5.15
2005	5.1	5.15
2006	4.6	5.15

Sources: Unemployment rate is from Council of Economic Advisers, *Economic Report of the President, 2007.* Washington, DC: U.S. Government Printing Office, 2007, Table B42, p. 280. Minimum wage is from U.S. Bureau of the Census, *Statistical Abstract of the United States, 2007,* 126th ed. Washington, DC: U.S. Government Printing Office, Table 633, p. 417.

Notes: Unemployment rate in percent, minimum wage in current dollars.

data must be adjusted in order to match the years in which the minimum wage was increased to the appropriate year in which the unemployment rate finally increased. After adjustment, we find that sometimes the lag is so short that cause and effect are simultaneous, occurring in the same year. This short lag happens in eight years: 1961, 1963, 1974, 1975, 1980, 1981, 1990, and 1991. In every episode, a rise in the minimum wage rate caused an immediate rise in the unemployment rate. Next, after continuing adjustment, we find that the lag was sometimes much longer. Starting in 1967, for example, the increased minimum wage does not cause unemployment to rise until 1970—three years later. Then the increased minimum wage in 1968 causes the unemployment rate to rise in 1971—again, a three-year lag. And even further adjustment shows that the lag may have temporarily lengthened in 1976. Although the minimum wage was increased in 1976, the rise in unemployment was not felt until 1980—four years later. The minimum wage was again increased in 1978 and 1979 with the rise in unemployment not felt until 1981 and 1982—three years later. The minimum wage was again increased in 1996 and 1997 but the unemployment rate showed no impact until 2001 and 2002—an exceptionally long lag of five years. In every single episode, a rise in the minimum wage was followed by a rise in unemployment after a variable lag.

Using the variable lag adjustment, the data have been forced to confess that the minimum wage increases unemployment. We could use the same torture to make our data confess that the minimum wage actually decreases unemployment. In fact, torturing the data can make them reveal whatever the researcher wants. The appropriate research approach is painfully clear. To obtain reliable evidence, researchers should not torture the data.

The appropriate public policy also is clear. To put abundance within reach, we propose changing the structure of the economy to generate more employment and production while raising the minimum wage in order to share the gains widely. We call our proposition universal employment.

Universal Employment: A Policy to Achieve Abundance

The goal is to achieve a zero rate of unemployment by using aggressive monetary and fiscal policies to continually expand aggregate demand in the economy and by encouraging structural changes in the economy, thereby generating more and more jobs and pushing down the unemployment rate closer and closer to zero. Everyone not in school, in custody, in the hospital, or in voluntary retirement should have a full-time job. If the community could achieve that goal, the unemployment costs of playing classist, racist, sexist, and nationalist games would be lowered dramatically and abundance would be within the grasp of everyone.

If the community could ensure that everyone of working age participates in using the joint stock of knowledge to produce goods or perform services, universal employment would put extreme pressure on the barriers raised by classism, racism, sexism, and maybe even nationalism. When the government has eliminated taxes and quasi-taxes on labor and when the minimum wage is set high enough, employers that are too inefficient, classist, racist, or sexist will be pushed out of business by universal employment, which will spare only those efficient enough to survive under the new conditions. In other words, we believe that universal employment will make it much harder for inefficient institutions—negative-sum games—to survive.

The concept of universal employment goes beyond both of the two employment goals usually suggested by economists. Keynesians usually suggest "full employment" as the appropriate goal, while neoclassicals usually suggest the "natural rate of unemployment." These unemployment goals were suggested a long time ago, and the best treatments can usually be traced back to Lerner (1951, 17–30). We reject both orthodox goals and propose universal employment instead. For further discussion of unemployment and macroeconomics, see Cohn (2007, 163–187).

For the United States, orthodox economists guesstimate that the full employment rate of unemployment is somewhere between a 4 and 8 percent rate of unemployment. Although the concept is a bit fuzzy, full employment generally means the lowest sustainable rate of unemployment, given the structure of the economy (James Galbraith 2000).

The given structure of the economy is where we part company with full employment as the goal. We do not accept the given structure of the economy because we know how it was given and what it contains. It was given by tradition and it contains the negative-sum games of inequality: racism, sexism, classism, and nationalism. We wish to substitute the goal of universal employment because we wish to change the structure of the economy. We reject these inefficient institutions of inequality. We wish to change the structure of the economy to make it compatible with full participation and incompatible with any of these isms. Marc Tool used the ism concept to explain how a rigidly held belief in an ideological system would lead the believer to follow ineffective policies. He used it to critique the rigid, ideological belief in capitalism, communism, and fascism. We follow Tool's basic treatment of ism but we extend its use to include critique of racism, sexism, nationalism, and classism (1979, 25–31).

Economic abundance will require the efforts of everyone, not just a self-selected few. The structure of the economy and the social fabric of society cannot be accepted as givens because they do not allow everyone to participate. They hold significant numbers of people back, as we have shown. The given structure of the economy and the given social fabric of the society cannot sustain a zero rate of unemployment. If the unemployment rate is to be pushed down toward zero, the structure of the economy must change. As the rate moves closer and closer to zero, the racism, sexism, classism, nationalism, and other structural deformities will be forced to change. That is why we propose universal employment as our goal. Full employment is compatible with unacceptable economic structure and unacceptable social fabric. Clearly, we have just made a value judgment: the given economic structure and the given social fabric are unacceptable. Orthodox economists claim that economists should not make value judgments, but they do it themselves by accepting the economic structure and the social fabric as given. Acceptance is as much a value judgment as nonacceptance. If orthodox economists can accept the existing structure, then unorthodox ones can reject it. The former, of course, do not consider themselves orthodox, simply correct. The latter consider themselves correct as well. The latter also do not think of themselves as unorthodox, but heterodox. Those who refrain from taking a position one way or the other consider themselves unbiased but are merely irrelevant (Tool 1979, 1986).

We also reject the natural rate of unemployment as our goal. The natural rate of unemployment is that rate toward which the economy tends to move in the long run if not interfered with by aggressive, governmental monetary and fiscal policies to reduce unemployment. It is similar to the full employment rate in the absence of government policy. Without government distortion, the natural rate of unemployment will eventually emerge by itself. It is the labor market in equilibrium. The natural rate has proven impossible to observe, so estimates of it keep changing (James Galbraith 2000, 171–182). In fact, the natural rate of unemployment does not exist. There is no natural rate of unemployment in an economy because an economy is not a natural thing in the first place. A national economy is the product of a nation's government policies, past and present, along with the conditions under which the nation started and the actions along the way of other powerful human forces. Economies are not natural things like the Grand Canyon. Economies are human-made things like the Grand Coulee Dam. The American economy, like other national economies, did not spring up spontaneously, nor did it evolve naturally. It was created through years of constitutional construction, legislation, administration, and adjudication. See Bourgin (1990) for an excellent discussion of the American case, with emphasis on the early period of nation making.

Both full employment and the natural rate of unemployment can be reconciled with nationalism, classism, sexism, and racism. Universal employment, in contrast, cannot be reconciled with any system of inequality, with any of the negative-sum games and their rationalizations. Universal employment requires full participation while systems of inequality limit it. Universal employment forces people to stop playing the negative-sum games. It promotes inclusion instead of exclusion and is a powerful antidote for all the isms, respecting none of them.

Economic structure is not to be respected, but replaced as needed by democratically determined economic policy. The economic structure is replaceable while the economic process is developmental. The structures of modern national economies have been adjusted to scarcity and negative-sum games—to the preservation of power, status, and wealth. Universal employment is aimed at abundance—at the full participation of everyone in the use of the community's joint stock of knowledge. The goal of universal employment has another extremely important attribute. Proposing a goal for the economy replaces proposing a blueprint for the economy. Instead of insisting on following the blueprint for a free market system or for a planned system, we have no economic blueprint. In fact, proposing economic blueprints is a demonstrably bad idea, since the proposed blueprint has a tendency to become a straitjacket for future generations. Instead of a blueprint and a straitjacket, we suggest a goal and a faith that succeeding generations will work out their own practical policies for pursuing it. We would not be true to the traditions of policy wonks, however, if we did not make some practical suggestions for policies to experiment with in the future. We make our suggestions under five related headings: stimulating the economy, restraining power, strengthening political resolve, facilitating structural change, and globalizing abundance.

Many of our suggestions are controversial. Most of them are fun to discuss. The whole thrust of this book, however—toward abundance and away from scarcity—does not stand or fall along with any of the suggestions. They stand or fall on their own merits.

Suggestions for Stimulating the Economy

Lawmakers can stimulate the economy by cutting taxes, raising government spending, and making it easier and cheaper for various groups to borrow. Which combination of stimulants is used makes a big difference in terms of equality and abundance. In recent years, equality of income distribution has been falling in the United States. The figures were given in Table 5.1 in Chapter 5 (see page 89). Therefore, we suggest that the economy be stimulated in ways that also increase equality.

A stern warning is in order at this point. The pursuit of equality will be difficult until the current influence of private money in financing election campaigns is eliminated. Public financing must replace private. Other political reforms will be needed as the community moves forward in pursuit of universal employment.

Cuts in income, inheritance, and capital gains taxes, particularly in the highest tax brackets, should be avoided since they are paid by those with high incomes. When taxes are cut to stimulate the economy, we suggest cutting payroll taxes to help get the price of labor right and cutting taxes paid by poorer taxpayers. Prominent among taxes paid by poorer taxpayers are sin taxes, sales taxes, and payroll taxes. We already discussed cutting payroll taxes as very promising. Sin taxes are those on alcohol and tobacco, but we do not want to encourage alcoholism and lung cancer so cutting them is not a high priority. Sales taxes, particularly on prescription medicines and food staples, should be high on the list for cutting. Since state and local governments are highly dependent on revenues from sales taxes, federal revenue-sharing programs will need to be arranged to compensate state and local governments that cut sales taxes.

Government spending stimulates the economy, including the private sector. Such spending should be devoted to projects that provide the widest distribution of benefits, particularly to the excluded. Government spending can even subsidize efforts in the private, for-profit sector and in the private, not-for-profit sector. Spending to maintain the American Empire should be a low priority. Imperial wars and police actions may provide employment opportunities in the military, profiteering opportunities in government contracting, and showing-off opportunities in the presidency, but the costs in life and health are unacceptable. Besides, the really big benefits of empire go to U.S. multinational corporations profiteering in Middle Eastern oil and in outsourcing jobs to China, not to the men and women in uniform.

When more government spending is needed to keep pushing the unemployment rate closer to zero, we suggest that high priority be given to the following four areas, with the actual details worked out and additions made as the community feels its way forward.

1. **Environmental quality.** This includes a very wide range of deep needs, including carbon and other emission-reduction projects, alternative energy sources and experiments, energy conservation, water quality, and projects improving environmental quality in the neighborhoods, schools, parks, and workplaces of everyone, always putting emphasis on the underdogs. The work needed to improve environmental quality is on such a monumental and global scale that no chance exists of running out of high-priority projects for the foreseeable future. No one's time should be wasted in unemployment or nonparticipation. The world cannot afford the opportunity cost.

2. **Transportation restructuring.** This requires replacing the existing transportation system so that people can get to work and wherever else they want to go without using automobiles or buses or airplanes powered by internal combustion engines. It also includes significant improvements and expansion in existing mass transit systems and experimentation with new and alternative systems. The numbers of new jobs and work-years of employment building, maintaining, and operating new and improved transportation systems should be very large. No one's time can be wasted.

3. **Universal health care.** This will probably include some combination of private and public provision of care as well as insurance and other forms of managed and regulated private and public payment for services. The health care system should take care of anyone who is already hurt or sick, but prevention of accidents and illnesses needs more emphasis. Health care for children should be aggressively and continually expanded. The world cannot afford wasting any of the next generation.

4. **Universal education.** This should start by replacing student loans with student grants and include improvement in all areas: religious and secular as well as public and private; higher education as well as primary and secondary education; and continuing adult education with emphasis on lifelong learning, vocational retraining, and English as a second language. There is plenty of work to do for everyone, including the so-called disabled. The world cannot afford to waste anyone's abilities.

Set-aside programs and affirmative action plans that direct a minimum share of spending to different underdog groups and to different geographical areas with special needs should be used aggressively. Ways to do so within constitutional constraints should be found. Surely a community that is trying to increase the participation of all should be able to find appropriate ways of doing so.

Monetary policy has to do with money, credit, and interest rates. It can be used to supplement fiscal policy in stimulating the economy to grow and provide more jobs. First, an unfortunate though temporary structural deformity in the U.S. political economy needs to be repaired. That deformity has to do with control of the nation's central bank, the Federal Reserve System (the Fed). The Fed was made independent of the central government in two major steps. First, during the Great Depression of the 1930s, the president's authority over the Fed was reduced when new legislation removed the secretary of the Treasury from the Fed's board of governors. The secretary is a member of the president's cabinet and serves at the pleasure of the president, who is democratically elected. Before being removed from the board, the secretary was also the ex officio head of the Fed—the president's agent. The legislation reduced the democratically elected President's authority to make and implement monetary policy. Even so, the U.S. Treasury maintained considerable influence over the Fed, particularly in times of war when the central government relied on the central bank to facilitate financing war spending. The influence was ended when a second major step was taken in the early 1950s in what is called the "Accord." This was an agreement reached between the Treasury and the Fed in which the Treasury agreed that the Fed did not have to keep interest rates low to facilitate Treasury financing (Greider 1987).

Today the Fed does not have to work in cooperation with the president, the Treasury, or any other part of the central government. The Fed can and at some junctures does oppose the central government. Opposition occurs usually when the central government is stimulating economic growth while the central bank is restraining it.

Central governments, elected democratically, need to be able to control their central banks. Japan and the United Kingdom are two examples of central governments that do control their central banks. In political systems such as theirs, the head of the country's central bank is the minister of finance or a similar official, appointed and directed by the prime minister of the central government. The prime minister can replace the minister of finance, if need arises.

The United States has a presidential system rather than a parliamentary one, but the democratically elected president can regain control over the independent central bank. The authority to replace the head of the central bank as needed should be returned to the president. Also, the presidential appointment and dismissal power should be extended to include all the members of the board of governors of the Fed. Today, the head of the central bank is not a member of the president's cabinet but is a member of the board of governors. The board has seven members, each appointed by the president for a fixed fourteen-year term. Instead, the term of office for the members should be changed to service at the pleasure of the president. New legislation would make it possible for the president to have such increased authority over the central bank. The central bank should be brought back into the democratic fold where it belongs as a cooperating part of the central government.

Once democratic control over monetary policy has been reestablished, it can be used to facilitate pursuit of universal employment. Interest rates and other costs of credit need to be pushed lower and lower to keep the unemployment rate itself falling toward zero. The government should know what responses to expect and not be alarmed by them. While welcomed by those who will get new jobs, the monetary policy of universal employment will be condemned by those whose incomes are obtained largely from interest rates and other credit costs. To the former, universal employment will be part of their pursuit of the American Dream. To the latter, it will be a full assault on freedom. This is not to say that the interest rate paid to families on their small savings accounts should be squeezed down. But it is to say that the cost of financing new jobs, new housing, new infrastructure, new research, and new investment should be kept as low as required by universal employment.

Suggestions for Restraining Power

Those who benefit from racism, sexism, classism, and nationalism will resist universal employment. Nevertheless, their resistance can be restrained in the United States and other nations. In the immediate past, a number of restraints were put in place that held such vested interests in check, more or less successfully. The restraints holding back racists and sexists involved a number of new and existing laws, court decisions, and accepted norms of behavior. Extremely prominent roles were played by the enforcement of new Civil Rights and Women's Rights legislation plus the enforcement of existing Constitutional Rights. But then many of these restraints were weakened in the 1980s and later, usually following intense political efforts by the interests being restrained. Those restraints should be strengthened once again. The waves of economic deregulation that began sweeping over the economy so strongly during the presidency of Ronald Reagan removed many restraints on the exercise of class power. Economic regulation can be reconsidered. American imperialism can be abandoned. The United States can begin peacefully disengaging from its unilateral exercise of military power all over the globe and return to a multilateral approach to peace and security.

The past restraints on the isms cannot provide ready-to-use policies that can simply be snipped out of the history books and applied to the current situation. However, the past can provide insight into what to expect in the future and what to think about right now.

For one thing, as the new policy stimulates the economy to grow faster and provide more jobs, inflation can be expected to go up. For another thing, some workplace incentives will lose their influence. To deal with inflation, wage and price controls have been tried a number of times in the past, with mixed results (Pohlman 1976). The government will need to apply such controls again, learning from previous experience and adapting new policies to deal with new situations as they arise. The power to raise prices when aggregate demand is rising and the economy is growing is a difficult power to deal with, but it is essential in order to get closer and closer to a zero unemployment rate. The government may end up controlling wages better than prices, putting working families in a squeeze as their wages fall further and further below the prices they have to pay. Nevertheless, as John Kenneth Galbraith pointed out years ago, fixing prices in a system of price controls is not as daunting a task as one might expect, particularly if the system of controls is restricted to prices that are already fixed. Prices are often fixed or nearly so in areas of production and distribution dominated by large multinational corporations ([1952] 1975, 245–449).

To deal with workplace incentives that lose their influence as the unemployment rate falls, employers will need to replace them with new incentives. It is the threat of being fired that loses its influence as unemployment falls. Workplace discipline based on this threat needs to be replaced in the future. More emphasis can be placed on forms of incentives that include pride of workmanship, pride in serving others, and the reward of helping those who need it. The not-for-profit sector of the economy already relies heavily on these kinds of incentives to make schools, hospitals, churches, universities, and many other organizations operate effectively.

Affirmative action and set-aside programs are two more features of the past that offer insight for the future. Unfortunately, the U.S. Supreme Court on June 28, 2007, overturned earlier decisions and decided that race could not be used as an admission criterion to help particular schools achieve racial diversity (Lewin 2007). Rectifying this ruling may take some fancy legal footwork or new legislation to change the number of justices in the Supreme Court. When school integration, set-asides, and affirmative action can once again be implemented, one lesson from experience must be kept in mind: it is much easier to integrate schools when student opportunities in them are expanding. In the same way, it is much easier to set aside parts of public programs for specified underdogs when the whole set of public programs is expanding and to implement affirmative action plans when opportunities in the areas involved are expanding. Expansion is the key to easier implementation, and continual pursuit of universal employment is the key to expansion.

Suggestions for Strengthening Political Resolve

Continued pursuit of universal employment will test the community's democratic resolve. As the unemployment rate falls, induced structural changes will begin to cost the top dogs more and more. Their control of workplace discipline will weaken. Their taxes will go up. The privileges in labor markets and in schools once enjoyed by their children will be challenged. Fearing the worst, many of them will object. This reaction should be expected. The volume and the pitch of their rhetoric will intensify. In the name of "freedom of the press," the radio, television, and print media will all be made less free by the reactions of powerful interests that have come to exert more and more influence through them.

To offset the howling from the top dogs, two important policies that worked to a limited extent in the past must be resurrected and improved: the fairness doctrine in radio and television broadcasting and antitrust limitations on media ownership. The old fairness doctrine was an attempt to get radio and television broadcasters to present different views on public issues. Doing so was difficult but certainly worthy of the effort. Basically, radio and television stations could broadcast what they wanted as long as they did not cause members of their audience to object to the Federal Communications Commission (FCC). If it received objections, the FCC would investigate, and if the station had been providing nonstop, one-sided coverage of an issue, the station would be instructed to provide comparable airtime to different views. Equal time was not required, only some roughly equivalent time and not necessarily in the same format as the original presentations. The fairness doctrine was formally adopted by the FCC in 1949. The rule was applied to broadcasters with a license to use the public airwaves. It never applied to cable radio or television. It was repealed in 1987 during President Ronald Reagan's push for deregulation. The fairness doctrine must be reinstated and improved, with emphasis on giving new voice to the underdogs. More is needed than a few token appearances by advocates of alternative views. The underdogs must acquire new voices of their own—their own radio and television stations and networks, along with their own newspapers, magazines, and Internet influences. They need more than a piece of the old cake. They need to be baking their own new cakes.

Consolidation in the newspaper industry has left many major cities with just one major daily paper, and consolidation in radio and television broadcasting has drastically increased the concentration of ownership in both. Diversity needs to be reestablished by applying new antitrust laws to break up media empires and creating numerous new and innovative newspapers and other forms of news systems. Of course, if democratic political resolve is to be strengthened, in order to withstand the backlash of the top dogs, private money must be replaced with public money in campaign finances. It does not take elaborate analysis to understand why. As long as public office is for sale through private financing of campaigns, the country will get the best public servants money can buy.

Suggestions for Facilitating Structural Change

As the economy moves toward zero unemployment, great structural pressures will be exerted on production enterprises, financial institutions, and patriarchal families. We offer no blueprints to which the family, the enterprise, or the financial institution should conform. Instead, we have some suggestions to facilitate structural change as these basic social building blocks struggle to adapt to universal employment.

The principal production enterprise now operating in the economy is the for-profit corporation. Partnerships and individual proprietorships are large in number, but the commanding heights of the national economy and the global economy are held by the large corporation. It can expand production rapidly by adding workers and contract production just as rapidly by laying off workers. In its ability to shed workers quickly lies a great strength in times of cyclical recession. As long as the economy in which it operates cycles through periods of boom and bust, the corporation can grow and prosper over the long run. In the boom it quickly adds workers. In the bust, it quickly subtracts them. It can thrive during the good times and survive the bad times. It can also expect to hire disciplined workers at all times. The workers are disciplined by fear of losing their jobs. This will all change with the persistent pursuit of universal employment.

The corporate enterprise is a hierarchical organization. Orders flow down from the top, the chief executive officer. So when the economy is in a recession, the corporation can quickly fire workers. The order to do so comes from the top and goes down: "Good-bye. Security will escort you out." In more participatory enterprises, it is harder to fire workers because it is hard for the participating rank and file to fire friends, co-workers, and themselves. The bosses have less personal attachment to the rank and file, finding it easier to fire them because the boss is not a part of them. This gives hierarchical enterprises a very big advantage in cyclical economies. Participatory forms of enterprise have never been able to gain a permanent foothold in economies that cycle through boom and bust because in the bust they find it so hard to lay off workers that they usually collapse into insolvency before managing to do so. Worker-owned and -managed enterprises bleed to death in recessions. Corporations do not; they fire their workers, who bleed for them.

If, however, recessions were eliminated by pushing unemployment ever closer to zero, the economic situation would change. Corporations would lose their traditional control of their workers because workers would no longer fear unemployment. New incentives will need to evolve—a perfect chance for economic innovation. Corporations can change. With appropriate help, the worker-owned and -managed enterprise may come into its own. No longer subject to bleeding to death during recessions, and with its powerful corporate rival struggling to develop new forms of incentives, could tiny David overcome giant Goliath? Could the almost nonexistent worker-owned and -managed enterprises do better than giant corporations in an environment characterized by virtually zero unemployment? After all, when unemployment is zero, getting new workers means they have to be coaxed out of their current jobs. How to do it? By making them co-owners of the new enterprise and giving them co-management status. How to keep them from taking jobs elsewhere? By making them co-owners and co-managers. How to give them more incentive? By making them and their co-workers all co-owners and co-managers. (Can you say "universal stock option"?) The literature on worker-owned and worker-managed enterprises is large and generally positive. A small number do actually exist and have for a long time. For an interesting historical treatment of such enterprises in the United States, see Gunn (1984); for a broad treatment, see Hahnel (2005).

Experimentation with new forms of corporate management and with worker-owned and worker-managed enterprise warrants a very serious social effort. Universal employment offers the perfect Petri dish. If such a policy could get more progressive firms to prosper, it would be implanting democracy into the economy, a feat as important to full social participation for everyone as what America's forefathers and foremothers did when they implanted democracy into the polity.

Experimentation with alternative enterprises will require parallel experimentation with alternative financial and technical institutions. Banks specially chartered to finance worker-owned and -managed enterprises and other experimental forms could be established at both state and national levels. Special investment banks could also be established to provide early financing and technical assistance for such enterprises. Such specialized financial institutions would be greatly strengthened if they were provided with their own oversight and regulatory agency possessed of the power to be a lender of last resort to its charges. Of course, these banks would have to expect a backlash from established banks and financial institutions.

Another excellent source for technical assistance could be established at universities by modeling them after the agricultural extension services that have been so successful at the numerous land grant colleges and universities in the United States.

Universal employment will put families as well as enterprises under stress. Husbands who are slackers will find the pressure to do their fair share at home rising as more and more women take advantage of the opportunities offered by a high-pressure labor market and a high minimum wage. In other words, as the unemployment rate approaches zero, the participation rate of women will approach that of men. One such opportunity offered to women by a high-pressure labor market is to support themselves with a good job and divorce a husband who is a slacker. Men who want to keep their wives, particularly those wives who can get a job paying a minimum of $10 an hour, will have to shape up as the high pressure in the labor market moves through the family to the husband. Innovative new family structures may very well evolve as women find alternatives to raising children on their own and living with slackers disguised as fathers and husbands. Courts may find innovative new ways to collect child support from the same. Even more radical structural change could lift from women's backs the almost exclusive responsibility for childcare in the first place. Women should not necessarily be responsible for the primary care of children. Their primary responsibility for childcare is what makes it so hard for them to enter the job market. Married or divorced men should not just have to pay up. Perhaps they should have the personal responsibility for the primary care of children. Perhaps, they should stand and deliver instead of put a check in the mail and run off.

Churches and other not-for-profits will find greater opportunities for service in the growing need for traditional day care and new forms of care provision. Government can help with grants to cover start-up costs and subsidies for nutritious meals. Furthermore, both government grants and regulations will be needed to encourage the provision of professional medical, educational, recreational, and rehabilitation services to the children and the elderly The human need for care and for care-giving will provide plenty of opportunity for service to others. Of course, there will be great outcries from the self-appointed guardians of traditional family values (male dominance and laziness).

Suggestions for Globalizing Abundance

The orthodox experts on economic development emphasize the near impossibility of abundance for the global majority. They are wrong. They make much of the need to do more for poor nations: send economic experts, technical assistance, multinational investment, government financing, and a seemingly endless list of such "help." However, the point is not what the rich and powerful of the world should start doing; it is what they should stop doing, instead. To globalize abundance, here are some very simple and fundamental things to stop doing.

Developed countries should stop subsidizing their agricultural exports to underdeveloped countries because the subsidies harm poor farmers there. The United States should stop building an empire and dismantle what it has already built. It should close its military bases and bring its soldiers home. It should support a democratic United Nations instead and lead by example, not force. It should stop trying to enforce intellectual property rights in poor countries. Just as the United States was before them, poor countries should be free to make their own cheap patented drugs with no royalties paid on their production or to import cheap knock-offs of such drugs. Poor countries should also be free to churn out cheap knock-offs of copyrighted works for domestic sale. The pharmaceutical companies and the mass media will cope—or not. Drug researching, writing, moviemaking, and all the creative arts will continue even if the structure of the leading organizations in each field is forced to change.

The developed nations should stop using the World Bank, International Monetary Fund, and World Trade Organization to dominate the poor and the weak countries. These institutions should be replaced by new global institutions operated on the democratic principle and charged with aiding the poor and excluded in their drive toward universal employment.

By operating on democratic principles, the new organizations will be run by the world's poor people, who constitute a clear majority. What will they do? In the following, we perform some "what if" mind experiments. What if the Bretton Woods institutions were managed according to the democratic principle of majority rule (Baran 1957; Chang 2003; Chua 2004; Stiglitz 2003; Tabb 2002; Wallach and Woodall 2004)?

Fate of the World Bank? It will be closed. Its loans to the poor will be written off as uncollectible. Loans to others will be paid up and not renewed. The transfer of funds from the developed countries to the underdeveloped countries will be continued if possible, but as unilateral transfers—gifts, not commercial loans. The poor nations should never have been lent money in the first place. They needed aid, not loans to be repaid to the World Bank with interest. They should have been given the funds as a gesture of human solidarity, not as a commercial transaction. A grant-administering institution should have been established instead of a loan-making one. Then, the poor nations would have a smaller debt burden.

Fate of the International Monetary Fund? If democracy befalls it, majority rule will close it. It has done what developed countries set it up to do. It discouraged competitive devaluations of national currencies to promote exports and discourage imports, it protected commercial banks and other investors in developed countries from currency collapses in the underdeveloped world, and it used its power as a battering ram to knock down barriers erected by poor countries to control foreign investment and foreign trade for the benefit of the home economy. It did all this in the name of stability and development for the poor nations of the earth.

Fate of the World Trade Organization? If it falls into the hands of the majority, they will end it. Its purpose is to deregulate the foreign trade and foreign investment sectors of the poor countries in favor of large multinational corporations from the rich countries. The rich countries have tried to convince the poor that adopting free trade and free foreign investment policies is the best way to develop. However, that is not the way the rich countries did it themselves. They did not follow strict strategies based on free trade and free foreign investment. Instead, they industrialized behind high tariff walls and regulatory barriers and they welcomed foreign investors with less than open arms (Chang 2003, 2008).

One last practice should be stopped. The United States should stop collaborating with the current Chinese government in the blatant exploitation of Chinese and U.S. workers. This collaboration began during the Nixon administration when President Richard Nixon "played the China card" in his attempt to end the Vietnam War. China was granted significant trade advantages and quickly began using them to expand its industrial production through partnering with multinational corporations. The multinationals quickly gained access to an immense supply of low-wage Chinese workers for outsourcing production from high-wage U.S. workers. The Chinese Communist Party used its complete control of the Chinese government to keep its people pouring into the growing production facilities. Much of the output was exported and the vast majority of the Chinese workers earned too little to buy what they produced. Internal dissent was brutally squashed in the massacre at Tiananmen Square. But China's economy grew at an astonishing rate and its cheap exports to the United States kept both the U.S. working class and the U.S. price level under control.

This collaboration came about largely by accident. None of the leaders from either country had such a grand design in mind when reaching the incremental decisions that made these arrangements all congeal. No grand conspiracy was involved. Nevertheless, the collaboration has worked against the interests of the industrial workers in both China and the United States. It has become a new and strange form of imperialism in which Chinese Communist Party members (the ruling class of China) and selected Chinese government officials sell out their people to work at low wages for multinational U.S. corporations that outsource the work that used to be done by U.S. workers at high wages. Numerous opportunities for graft and profiteering are opened up to the lucky Chinese who are participating in the industrialization of China. Now that they are multinational and span the globe, most big U.S. corporations have no economic interest in keeping production in the United States. They do have an interest in keeping their wage bill down, however. So on one side of the Pacific Ocean, U.S. workers lose good jobs as the U.S. economy is deindustrialized. On the other side of the ocean, Chinese workers do not get good jobs during the industrialization of the Chinese economy because of the continued repression applied by the Chinese ruling class. The capitalists and the communists win big-time. Abundance for working people in both countries loses. For an extensive but generally orthodox analysis of Chinese development, see Naughton (2007).

Conclusion

Universal employment is a noble goal. It is not a panacea and it is not a blueprint. Many problems will remain, even if the unemployment rate is finally reduced all the way down to absolute zero. The United States could achieve abundance and perhaps even help the other people who live on the planet to grasp it, too. But they must expect massive and prolonged objection.

The top dogs will howl. They may bite. They will try to hold back abundance. We do not know if they will succeed. But we are convinced that economic abundance cannot be achieved in societies bound by the inequalities we have discussed. As sure as Chinese women could not run with bound feet, we cannot achieve abundance when bound by counterproductive institutions.

Reflection and Conclusion

Review of the Theme

Economics is not just about scarcity. It is also about abundance. The evidence strongly supports the proposition that abundance is possible. Some economists have known it all along, but scarcity economics has denied abundance economics the attention it deserves. The result is a mutilation of the "Queen of the Social Sciences" (economics) into the "dismal science." We love the old Queen and wish to make her whole.

Abundance means the full participation of everyone in the use of the community's joint stock of knowledge; it does not mean free goods and services for everyone. This means that abundance is the economics of productive work, and we have devoted most of this book to it, focusing on the costs of unemployment and low labor force participation and proposing to change the economy by pursuing the goal of universal employment.

Abundance is blocked by the inequalities that groups of people impose on each other. Abundance is not blocked by too much equality or by insufficient resources, insufficient government, or imminent environmental collapse. Abundance is not blocked by external factors. Mother nature is not a miser. Social relationship is where the scarcity shoe pinches. That is where abundance is denied—in the struggles between the top dogs and the underdogs of class, race, sex, and nation.

Review of the Chapters

A wide range of economists have recognized and discussed the possibility of abundance. In our first chapter we survey the many economists from different schools of thought who have argued that economic abundance is possible. There are many important abundance economists, even though scarcity economists have been able to exclude their views on abundance from the mainstream of economics.

In our second chapter, "The Meaning of Abundance," we show that abundance means full and equal access to the community's stock of knowledge. Abundance is relative to the level of knowledge, with abundance meaning more in the Space Age than the Stone Age. Neither scarcity nor abundance is inevitable. Instead, they are institutional. Humans make choices and communities make policies. These choices and policies become institutions. The human-made institutional order, not an inevitable natural order, generates either equality and abundance or inequality and scarcity.

In Chapter 3 we show that excessive human population is not a limit to economic abundance. The relations between demographic and economic factors are numerous and complex. We find that the population and its growth rate are important factors and have been stressed in different ways by economists, but we could not find solid ground to argue that the population and its growth rate hindered abundance or that they promoted it, either. However, it may be that abundance, measured by high per capita gross domestic product (GDP), promotes a low population growth rate under current conditions. That is, it could be that the causal relation between population and economy runs in the opposite direction; instead of population factors affecting economic ones, economic factors may affect population ones. In highly developed industrial economies with high incomes, fertility rates are low. In underdeveloped economies with low incomes, fertility rates are higher. The former increasingly rely on the latter to provide immigrant labor. Perhaps abundance itself is a form of population control.

The full participation of women in all social activities, including employment outside the home, gives them more choices. Many of those choices involve having fewer children. Abundance will not generate excessive population growth. It will do quite the opposite. In the future, there may be too few people, not too many. In parts of Europe and Japan, this problem is already showing up as an aging of the population and a financial crunch in social security systems. With women having fewer children and with people living longer, both the average age of the population and the number of retirees per active worker have been rising. In this sense, high-income Europe and Japan do not produce enough people. Abundance will not result in overpopulation.

In Chapter 4 we show that natural resources and environmental quality are not barriers to economic abundance. Exploring the environmental Kuznets curve, doomsday models, and much else, we do not find hard evidence supporting limited resources or environmental deterioration as inevitable barriers to economic abundance. On the contrary, we strongly suspect that, as with population, more important forms of causation may run counter to the conventional wisdom. The conventional wisdom indicates that excess population causes economic decline. Cause runs from population to economy. In the recent experience of humans, we find reason to believe that cause runs from economy to population. In recent times, most high-performing economies have low population growth rates because high GDP per person is accompanied by low fertility rates. The conventional wisdom also holds that excess economic production causes resource depletion and environmental deterioration, which will then bring economic production down, possibly with a crash. But in the recent experience of humans we find that high economic production makes it possible to afford environmental improvement and to enlarge the availability of resources through new knowledge and new practices.

If vast pools of poverty and inequality are allowed to remain in the world because the negative-gum games are allowed to continue, then the community will continue to experience population growth, environmental deterioration, and resource depletion. Further research is needed here, too. The older generation has left the younger generation with a lot of work to do.

In Chapter 5 we stop looking at external factors—population hitting a ceiling, resources being depleted, environment deteriorating—and we start looking internally. We start looking at the games people play with each other, in which one group exploits another one. These are the real barriers to abundance. In particular, we look at racism, sexism, classism, and nationalism as negative-sum games. We encourage you, the reader, to make careful empirical estimates of the gains and losses from playing these games. In the following chapters, we concentrate on unemployment and underparticipation in the workforce. We explain how to measure inequality in terms of the Gini ratio and we debunk the conventional wisdom of the trickle-down theory, which suggests that economic performance improves when inequality is allowed to rise. It does not.

The alternative argument that economic performance is improved when equality is increased is only weakly supported by the evidence, but the conventional wisdom is not supported by the evidence at all.

Here too is room for the flowering of many rewarding careers in empirical research—challenging investigations that pay more attention to the empirical record than to the conventional wisdom.

In Chapter 6 we show that the class game is a barrier to abundance. Several minor classes use their power to pursue their class interest at the cost of others. Bankers, farmers, and managers may be the best-known top dogs who play this game at the expense of the community. However, the major classes are the ones that impose the most cost on the community. Slave masters and feudal lords left their marks of fire and destruction, heartbreak and waste. With capitalism and capitalists, major costs are different in kind. The cost of the capitalist game that we concentrate on is the unemployment of workers. The enormous cost of unemployment under capitalism is a clear barrier to abundance. There is nothing natural about the rate of unemployment. The historical record shows that the community can reduce unemployment. Now the test is whether the community can eliminate it altogether. Perhaps capitalism will survive the elimination of unemployment. Perhaps not.

In Chapter 7 we explore nationalism, not the patriotism that comes from honest pride in honest accomplishments but the chauvinism that comes from dominating other countries. This latter kind of nationalism is another barrier to abundance. When one nation dominates others, it molds them into an empire. At one time, about a century ago, all but a few countries had been brought under the imperial control of European nations. The dominant European nations developed industrial economies that generated high incomes for their citizens. The dominated nations became underdeveloped colonial backwaters that generated low incomes for theirs.

The United States and most of Latin America broke free of the imperial dominance of Europe before the other colonial countries. Finally, two world wars and many wars of national liberation later, most of the empires collapsed or were defeated. By the end of the 1960s European imperialism was essentially gone, even from most of Africa. The newly independent countries have been unsteadily but persistently trying to find their own ways forward since then.

And now, in 2008, it should be no surprise that much foreboding is felt all over the globe at what looks like the attempt to construct a new imperial order—that of the United States.

In his three books in the American Empire Project, Chalmers Johnson lays out the dynamics of American imperialism in more detail than we have done. He emphasizes the internal distortions and costs imposed on the United States by its imperial misadventure (Johnson 2000, 2004, 2006). Abundance requires that a path to peaceful cooperation be taken. Imperial domination will deny abundance to the dominated countries. The resistance movements that spring up will deny abundance to the dominators, as both sides are doomed to make swords instead of plowshares and to die by them.

In Chapter 8 we discuss sexism, which also denies abundance. Half or more of the population is female. Reducing women's economic contribution to the community by discouraging their participation in the labor market is very costly. By eliminating such waste, the community could move much closer to abundance. Beyond the economics of it, sexism is cruel and violent. It should be eliminated, even if it did not harm the economy at all.

In Chapter 9 we dig into racism, first by exposing the myths of race, then by exposing the myths of the new racism in the United States. We also calculate the costs of racism in the United States in terms of lost GDP and we calculate the economic burden put on black workers and black families. The costs and burdens are substantial. The civil rights movement still has work to do. Racism is alive and harming the entire country still, after some four centuries.

In Chapter 10 we look back at these negative-sum games and we criticize orthodox economists for ignoring them. These isms are not temporary deviations from equilibrium. They are profound economic problems that keep the community from attaining abundance.

Chapter 11 is devoted to universal employment. If all poor adults were working at a high minimum wage or above, they would pull themselves out of poverty and the nation into abundance. The poor are their own salvation, their own best friends. They need high-paying jobs, not charity. Rather than a frontal attack on racism, sexism, nationalism, and classism, we propose universal employment, which would drive the aggregate unemployment rate down closer and closer to zero. Then, those negative-sum games that cannot be played in a zero-unemployment environment would go the way of the thumbscrew and the noose. The community would move closer to abundance.

The Last Word: Veblen's Game

It may seem odd that we place our discussion of Thorstein Veblen's theory of conspicuous consumption and conspicuous waste at the end of the last chapter of our book. We put it here to emphasize how important it is and to give Veblen the last word. After all, he certainly will have the last word on the current world civilization if we continue conspicuously consuming and conspicuously wasting. In a zero-unemployment environment, the world would remain in scarcity if it allowed conspicuous consumption and conspicuous waste to continue unrestrained. All the participation and all the extra goods and services could easily be wasted in a Veblenian orgy of conspicuous display. We call this Veblenian orgy "Veblen's game." We put this at the end of our book to emphasize our warning that his could be the End Game.

Thorstein Veblen described and analyzed conspicuous consumption and conspicuous waste ([1899] 1975). What he explained can be understood best in the terms of game theory. But make no mistake about it. This game is serious. It causes enormous harm. By using game theory terms, we do not mean to trivialize it in the least. Even if people succeeded in providing for the full participation of all in the economy and reaped a tremendous increase in production, they still might be trapped in a kind of scarcity—relative scarcity. This could easily come to pass through playing Veblen's game. The game is a special case of showing off: one player shows off and one or more opposing players watch the performance. The performer's objective is to raise his or her own status relative to the status of the players watching. The objective of the observers is to maintain their status by avoiding envy of the performer's display. Veblen's game of relative status is played over and over again, with performer becoming observer and observer becoming performer in successive rounds of the game. In real life, the play becomes continuous.

In general, showing off does not seem to raise a public outcry, although it is commonly viewed with a mildly condemnatory air, as when grown-ups see little boys showing off to impress their mates. Veblen's game may appear to be a zero-sum game, in which what the winner gains in relative status is equivalent to what the observer loses in relative status, so the sum of the gains and losses is zero. Nevertheless, Veblen showed that this is actually a negative-sum game. It involves more than the status gained and the status lost. There is also the cost of all the effort expended by the performer to impress the observer and the cost of all the effort expended by the observer to avoid being impressed. Furthermore, since this is an economic game, there is an opportunity cost—the diversion of what could be productive effort into frivolous and even meretricious display and into deflecting the same.

People play Veblen's game by displaying that their new car or golf swing is better than other people's. The members of the audience try to avoid that judgment. They may then try to show that their new car or golf swing is better than the first performer's. In Veblen's game, better means more expensive. What the game is really displaying is the ability to pay. The winners puff themselves up with pride while the losers slink away in defeat. Watching male peacocks displaying their tails gives the general idea of the game. Each tries to display a tail larger than anybody else's. Mine is bigger than yours—tail envy. Of course, humans are more sophisticated than peacocks. They have no tails.

Humans play Veblen's game on two fronts simultaneously, through conspicuous consumption and conspicuous leisure, with the relationship between the two being quite sophisticated. Conspicuous consumption without conspicuous leisure is embarrassing. A person who merely consumes on a vast scale will be placed on the status level of an autoworker who wins the lottery and tries to buy a way into higher circles—how very gauche. While displaying lavish consumption, the players of Veblen's game must also be able to show that they do not have to work for money, so they are free to spend vast blocks of time on leisure, instead. Leisure must be conspicuously vast to match consumption.

Here is where the autoworkers who win the lottery give themselves away. Their bodies show that they have not patronized a personal trainer at the gym nor a plastic surgeon at the clinic. Their vacation stories show that they have been to Disneyland but not the south of France. Their school stories are about Wayne State, not Harvard. They display frequent familiarity with beer but little knowledge of fine wine. Acquiring the appropriate knowledge of fine wine takes more time and money than acquiring the same knowledge of beer. So wine is better than beer for the simultaneous display of conspicuous consumption and conspicuous leisure.

Another complication arises in Veblen's game, making play extremely sophisticated. Mere consumption does not count in Veblen's game; it must be *conspicuous* consumption—that is, consumption on display. Leisure does not count unless it is *conspicuous* leisure. However, while both must be conspicuous, neither can be obvious. This rule puts Veblen's game on a higher plane than the showing-off of little boys or the strutting of peacocks. In Veblen's game, performers must try to show off without their audience readily recognizing it. Showing off without people realizing that you are doing so is not an easy thing to do. If members of the audience know that the performer is showing off, then they also know that the performer secretly feels inadequate. The show-off therefore loses status, thus defeating the purpose of the game, which is to elevate the performer's status and depress the status of the audience. This cannot be done with experienced adult players if it becomes obvious that the performer is trying to show off.

In Veblen's game, players come to continuously compare their consumption and leisure to everyone else's. Unless players can make a favorable comparison, can conspicuously consume and display conspicuous leisure more than everybody else, they will feel like a loser. But since only one consumer out of all the players can consume the most and display the most leisure, all players except for that one will feel like losers. This is not abundance. Even with full participation and universal employment, if everybody is playing Veblen's game, everybody will feel like a loser, except for one person. This game must be stopped. Otherwise, Veblen argues, "the conspicuous consumption of goods [and leisure would] gradually gain in importance, both absolutely and relatively, until it had absorbed all the available product, leaving nothing over beyond a bare livelihood" ([1899] 1975, 91).

You do not have to carry the baggage of scarcity and inequality forward with you into the future. Choose abundance, reject scarcity. Reduce the inequalities groups of people impose on each other. Reject conspicuous consumption and conspicuous waste. Measure the alternatives for yourselves. Do better than earlier generations have done.

References

Preface

Dugger, William M., and Howard J. Sherman. 2000. *Reclaiming Evolution: A Dialogue Between Marxism and Institutionalism on Social Change.* London: Routledge.

Gruchy, Allan G. 1987. *The Reconstruction of Economics: An Analysis of the Fundamentals of Institutional Economics.* Westport, CT: Greenwood Press.

International Labor Office. 2007. *Key Indicators of the Labour Market.* 5th ed. Geneva, Switzerland: International Labor Office.

Phillips, Ronnie J., ed. 1995. *Economic Mavericks: The Texas Institutionalists.* Greenwich, CT: JAI Press.

Chapter 1

Ayres, Clarence E. [1944] 1962. *The Theory of Economic Progress: A Study of the Fundamentals of Economic Development and Cultural Change.* 2nd ed. New York: Schocken Books.

Baran, Paul A., and Paul M. Sweezy. 1966. *Monopoly Capital: An Essay on the American Economic and Social Order.* New York: Monthly Review Press.

Blaug, Mark. 1978. *Economic Theory in Retrospect.* 3rd ed. Cambridge: Cambridge University Press.

Chase, Stuart. 1934. *The Economy of Abundance.* New York: Macmillan.

Commons, John R. [1934] 1961. *Institutional Economics: Its Place in Political Economy.* Madison: University of Wisconsin Press.

Domar, Evsey. 1957. *Essays in the Theory of Economic Growth.* New York: Oxford University Press.

Dugger, William M. 1990. "From Utopian Capitalism to the Dismal Science: The Effect of the French Revolution on Classical Economics." In *Research in the History of Economic Thought and Methodology*, ed. Warren J. Samuels, 8: 153–173. Greenwich, CT: JAI Press.

Galbraith, John Kenneth. 1969. *The Affluent Society.* 2nd ed. Boston: Houghton Mifflin.

Gruchy, Allan G. 1987. *The Reconstruction of Economics.* Westport, CT: Greenwood Press.

Hobson, John A. [1902] 1948. *Imperialism*. London: Allen and Unwin.

———. 1976. *Confessions of an Economic Heretic: The Autobiography of John A. Hobson*. Ed. Michael Freeden. Sussex, England: Harvester Press.

Hunker, Henry L., ed. 1964. *Erich W. Zimmermann's Introduction to World Resources*. New York: Harper and Row.

Keynes, John Maynard. 1963. "Economic Possibilities for Our Grandchildren." In *Essays in Persuasion*, 358–374. New York: Norton Library.

Malthus, Thomas Robert. [1798] 1926. *An Essay on the Principles of Population*. London: Macmillan.

Marx, Karl. [1848] 1988. *The Communist Manifesto*. Ed. Frederic L. Bender. New York: W.W. Norton.

Mill, John Stuart. 1848. *The Principles of Political Economy with Some of Their Applications to Social Philosophy*. London: Longmans, Green.

O'Hara, Phillip Anthony, and Howard J. Sherman. 2004. "Veblen and Sweezy on Monopoly Capital, Crises, Conflict, and the State." *Journal of Economic Issues* 38 (December): 969–987.

Ricardo, David. [1817] 1963. *The Principles of Political Economy and Taxation*. Homewood, IL: Irwin Paperback Classics in Economics.

Rostow, Walt W. 1960. *The Stages of Economic Growth: A Non-Communist Manifesto*. Cambridge, MA: Harvard University Press.

Sachs, Jeffrey D. 2005. *The End of Poverty*. New York: Penguin.

Schumpeter, Joseph A. [1942] 1950. *Capitalism, Socialism, and Democracy*. 3rd ed. New York: Harper Torchbooks.

Sen, Amartya K. 1999. *Development as Freedom*. New York: Random House.

Sherman, Howard J. 1991. *The Business Cycle: Growth and Crisis under Capitalism*. Princeton, NJ: Princeton University Press.

Smith, Adam. [1776] 1937. *An Inquiry into the Nature and Causes of the Wealth of Nations*. New York: Modern Library.

Tawney, R.H. [1920] 1948. *The Acquisitive Society*. New York: Harcourt, Brace.

Veblen, Thorstein. [1899] 1975. *The Theory of the Leisure Class*. New York: Augustus M. Kelley.

———. [1904] 1975. *The Theory of Business Enterprise*. Clifton, NJ: Augustus M. Kelley.

———. [1919] 1964. *The Vested Interests and the Common Man*. New York: Augustus M. Kelley.

———. [1921] 1965. *The Engineers and the Price System*. New York: Augustus M. Kelley.

Zimmermann, Erich W. 1951. *World Resources and Industries*. Rev. ed. New York: Harper and Brothers.

Chapter 2

Ayres, Clarence E. [1944] 1962. *The Theory of Economic Progress: A Study of the Fundamentals of Economic Development and Cultural Change*. 2nd ed. New York: Schocken Books.

Childe, V. Gordon. 1942. *What Happened in History*. London: Penguin.

Commons, John R. [1924] 1968. *Legal Foundations of Capitalism*. Madison: University of Wisconsin Press.

Conner, Clifford D. 2005. *A People's History of Science: Miners, Midwives, and "Low Mechanicks."* New York: Nation Books.

Davis, David Brion. 2006. *Inhuman Bondage: The Rise and Fall of Slavery in the New World.* New York: Oxford University Press.

Diamond, Jared. 1997. *Guns, Germs and Steel.* New York: W.W. Norton.

————. 2005. *Collapse.* New York: Viking.

Forde, C. Daryll, ed. 1963. *Habitat, Economy and Society.* New York: E.P. Dutton.

Harris, Marvin. 1974. *Cows, Pigs, and Witches.* New York: Random House.

————. 1977. *Cannibals and Kings.* New York: Random House.

Maril, Robert Lee. 2000. *Waltzing with the Ghost of Tom Joad: Poverty, Myth, and Low-Wage Labor in Oklahoma.* Norman: University of Oklahoma Press.

Sherman, Howard J. 2006. *How Society Makes Itself: The Evolution of Political and Economic Institutions.* Armonk, NY: M.E. Sharpe.

Tool, Marc R. 1996. "Choose Equality." In *Inequality: Radical Institutionalist Views on Race, Gender, Class, and Nation,* ed. William M. Dugger, 103–126. Westport, CT: Greenwood Press.

United Nations Development Program (UNDP). 2006. *Human Development Report, 2006: Beyond Scarcity: Power, Poverty and the Global Water Crisis.* New York: Palgrave Macmillan.

U.S. Bureau of the Census. 2004. *Statistical Abstract of the United States, 2004–2005,* 124th ed. Washington, DC: U.S. Government Printing Office.

United States Government Printing Office. U.S. Department of Labor. 2007. Bureau of Labor Statistics, Employment Situation Summary (July), Table A-5. www.bls.gov.

Veblen, Thorstein. [1904] 1975. *The Theory of Business Enterprise.* Clifton, NJ: Augustus M. Kelley.

————. 1919. *The Place of Science in Modern Civilization and Other Essays.* New York: B.W. Huebsch.

Widerquist, Karl, Michael Anthony Lewis, and Steven Pressman, eds. 2005. *The Ethics and Economics of the Basic Income Guarantee.* Burlington, VT: Ashgate.

Chapter 3

Alba, Francisco. 1984. *La Población de México: Evolución y dilemas.* Mexico, Distrito Federal: Centro de Estudios Económicos y Demográficos, El Colegio de México.

Blaug, Mark. 1962. *Economic Theory in Retrospect.* Homewood, Illinois: Richard D. Irwin.

Czech, Brian. 2000. "The Importance of Ecological Economics to Wildlife Conservation." *Wildlife Society Bulletin* 128, no 3: 2–3.

Daly, Herman. 1996. *Beyond Growth: The Economics of Sustainable Development.* Boston: Beacon Press.

Eberstadt, Nicholas. 1997. "World Population Implosion?" *Public Interest* 129 (Fall): 3–22.

Ehrlich, Paul. 1968. *The Population Bomb.* New York: Ballantine Books.

INEGI (Instituto Nacional de Estadística Geografia y Informatica). 1990. *Estadistícas Históricas de México. Vol. I.* Mexico Distrito Federal: INEGI.

Lee, Ronald. 2003. "The Demographic Transition: Three Centuries of Fundamental Change." *Journal of Economic Perspectives* 17, no. 4 (Fall): 167–190.

Malthus, Thomas Robert [1798] 1965. *First Essay on Population with notes by James Bonar*. New York: Augustus M. Kelley, Reprints.

Meadows, Dennis L., et al. 1974. *Dynamics of Growth in a Finite World*. Cambridge, MA: Wright-Allen Press.

Myrdal, Gunnar. [1944] 1962. *An American Dilemma: The Negro Problem and Modern Democracy*. New York: Harper and Row.

Pasinetti, Luigi. 1974. *Income Distribution and Growth*. London: Cambridge University Press.

Rostow, Walt W. 1998. *The Great Population Spike and After: Reflections on the 21st Century*. London: Oxford University Press.

Smith, Adam. [1776] 1937. *An Inquiry into the Nature and Causes of the Wealth of Nations*. New York: Modern Library.

Simon, Julian. 1996. *The Ultimate Resource 2*. Princeton, NJ: Princeton University Press.

United Nations, Population Division, Department of Economic and Social Affairs. 2005. *World Population Prospects: The 2004 Revision*, vol. 1, *Comprehensive Tables*. New York: United Nations. www.un.org/popin/data.html.

U.S. Bureau of the Census. 2003. *Statistical Abstract of the United States, 2003*, 123rd ed. Washington, DC: U.S. Government Printing Office.

———. 1967. *Absentee Ownership: The Case of America*. Boston: Beacon.

Weeks, John R. 1999. *Population: An Introduction to Concepts and Issues*. 7th ed. Belmont, CA: Wadsworth.

———. 2000. "Population Growth as a Ponzi Scheme." 36th Phi Beta Kappa lecture at San Diego State University (mimeo).

Chapter 4

Beckerman, Wilfred. 2003. *A Poverty of Reason: Sustainable Development and Economic Growth*. Oakland, CA: Independent Institute.

Boulding, Kenneth. 1961. *The Collected Works of Kenneth Boulding*, vol. 2. Boulder: Colorado Associated Press, 1971. Reprinted from "Where Do We Go From Here?" In *Proceedings, Fourth National Conference, Administration of Research*, 66–72. University Park: Penn State University Press.

———. 1966. "The Economics of the Coming Spaceship Earth." In *Environmental Quality in a Growing Economy*, ed. Henry Jarrett, 3–14. Baltimore: Johns Hopkins University Press.

Bush, George W. 2002. "President Announces Leader of Delegation to World Summit on Sustainable Development." Press release, August 19. www.whitehouse.gov/news/releases/2002/08/20020819.html.

Ehrlich, Paul R., and Anne H. Ehrlich. 1990. *The Population Explosion*. New York: Simon and Schuster.

Gore, Al. 2006. *An Inconvenient Truth*. Emmaus, PA: Rodale Press.

Hollander, Jack M. 2003. *The Real Environmental Crisis: Why Poverty, Not Affluence, Is the Environment's Number One Enemy*. Berkeley: University of California Press.

Kuznets, Simon. 1955. "Economic Growth and Income Inequality." *American Economic Review* 49: 1–28.

Lomborg, Bjorn. 2001. *The Skeptical Environmentalist: Measuring the Real State of the World*. London: Cambridge University Press.

Meadows, Donella H., Dennis L. Meadows, Jorgen Randers, and William W. Behrens III. 1972. *The Limits to Growth: A Report for the Club of Rome's Project on the Predicament of Mankind.* New York: Universe Books.

Meadows, Donella H., Dennis L. Meadows, and Jorgen Randers. 2004. *Limits to Growth: The Thirty-Year Update.* White River Junction, VT: Chelsea Green.

Newsweek. 1975. "The Cooling World." April 28. www.globalclimate.org/Newsweek.htm.

Rifkin, Jeremy. 2002. *The Hydrogen Economy: The Creation of the Worldwide Energy Web and the Redistribution of Power on Earth.* New York: Tarcher/Penguin.

Simon, Julian. 1996. *The Ultimate Resource 2.* Princeton, NJ: Princeton University Press.

Swaney, James A. 2003. "Are Democracy and Common Property Possible on Our Small Earth?" *Journal of Economic Issues* 37, no. 2: 259–288.

Todaro, Michael P., and Stephen C. Smith. 2003. *Economic Development.* 9th ed. New York: Addison Wesley.

United Nations, General Assembly. 1987. *Report of the World Commission on Environment and Development: Our Common Future.* New York: United Nations. www.are.admin.ch/are/en/nachhaltig/international_uno/unterseite02330/

U.S. Environmental Protection Agency. 2005. Global Warming Web site. http://yosemite.epa.gov/oar/globalwarming.nsf/content/index.html.

Wingo, Dennis. 2004. *Moonrush: Improving Life on Earth with the Moon's Resources.* Burlington, Ontario, Canada: Apogee Books.

World Bank. 2003. *Sustainable Development in a Dynamic World: Transforming Institutions, Growth, and Quality of Life: World Development Report, 0163–5085.* Washington, DC: World Bank.

Yergin, Daniel. 1992. *The Prize: The Epic Quest for Oil, Money and Power.* New York: Simon and Schuster.

Zimmermann, Erich W. 1951. *World Resources and Industries.* Rev. ed. New York: Harper and Row.

Chapter 5

Alesina, Alberto F., and Dani Rodrik. 1994. "Distributive Politics and Economic Growth." *Quarterly Journal of Economics* 109, no. 2: 465–490.

Beauvoir, Simone de. [1952] 1989. *The Second Sex.* Trans. and ed. H.M. Parshley. New York: Random House.

Benabou, Roland. 2000. "Unequal Societies: Income Distribution and the Social Contract." *American Economic Review* 90, no. 1: 96–129.

Clark, Charles M.A. 1996. "Inequality in the 1980s: An Institutionalist View." In *Inequality: Radical Institutionalist Views on Race, Gender, Class, and Nation,* ed. William M. Dugger, 197–222. Westport, CT: Greenwood Press.

DeMott, Benjamin. 1990. *The Imperial Middle: Why Americans Can't Think Straight About Class.* New York: William Morrow.

———. 1995. *The Trouble with Friendship: Why Americans Can't Think Straight about Race.* New York: Atlantic Monthly.

———. 2000. *Killer Woman Blues: Why Americans Can't Think Straight About Gender and Power.* Boston: Houghton Mifflin.

Dugger, William M., ed. 1996. *Inequality: Radical Institutionalist Views on Race, Gender, Class, and Nation.* Westport, CT: Greenwood Press.
———. 1998. "Against Inequality." *Journal of Economic Issues* 32 (June): 287–303.
———. 2000. "Deception and Inequality: The Enabling Myth Concept." In *Capitalism, Socialism and Radical Political Economy: Essays in Honor of Howard J. Sherman*, ed. Robert Pollin, 66–80. Cheltenham, UK: Edward Elgar.
———. 2005. "Dugger's Theorem: The Free Market Is Impossible." *Journal of Economic Issues* 39 (June): 309–324.
Friedman, Milton. 1962. *Capitalism and Freedom.* Chicago: University of Chicago Press.
Friedman, Milton, and Rose D. Friedman. 1980. *Free to Choose.* New York: Avon Books.
Mills, Charles W. 2003. *Race: Essays in White Marxism and Black Radicalism.* Lanham, MD: Rowman and Littlefield.
Mills, C. Wright. 1943. "The Professional Ideology of Social Pathologists." *American Journal of Sociology* 49, no. 2: 165–180.
Moynihan, Daniel P. 1965. *The Negro Family: The Case for National Action.* Washington, DC: U.S. Department of Labor (Office of Policy Planning and Research).
Okun, Arthur. 1975. *Equality and Efficiency: The Big Tradeoff.* Washington, DC: Brookings Institution.
Peach, James. 1996. "Regional Income Inequality Revisited: Lessons from the 100 Lowest-Income Counties in the United States." In *Inequality: Radical Institutionalist Views on Race, Gender, Class, and Nation*, ed. William M. Dugger, 237–250. Westport, CT: Greenwood Press.
Pressman, Steven. 2005. "Income Guarantees and the Equity-Efficiency Tradeoff." In *The Ethics and Economics of the Basic Income Guarantee*, ed. Karl Widerquist, Michael Anthony Lewis, and Steven Pressman, 163–182. Burlington, VT: Ashgate.
Roszak, Theodore. 1969. *The Making of a Counter Culture.* Garden City, NY: Anchor Books.
Ryan, William. 1976. *Blaming the Victim.* Rev. ed. New York: Vintage.
Wright, Erik Olin, ed. 2005. *Approaches to Class Analysis.* Cambridge: Cambridge University Press.
Zweig, Michael, ed. 2004. *What's Class Got to Do with It? American Society in the Twenty-First Century.* Ithaca, NY: Cornell University Press.

Chapter 6

Anderson, S.E. 1995. *The Black Holocaust for Beginners.* New York: Writers and Readers Publishing.
Ayres, Clarence E. [1944] 1962. *The Theory of Economic Progress: A Study of the Fundamentals of Economic Development and Cultural Change.* 2nd ed. New York: Schocken Books.
Beard, Charles A. 1957. *The Economic Basis of Politics.* Ed. William Beard. New York: Vintage.
Bebchuk, Lucian, and Jesse Fried. 2004. *Pay Without Performance: The Unfulfilled Promise of Executive Compensation.* Cambridge, MA: Harvard University Press.

Berle, Adolf A., and Gardiner C. Means. 1968. *The Modern Corporation and Private Property*. Rev. ed. New York: Harcourt, Brace and World.

Braverman, Harry. 1974. *Labor and Monopoly Capital*. New York: Monthly Review Press.

Bryce, Robert. 2002. *Pipe Dreams*. New York: Perseus Books.

Conner, Clifford D. 2005. *A People's History of Science*. New York: Nation Books.

Curtin, Philip D. 1969. *The Atlantic Slave Trade: A Census*. Madison: University of Wisconsin Press.

Davis, David Brion. 1966. *The Problem of Slavery in Western Culture*. Ithaca, NY: Cornell University Press.

———. 2006. *Inhuman Bondage: The Rise and Fall of Slavery in the New World*. New York: Oxford University Press.

Debo, Angie. 1943. *Tulsa: From Creek Town to Oil Capital*. Norman: University of Oklahoma Press.

———. [1944] 1998. *Prairie City: The Story of an American Community*. Norman: University of Oklahoma Press.

———. 1961. *The Rise and Fall of the Choctaw Republic*. 2nd ed. Norman: University of Oklahoma Press.

Dobbs, Lou. 2006. *War on the Middle Class: How the Government, Big Business, and Special Interest Groups Are Waging War on the American Dream and How to Fight Back*. New York: Viking Penguin.

Dugger, William M. 1984. "The Nature of Capital Accumulation and Technological Progress in the Modern Economy." *Journal of Economic Issues* 18 (September): 799–823.

———. 2005. "Dugger's Theorem: The Free Market Is Impossible." *Journal of Economic Issues* 39 (June): 309–324.

Fogel, Robert William, and Stanley L. Engerman. 1974. *Time on the Cross*. Boston: Little, Brown.

Forder, James. 2005. "Why Is Central Bank Independence So Widely Approved?" *Journal of Economic Issues* 39 (December): 843–865.

Goolsbee, Austin. 2006. "Count Ethnic Divisions, Not Bombs, to Tell If a Nation Will Recover from War." *New York Times,* July 20.

Gordon-Reed, Annette. 1998. *Thomas Jefferson and Sally Hemings: An American Controversy*. Charlottesville: University Press of Virginia.

Greider, William. 1987. *Secrets of the Temple: How the Federal Reserve Runs the Country*. New York: Simon and Schuster.

Kindleberger, Charles P. 1996. *Manias, Panics, and Crashes*. 3rd ed. New York: John Wiley.

Lekachman, Robert. 1966. *The Age of Keynes*. New York: Random House.

Low, Augustus, and Virgil A. Clift, eds. 1981. *Encyclopedia of Black America*. New York: McGraw-Hill.

Mellon, James, ed. 1988. *Bullwhip Days: The Slaves Remember; An Oral History*. New York: Avon Books.

Morton, A.L. 1979. *A People's History of England*. New York: International Publishers.

O'Sullivan, Mary A. 2000. *Contests for Corporate Control*. New York: Oxford University Press.

Pirenne, Henri. 1937. *Economic and Social History of Medieval Europe*. Trans. I.E. Clegg. New York: Harcourt, Brace.

Roemer, John. 1982. *A General Theory of Exploitation and Class.* Cambridge, MA: Harvard University Press.

Sciolino, Elaine. 2005. "Immigrants' Dreams Mix with Fury in a Gray Place Near Paris." *New York Times,* December 12.

Sherman, Howard J. 1991. *The Business Cycle.* Princeton, NJ: Princeton University Press.

Smith, Adam. [1776] 1937. *An Inquiry into the Nature and Causes of the Wealth of Nations.* New York: Modern Library.

United Nations Development Program (UNDP). 2005. *Human Development Report, 2005: International Cooperation at a Crossroads; Aid, Trade, and Security in an Unequal World.* New York: Oxford.

Veblen, Thorstein. [1919] 1964. *The Vested Interests and the Common Man.* New York: Augustus M. Kelley.

Vestal, Stanley. [1932] 1957. *Sitting Bull: Champion of the Sioux.* Norman: Oklahoma University Press.

Waldman, Amy. 2002. "Poor in India Starve as Surplus Wheat Rots." *New York Times,* December 2.

Wright, Erik Olin. 1985. *Classes.* London: Verso.

Zinn, Howard. 2003. *A People's History of the United States.* New York: HarperCollins.

Chapter 7

Food and Agricultural Organization of the United Nations. FAOSTAT www.fao.org/corp/statistics/en/

Commodity Research Bureau. 2003. CRB Commodity Yearbook. Chicago, Illinois: Commodity Research Bureau. www.crbtrader.com/ addis.

Gaddis, John Lewis. 2005. *The Cold War: A New History.* New York: Penguin.

Gorbachev, Mikhail. 1987. *Perestroika: New Thinking for Our Country and the World.* Updated ed. New York: Harper and Row.

Ichino, Andrea, and Rudolf, Winter-Ebmer. 2001. "The Long-Run Education Cost of World War II: Example of Local Average Treatment Effect Estimation." European University Institute, Economics Working Papers, http://ideas.repec.org/p/eui/euiwps/ec098–10.html.

Jansson, Bruce S. 2001. *The Sixteen Trillion Dollar Mistake: How the U.S. Bungled Its National Priorities from the New Deal to the Present.* New York: Columbia University Press.

Kennedy, Paul. 1989. *The Rise and Fall of the Great Powers.* New York: Random House.

Myrdal, Alva. 1976. *The Game of Disarmament: How the United States and Russia Run the Arms Race.* New York: Pantheon.

Sato, Kazuo. 2001. "Japan's Potential Output and the GDP Gap: A New Estimate." *Journal of Asian Economics* 12:183–196.

Stockholm International Peace Research Institute (SIPRI). August 22, 2007. www.sipri.org/contents/milap/milex/mex_trends.html.

U.S. Bureau of the Census. 2005. *Statistical Abstract of the United States, 2004–2005,* 124th ed. Washington, DC: U.S. Government Printing Office.

World Bank. 2007. World Development Indicators: WDI Online. Washington, DC: World Bank. https://publications.worldbank.org/

Ziemke, Earl F. 2007. "World War II." Microsoft Encarta Online Encyclopedia. http://encarta.msn.com.

Chapter 8

Beauvoir, Simone de. [1952] 1989. *The Second Sex*. Trans. and ed. H.M. Parshley. New York: Random House.

Council of Economic Advisers. *Economic Report of the President*, 2007. Washington, DC: U.S. Government Printing Office, 2007.

Faludi, Susan. 1991. *Backlash: The Undeclared War Against American Women*. New York: Crown Publishers.

Figart, Deborah M. 1997. "Gender as More Than a Dummy Variable: Feminist Approaches to Discrimination." *Review of Social Economy* 55 (Spring): 1–32.

Heise, Lori L., Jacqueline Pitanguy, and Adrienne Germain. 1994. *Violence Against Women: The Hidden Health Burden*. World Bank Discussion Paper no. 255. Washington, DC: World Bank.

Hite, Shere. 1987. *Women and Love: A Cultural Revolution in Progress*. New York: Knopf.

Hochschild, Arlie Russell, with Anne Machung. 2003. *The Second Shift*. Updated ed. New York: Penguin.

Laurence, Louise. 1999. "Domestic Abuse." In *The Elgar Companion to Feminist Economics*, ed. Janice Peterson and Margaret Lewis, 121–126. Cheltenham, UK: Edward Elgar.

Miles, Rosalind. 1989. *The Women's History of the World*. New York: Harper and Row.

Montagu, Ashley. 1974. *The Natural Superiority of Women*. Rev. ed. New York: Macmillan.

Olson, Paulette. 1994. "Feminism and Science Reconsidered: Insights from the Margin." In *The Economic Status of Women under Capitalism*, ed. Janice Peterson and Doug Brown. Brookfield, VT: Edward Elgar.

U.S. Bureau of the Census. 2005. *Statistical Abstract of the United States, 2004–2005*. 124th ed. Washington, DC: U.S. Government Printing Office.

U.S. Council of Economic Advisers. 2007. *Economic Report of the President*. Washington, DC: U.S. Government Printing Office.

Chapter 9

Allport, Gordon W. 1958. *The Nature of Prejudice*. Abridged. Garden City, NY: Doubleday Anchor.

Cox, Oliver Cromwell. [1948] 2000. *Race: A Study in Social Dynamics*. 50th anniversary edition of *Caste, Class, and Race*. New York: Monthly Review Press.

Gitlitz, David M. 1996. *Secrecy and Deceit: The Religion of the Crypto-Jews*. Albuquerque: University of New Mexico Press.

Memmi, Albert. [1967] 1991. *The Colonizer and the Colonized*. Expanded ed. Boston: Beacon Press.

Myrdal, Gunnar. 1944. *An American Dilemma: The Negro Problem and Modern Democracy*. New York: Harper and Row.

Shirer, William L. 1959. *The Rise and Fall of the Third Reich.* New York: Simon and Schuster.

U.S. Bureau of the Census. 2001. *Overview of Race and Hispanic Origin, Census 2000 Brief.* Washington, DC: U.S. Bureau of the Census. www.census.gov /prod/2001pubs/c2kbr01–1.pdf.

U.S. Bureau of the Census. 2006. *American Community Survey Subject Definitions*, p. 29. Washington, DC: U.S. Bureau of the Census. www.census.gov/acs/www /Downloads/2006/usedata/Subject_Definitions.pdf.

Chapter 10

Cypher, James M. 2007. "From Military Keynesianism to Global Neoliberal Militarism." *Monthly Review* 59 (June): 37–56.

Devine, James. 2004. "The 'Natural' Rate of Unemployment." In *A Guide to What's Wrong with Economics*, ed. Edward Fullbrook, 126–132. London: Anthem Press.

Dugger, William M. 1984. *An Alternative to Economic Retrenchment.* New York: Petrocelli.

———. 1992. *Underground Economics: A Decade of Institutionalist Dissent.* Armonk, NY: M.E. Sharpe.

Haywood, William D. [1929] 1966. *The Autobiography of Big Bill Haywood.* New York: International Publishers.

Hochschild, Arlie Russell, with Anne Machung. 2003. *The Second Shift.* Updated ed. New York: Penguin.

Okun, Arthur M. 1975. *Equality and Efficiency: The Big Tradeoff.* Washington, DC: Brookings Institution.

Salvatore, Nick. 1982. *Eugene V. Debs: Citizen and Socialist.* Urbana: University of Illinois Press.

Taylor, Nick. 2008. *American-Made: The Enduring Legacy of the WPA; When FDR Put the Nation to Work.* New York: Bantam Books.

Terkel, Studs. 1984. *The Good War: An Oral History of World War Two.* New York: Pantheon.

U.S. Bureau of the Census. 2007. *Statistical Abstract of the United States, 2007*, 126th ed. Washington, DC: U.S. Government Printing Office.

Veblen, Thorstein. [1899] 1975. *The Theory of the Leisure Class.* New York: Augustus M. Kelley.

Chapter 11

Baran, Paul A. 1957. *The Political Economy of Growth.* New York: Monthly Review Press.

Bourgin, Frank. 1990. *The Great Challenge: The Myth of Laissez-Faire in the Early Republic.* New York: Harper and Row.

Bowles, Samuel. 2004. *Microeconomics: Behavior, Institutions, and Evolution.* Princeton, NJ: Princeton University Press.

Chang, Ha-Joon. 2003. *Kicking Away the Ladder: Development Strategy in Historical Perspective.* London: Anthem.

———. 2008. *Bad Samaritans: The Myth of Free Trade and the Secret History of Capitalism.* New York: Bloomsbury Press.

Chua, Amy. 2004. *World on Fire: How Exporting Free Market Democracy Breeds Ethnic Hatred and Global Instability.* New York: Random House.

Cohn, Steven Mark. 2007. *Reintroducing Macroeconomics: A Critical Approach.* Armonk, NY: M.E. Sharpe.

Galbraith, James Kenneth. 2000. "The Keynesian Economics of Unemployment and Inequality." In *Commitment to Full Employment: The Economics and Social Policy of William S. Vickrey,* ed. Aaron W. Warner, Mathew Forstater, and Sumner M. Rosen, 182–188. Armonk, NY: M.E. Sharpe.

Galbraith, John Kenneth. 1952. *A Theory of Price Control.* Cambridge, MA: Harvard University Press.

———. 1975. *Money: Whence It Came, Where It Went.* Boston: Houghton Mifflin.

Greider, William. 1987. *Secrets of the Temple: How the Federal Reserve Runs the Country.* New York: Simon and Schuster.

Gunn, Christopher Eaton. 1984. *Workers' Self-Management in the United States.* Ithaca, NY: Cornell University Press.

Hahnel, Robin. 2005. *Economic Justice and Democracy: From Competition to Cooperation.* London: Routledge.

Lerner, Abba P. 1951. *Economics of Employment.* New York: McGraw-Hill.

Levin-Waldman, Oren and Charles Whalen. 2007. "The Minimum Wage Is a Middle Class Issue." *Challenge: The Magazine of Economic Affairs* 50, no. 3 (May–June): 59–71.

Lewin, Tamar. 2007. "Justices, 5–4 Limit Use of Race for School Integration Plans." *New York Times,* June 29.

Naughton, Barry. 2007. *The Chinese Economy: Transitions and Growth.* Cambridge, MA: MIT Press.

Pohlman, Jerry E. 1976. *Inflation Under Control?* Reston, VA: Reston Publishing.

Stiglitz, Joseph E. 2003. *Globalization and Its Discontents.* New York: W.W. Norton.

Tabb, William K. 2002. *Unequal Partners: A Primer on Globalization.* New York: New Press.

Tool, Marc R. 1979. *The Discretionary Economy: A Normative Theory of Political Economy.* Santa Monica, CA: Goodyear.

———. 1986. *Essays in Social Value Theory: A Neoinstitutionalist Contribution.* Armonk, NY: M.E. Sharpe.

Wallach, Lori, and Patrick Woodall. 2004. *Whose Trade Organization? A Comprehensive Guide to the WTO.* New York: New Press.

Chapter 12

Johnson, Chalmers. 2000. *Blowback: The Costs and Consequences of American Empire.* New York: Metropolitan Books.

———. 2004. *The Sorrows of Empire: Militarism, Secrecy, and the End of the Republic.* New York: Metropolitan Books.

———. 2006. *Nemesis: The Last Days of the American Republic.* New York: Metropolitan Books.

Veblen, Thorstein. [1899] 1975. *The Theory of the Leisure Class.* New York: Augustus M. Kelley.

Index

About the Authors

William M. Dugger is Professor of Economics at the University of Tulsa. **James T. Peach** is Regents Professor of Economics at New Mexico State University. Both earned PhDs at the University of Texas in the 1970s and have been friends ever since.